SMALL TOWN PROSECUTOR

TRIALS OF KILLERS, CON MEN, AND A PRIEST

BOB SIMPSON

ONION RIVER PRESS

Burlington, Vermont

Onion River Press
89 Church Street
Burlington, VT 05401
info@onionriverpress.com
www.onionriverpress.com
ISBN: 978-1-966607-06-9 Paperback / 978-1-966607-07-6 eBook
Library of Congress Control Number: 2025905612

This book is dedicated to my wife Toni and our sons Joe and Mike.

CONTENTS

AUTHOR'S NOTE

The trials described in this book took place decades ago in the latter part of the 20th century and early in the 21st century. I have distinct memories of these cases, but to ensure the book's accuracy, I reviewed Vermont Supreme Court decisions affirming the jury's verdicts as well as newspaper articles describing the trials as they happened, my own records of trial exhibits, and notes I took while I was preparing for trial. Those sources are detailed in the book's endnotes.

I have not used the full names of victims of the brutal killings described in the book. The victims' last names would add nothing substantive to the description of these crimes. I also excluded them to respect the privacy of friends and families of the victims of these crimes—people who are likely to still have agonizing memories of the loss of their loved ones, even after many years.

Warning: This book contains descriptions of several disturbing crimes, including crimes against children. Most graphic details were removed, but some passages may still be upsetting and difficult to read.

INTRODUCTION

This book is about jury trials in criminal cases, many of which rocked Vermont in the 1980s. It's mainly about trying cases before juries, but it is also about investigating and preparing cases for trial. Some of the cases might be hard to read, but they are part of the history of Vermont and have, at times, shaped the law in this state.

Part I of the book deals with the work I did with other prosecutors and police on five brutal murders. This work ranged from trying four killers before juries to working side by side with detectives to identify the two teenagers who had raped and murdered a 12-year-old girl as she walked through a park on her way home from school.

From there, I've included a description of the trials of two longtime con men who cheated a 93-year-old woman out of $1,800. There is also a review of preparation for a murder trial where the defendant who had shot and killed a woman in 1985 raised an insanity defense—a defense that had worked for him 21 years earlier when he had escaped criminal responsibility for shooting and killing his young wife.

Then there is a break from jury trials. I recount my memories of the controversial June 1984 "Raid at Island Pond." In that case, I filed a juvenile petition that resulted in the temporary seizure of 112 children from the Twelves Tribes religious community in Island Pond, a village of approximately 800 people located in the northeast corner of Vermont near the Quebec border.

Part II of the book deals with my work at the Chittenden County

State's Attorney's Office. In April 1994, I returned to the office as an entry-level deputy state's attorney, and I worked there until 2006, when I retired after serving four years as the elected state's attorney.

When I returned to the State's Attorney's Office, my focus returned to jury trials.

One of these trials was in 1995, and it resulted in the first criminal jury trial conviction in Vermont for manslaughter in a drug overdose death. I've also included a description of the 1998 trial that resulted in the first Vermont criminal jury trial conviction of a priest for sexually abusing a child.

There is also a description of the attempted murder trial of a man who attacked two of his fellow Vietnamese refugees with a meat cleaver. This intersects with my own service in Vietnam and my brief contact with the CIA's so-called "Secret War" in Laos—a war that resulted in the death of 10 percent (200,000) of the country's inhabitants.

But most of the second half of the book deals with the difficult issue of prosecuting "domestic violence" cases. I tried six jury trials in my last full year as state's attorney. Five of them involved men who had already been convicted of domestic violence. In this book, I describe four of those trials. This includes an attempted murder trial where jurors heard testimony that a man had attacked his ex-girlfriend three times in the preceding four months and was out of jail on bail when he broke into her apartment and stabbed her repeatedly. In another trial—a murder trial—the victim had been honored as a hero by the police for stepping in to protect a friend who was being savagely beaten by her boyfriend.

I practiced law for more than 40 years. Trying cases before juries was the most satisfying work I did as a lawyer.

A Balding "Boy Scout": Brief Background

With the exception of my service in the military, I have lived all of my adult life in the state of Vermont. I grew up in northeastern Rhode Island, but my parents moved to Vermont in 1966—the year before I went into the Army. I had been a Vermont resident for less than a year when I received my draft notice.

I served as an enlisted man[1] in the US Army as an intelligence analyst and spent two tours in Southeast Asia. One tour (1969–70) was in the northern part of what was then called South Viet Nam, roughly 50 miles south of the Demilitarized Zone (DMZ). The DMZ separated South Viet Nam, which the US was supporting, from North Viet Nam, which was supported by two Communist countries—the Soviet Union (Russia and satellite countries) and China. I served my second tour (1970–71) in Northeast Thailand not far from the Mekong River, which served as the border between Thailand and Laos.

I am now 79, and I suspect many men my age have vivid memories of their service in Vietnam and Southeast Asia in the 1960s and 1970s. I know I do. But I don't have the words to adequately describe the waste and slaughter caused by the "Vietnam War." More than three million Vietnamese—North and South, soldiers and civilians—died.[2] Although deaths of members of the American Military were small in comparison (58,300), the war still hit home for many American families, loved ones, and friends. Four of my teammates on my college lacrosse team were killed in action in Vietnam. Two of my teammates on my high school football team were killed there as well.

All for nothing.

When I got out of the Army in June 1971, I went back to Randolph, Vermont, where my parents lived. With kind help from people in Randolph, I found a job. I first started working for a farmer, then later as a laborer for a building contractor, and finally as a reporter for the *Barre-Montpelier Times Argus* newspaper.

It was at the *Times Argus* that I met my future wife, Antonia ("Toni") Webster, the love of my life. We were married by a local pastor in the home she rented in Washington, Vermont, on Thanksgiving, 1972. We have been married for over 50 years.

The *Times Argus* was a great place to work. I liked being a reporter. The people there were smart, fun, and interesting. But after about three years at the paper, I decided I wanted to be a lawyer. I had covered several criminal jury trials while working for the paper, and I found the prosecutor's work to be important and interesting. I especially admired the lawyers who did the jury trials.

Vermont Law School (VLS) in South Royalton had just been accredited. It was about 10 miles from where Toni and I were living at the time. Toni worked several jobs to put me through VLS. I also got help on tuition payments through the "GI Bill" (AKA the "Servicemen's Readjustment Act").

I graduated from VLS in 1978 and was admitted to the Vermont Bar in February 1979.

Later in 1979, I got my first full-time job as a lawyer as a deputy state's attorney in the Chittenden County State's Attorney's Office. Including me, there were five lawyers in the office. We were the busiest county prosecutor's office in Vermont. We prosecuted all criminal cases in Chittenden County from driving with a suspended license to rape, kidnapping, and murder. We also did all "juvenile delinquency" cases.

The office was located in Burlington, Vermont's largest city, which had a population of only 37,712 in 1980 (my first full year in the office).

Chittenden County is Vermont's most populous county. It contains more than a quarter of the state's population. Vermont is often thought of as rural farm country dotted with quaint villages. That is not Chittenden County, which has been described as a "chunk of suburbia surrounded by Vermont."

For me, though, Chittenden County has turned out to be a great place to live, work, and help raise a family. When I started work at the State's Attorney's Office, I would sometimes eat lunch with my coworkers at nearby Battery Park. I remember commenting to someone about how lucky I was to work in a place where I had daily beautiful views of the New York shore across Lake Champlain with the Adirondack mountains in the background.

Due to the eleven-year gap between my graduation from college and my graduation from law school,[3] I had the dubious distinction of being not only the oldest member of the office but also the least experienced.

I was happy to get the job as a Chittenden County deputy state's attorney for two basic reasons. First, I would be getting unique experience in doing jury trials—experience that I thought would help me later in getting better-paying work in private practice. Second, I would be doing what a friend, who later became a judge, called "honorable work"— working to help protect members of the community by enforcing criminal laws that the community members counted on for protection of their lives and property. (My wife, Toni, later teased that I was working as a "boy scout.")

At the time, the Chittenden County State's Attorney's Office was probably the best place in Vermont for a new lawyer to get experience doing jury trials.

I tried my first jury trial, a DWI (Driving While Intoxicated/Impaired), after I had been in the State's Attorney's Office for a little over a month. The state's attorney, Mark Keller, had me watch another deputy try a case from jury selection to verdict. After that, I began picking my own juries and trying my own cases. I eventually tried at least 30 jury trials in the 24 months (Sept. 1979–Sept. 1981) that I was at the Chittenden County State's Attorney's Office working for Keller.

I lost at least four cases in that first year I tried cases. I worked hard at it. But I was nervous about speaking in public and I'm sure that I didn't show much confidence at first. As I gained confidence, juries seemed to have more confidence in me. But there was seldom a year when I won all the cases I tried—even after I had been trying cases for many years.

If I lost, it might have been because a key witness didn't show up at trial. But more likely, it was because the defense simply did a better job explaining the evidence than I did. In other words, it was definitely not "the jury's fault."

There has been a sharp decline in jury trials. This is particularly true in state courts, where more than 90 percent of all criminal cases in the US are prosecuted. In 1976, an average of 3.4 percent of felonies in the 22 "most populous" states were resolved through jury trials. By 2002, that number had slipped to 1.3 percent.[4] In one "populous state"—New York—criminal jury trials dropped 61 percent between 1990 and 2019.[5]

But they were not on the decline in Vermont when I first started practicing law in 1979 and when I started work as a deputy state's attorney in Burlington.

Back then, nothing focused the mind of defendants, defense attorneys, and prosecutors like "jury draw day." There were usually at least 20 cases—misdemeanors and low-level felonies that were still not settled through plea bargains in the week before jury draw. Usually, all but three or four of the cases were settled with "plea agreements" by the time the actual process of "picking a jury" began.

I have set out (below) a summary of the jury trial process from selecting the jury ("jury draw") through the trial itself. My hope is that the summary will provide helpful context for the trials that I describe in the rest of the book.

Jury Draw

As I remember it, the county clerk would randomly select 40 to 50 people from the list of Chittenden County voters and notify them that they had been selected for "jury duty." These potential jurors were told to report to the Vermont District Court at 32 Pearl Street in Burlington on a particular date. On that day, they were likely to be selected to sit as jurors in at least one criminal trial.

The process began with the random selection of potential jurors. The names of all the potential jurors were put in a wooden box, and 20 names would be drawn at random by a court clerk. The first 14 people would then sit in the "jury box"—the place separated from the rest of the court by a waist-high wooden railing where the twelve jurors and two alternates would eventually sit and listen to the evidence.

The remaining six people whose names had been called would sit in chairs directly in front of the 14 people who were already sitting in the jury box. If one of the people sitting in the box was excused from sitting as a juror, then one of the people sitting in front would move up and take that person's place.

The overriding rule in criminal trials is the presumption of innocence. The judge would tell the jurors that they must presume that the defendant is innocent and that the presumption of innocence remains until the prosecutor proves the defendant is guilty of the crime they are charged with "beyond a reasonable doubt."

The judge would then usually tell the prospective jurors what type of case they would be considering (e.g., burglary, DWI, simple assault), and that the prosecution had the "burden of proof." That is, the prosecution had to prove the "essential elements" of the crime it had charged the defendant with—murder, for instance—"beyond a reasonable doubt." That is, "beyond any doubt based on reason."

For example, to prove essential elements of first degree murder,[6] the prosecution would have to prove: (1) the defendant, Mr. X, committed the acts charged; (2) that he caused the death of the victim; (3) that he acted "unlawfully"—he had no legal excuse or justification such as self-defense; (4) that the defendant acted "willfully"—his acts were intentional and he was aware of what he was doing; (5) that the defendant acted "deliberately"—he didn't act on impulse but instead thought about whether or not to do it; and (6) that he acted with "premeditation"—in addition to acting deliberately, he "planned" the act.

The prosecutor and the defense attorney would have already reviewed a "questionnaire" that had been filled out by each prospective juror. This would let the lawyers know what kind of job the person had, whether s/he had ever been convicted of a crime, whether the person was married, had children, etc.

It usually didn't take long to select the jurors who would hear the evidence and decide the case. Both the prosecution and defense each had the right to exclude up to six prospective jurors without giving a reason (peremptory challenges). I don't think I ever used all six—not even in murder trials.

I would rely on the jury questionnaire to identify people who might be unhappy with police and prosecutors, such as people with criminal records. We did not have a budget for hiring outside experts in jury selection. I tried to pick people who seemed smart and serious about listening carefully to the evidence and producing a fair verdict. I found that I tended to pick older men and women rather than young people because the older people were more likely to have been victims of a crime or have known someone who had been a crime victim.

There would be 14 people who would ultimately sit on the jury and hear the evidence. Twelve people would ultimately decide the case, but 14 jurors would hear the evidence. This was to try to ensure that there would still be twelve people available to deliberate and decide the case if a juror became ill or otherwise became unable to serve through the end of the trial. It was common practice to have all 14 hear the evidence and then draw two names by lot once the evidence was closed. The two people whose names were drawn would be excused and could go about their business.

Jury Trial

People who had been selected to sit as jurors in a particular case would show up at the Vermont District Court in Burlington at 8 a.m. on the designated day.

The judge would explain to the jurors that they were about to hear the lawyers' "opening statements," in which the prosecution and defense had an opportunity to lay out what each lawyer considered to be the key evidence the jurors were likely to hear from the witnesses in the upcoming trial.

The judge would emphasize that the opening statements, and the closing arguments the lawyers would make at the end of the case, were not evidence. The only evidence jurors could consider in deciding whether the prosecution had proven its case would come from witnesses who were sworn in and subject to cross-examination.

First, the prosecutor would make an opening statement. This was usually 10 to 15 minutes in which the prosecutor would outline the evidence they would introduce to prove "beyond a reasonable doubt" that the defendant was guilty of the crime he had been charged with. The goal was to outline the evidence that would come in through the witnesses while taking care not to promise too much.

The defense attorney would have the option of giving the defense opening statement right after the prosecution opening or waiting to give the defense opening until after the prosecution had "presented its case," i.e., called all of its witnesses.

Usually, though, the defense would go right after the prosecution. The defendant's lawyer would tell jurors that there was more evidence than the evidence that the prosecutor had just described, and that when jurors had heard all the evidence, they would have a reasonable doubt, and they would "have no choice" but to acquit the defendant.

Once opening statements were finished, the prosecution would call the witnesses it needed to prove its case. This, of course, was the "meat" of the trial. The prosecutor would go first with "direct examination"—questions that were designed to explain to jurors how the crime in question had taken place and, in the process, show why the defendant was guilty. "Leading questions" were not permitted on direct examination. An example of a leading question from the prosecution would be: "The defendant was angry and upset, wasn't he?" In other words, a question that suggests the answer.

The prosecutor would have met with witnesses before the trial. Each witness would be asked to go over the statement they made earlier to investigators before the meeting with the prosecutor. The prosecutor would then go over the questions the witness would be asked at trial. These questions would be based on the statement the witness had already given. The witness would then be asked to answer as they would answer at trial.

Not surprisingly, preparation is key to effective direct examination, just as preparation is the key to cross-examination—and just about anything else in the law, for that matter.

Over the roughly 20 years that I tried cases before juries, I always wrote down the facts I had to prove—e.g., identity, causation, unlawful killing, intent to kill. Then I identified the witnesses I would call to prove these elements. Once I had identified the witness, I wrote out all the questions I would have to ask the witness to prove the element(s) I needed to prove.

In the meeting with the witness before the trial, the prosecutor would emphasize that the witness must tell the truth and that there are no "wrong answers" as long as the witness told the truth. I often told nervous witnesses to "just tell the truth" as they remembered it. I told them not to worry about whether their answer would hurt my case. "Just tell the truth. If it hurts my case, that's my problem—not yours."

Once a witness had gone through direct questioning from the prosecutor, the witness was subject to cross-examination by the defense attorney, who would try to show that the witness was either suffering from a "misperception" or was lying.

"Leading questions" are permitted in cross-examination. For example: "Isn't it true you are legally blind?" (misperception) Or, "You told James Dean you would say anything if it would hurt my client. Didn't you?" (lying)

The prosecution would normally call at least seven witnesses. Once the prosecution had called all its witnesses—a process that usually took at least two days—the prosecution would "rest its case," meaning: "I am not calling any more witnesses."

The judge would tell the jurors that they would be excused while the judge and the lawyers went over "matters of law." Once the jurors had left the courtroom, the defense attorney would ask the judge to dismiss the prosecution's case. The defense would argue that even if the judge viewed the evidence the prosecution had presented "in the light most favorable to the prosecution" the evidence was still insufficient. That is, no reasonable juror could find the prosecution had proven its case.

This often led to some lively argument between the prosecutor and the defense attorney. But the judge almost always denied the motion.

The jury was then called back into the courtroom, and the defense puts in its case. It was the same process the jury had already seen when the prosecution put in its case. Only, the roles were reversed. That is, the defense attorney called witnesses and conducted "direct examination" of them. This time, it was the prosecutor who conducted the cross-examination.

Although the defense usually called witnesses who were intended to create a "reasonable doubt" as to whether the prosecution has proven its case, it was not unusual for the defendant to exercise his Fifth Amendment right and elect not to testify in his own defense.

Once the defense has rested, the judge often called for a recess, during which the judge would go over the instructions ("jury charge") on the law that the jurors must apply to the "facts"—facts such as did the defendant intend to kill or seriously injure the victim. (These instructions were usually sent to the prosecution and defense at least two days before the charge conference.)

This "charge conference" gave the attorneys an opportunity to raise any objections they might have to the judge's proposed instructions. Once it was over, the jurors were called back into the courtroom, and the lawyers gave their "closing arguments."

Jurors who were interviewed by investigators after they had completed their service often said that the closing arguments were the most important part of the trial for them.

The prosecution, which always has the "burden of proof," actually gets to make two closing arguments to the jury in criminal trials.

In the first "closing," the prosecutor goes through the essential elements of the crime that the prosecution must prove "beyond reasonable doubt" in order to convict the defendant. The prosecutor then goes through the evidence the jury has heard that the prosecutor claims proves conclusively, "beyond any doubt based on reason," that the prosecution has met its burden of proof and the defendant is "guilty" of the crime charged. This usually takes fifteen to twenty minutes.

Then it's the defense attorney's turn. The defense attorney generally focuses on the testimony of the key prosecution witnesses and argues why these witnesses cannot be believed, and because they cannot be believed, there is a "reasonable doubt." The argument here is: "Are you willing to convict this man based on the testimony of this weak, confusing, and often contradictory testimony? You cannot reasonably find that the prosecution has met its burden. Under the law, you have no choice but to find my client not guilty."

Defense attorneys are generally very good at making an argument that there is "reasonable doubt." In my experience, defense closings usually take no more than 30 to 40 minutes.

Once the defense attorney has finished, the prosecution has the opportunity to make a "rebuttal." In theory, because the prosecution has the burden of proof, they are allowed the "final word" to rebut any unanticipated claims the defense makes in its closing argument. In fact, though, prosecutors can normally anticipate the issues the defense will raise in its closing argument, and they have already prepared and rehearsed the rebuttal. They may save their most compelling points for rebuttal, knowing that these will be the last words the jury will hear in highlighting and interpreting the evidence that has been presented.

After the lawyers have finished their closing arguments, there is usually a brief recess, and then the judge will read the "instructions" that were approved earlier during the charge conference (e.g., the "essential elements" of the offense[s]). As I recall, it usually took 30 to 40 minutes for the judge to read the instructions. After that, the jury "retired to the jury room" to deliberate.

It typically took, on average, five to six hours for jurors to deliberate and reach a verdict. There were exceptions, of course. There is an example in this book where the jury took less than an hour to reach a verdict—and another where the period the jury deliberated was longer than the period it took to try the case itself.

Most of the trials lasted no more than three or four days, including deliberation and verdict. But trials of serious felonies like murder, sexual assault, and kidnapping often lasted more than a week.

PART I
1981–1987

A Young Killer

On a Sunday afternoon in January 1981, CH, a junior at the University of Vermont, decided to climb up the steep, rocky slope of Rock Point on Lake Champlain near North Beach in Burlington. As she was making her way up the slope, a stocky teenage boy—who she later learned was Louis ("Louie") Hamlin—asked her if she needed help. CH said "no," but Hamlin climbed up next to her anyway and walked with her as she climbed to the top.

Once they reached the top, she turned to leave, and Hamlin continued to follow her. She told him she was going to jog for a while. Hamlin followed her and suggested they follow nearby railroad tracks back into Burlington.

CH had been nervously making small talk with Hamlin. She grew more nervous when Hamlin stopped talking. "The next thing I knew, there's a knife at my throat." She moved his arm and slipped out of his chokehold, asking him what he thought he was doing. He told her to shut up and sit down. "Don't provoke me," he warned.

CH refused to sit down. Instead, she put both her hands on the hand that was holding the knife and convinced him to put his knife back in the sheath on his belt. She was able to calm him down, and they walked the mile or so back into Burlington. Hamlin apologized for his behavior.

After they parted company, CH went to the Burlington Police Department and reported the incident.

I was assigned to the Hamlin case in late February or early March, 1981.

Hamlin's conduct was bizarre and dangerous. But because CH was not physically injured, I could only charge Hamlin with simple assault—"attempting by physical menace to put CH in fear of imminent serious bodily injury."[7] The charge was a misdemeanor, with a maximum sentence of one year in prison.

Hamlin's was the only simple assault by a teenager that I ever charged or knew of being charged in criminal, or "adult," court. Any other simple assault involving a 16-year-old would have gone to juvenile court. But Louie Hamlin's case was different.

Hamlin had just turned 16, and he had no criminal record. If he had committed the assault when he was 15, his case would have gone to juvenile court, and any record of the case would have been sealed and kept from the public. But since he was 16, I had the option of either sending the case to juvenile court or "charging him as an adult" in criminal court. I chose to charge him as an adult in Vermont District criminal court. His actions—stalking and then holding a knife to the throat of a young woman he did not know—were so disturbing and dangerous that it made no sense to me to keep what Hamlin had done from the public.

Hamlin agreed to plead guilty to simple assault in late March, roughly two months after he'd held a knife to CH's throat. I recommended that he get a suspended sentence and get psychological counseling to address his dangerous impulses. But once Hamlin had pled guilty in criminal court, his lawyer asked Judge John Connarn to transfer Hamlin's case to juvenile court. He argued that Hamlin should not have a criminal record because of this one "stupid" act. I countered that Hamlin's act was more than "stupid," it was dangerous, and I said that Hamlin should be treated as an adult given his actions and that there should be a public record of what he had done.

Judge Connarn had served in the Army in World War II and had been wounded in action while fighting in France. He had later served in the Vermont Legislature and as Vermont's attorney general before being appointed to the bench. He refused to send Hamlin's case to juvenile court.

Judge Connarn told Hamlin's lawyer he'd made a persuasive argument: "But I don't buy it." He asked Hamlin what made him "so angry." Hamlin mumbled that he didn't know. "Just once in a while I get really mad."

The judge sentenced Hamlin to a 12-month sentence, which he "suspended." This meant that Hamlin would not serve any jail time but that he would be assigned a probation officer (PO) who would meet with him and monitor his conduct. He would be required to meet regularly with his PO and undergo any counseling the PO "deemed appropriate."

The judge told Hamlin that he had to learn to quell his anger:

> This young lady, if she hadn't been so brave—I guess she got the knife away from you somehow—I can imagine what may have happened. There may have been an aggravated assault or a murder here.[8]

"God Help You"

Two months later, on May 15, 1981, around 4 p.m. on a Friday afternoon, two 12-year-old girls were walking home from school on a path in Maple Street Park in Essex Junction. Suddenly they were approached by two young men they did not know. The men dragged the two sixth graders into the woods, where they threatened them with BB guns and forced them to strip off their clothes. The men bound the girls' wrists and gagged them. Then the men raped and stabbed the girls multiple times and left them for dead.[9]

One of the girls, MO, stumbled out of the woods near the railroad tracks that ran near the park. A railroad flagman who was working in the area spotted her. She was naked and "covered in blood from head to foot." He radioed for an ambulance. Then he picked her up and ran with her down the tracks to a point where another railroad man was waiting. He gave MO over to that man who, in turn, ran with her to a parking lot where an ambulance picked her up. From there, she was rushed to the Medical Center Hospital in Burlington in critical condition and taken to the Intensive Care Unit.

MO had a 24-hour police guard outside her hospital room from the time she arrived until the men who attempted to kill her were finally arrested.

MO was in pain. She had several stab wounds, including a deep wound to her chest. But she kept asking about her friend Melissa. She said they had both been attacked, and as far as MO knew, Melissa was still in the woods.

Not long after MO was taken to the hospital, police found Melissa's body in the woods.

Melissa had been 12 years old with "big blue eyes and blonde hair and a deep husky voice that was ages older than her little body." She had just started her own babysitting business. Her parents described her as "spunky." They said she'd loved to travel and had recently traveled to Florida with her grandmother. Her mother said that Melissa had wanted to "go to St. Thomas in the Virgin Islands and travel on her own money." MO told investigators that Melissa had resisted her attackers with "all her might."[10]

Melissa had been bound and gagged. The medical examiner counted 29 wounds on the child's body. She had been cut and stabbed with a knife. The stab wounds were deep, including one to her neck and a fatal wound to her heart. The cuts were "teasing" cuts across her neck and chest, meant to inflict pain. Significantly, as it turned out, she had been shot at least six times with a BB gun, including a shot directly into her left eye. Bottom line—the girls had been raped, tortured, and left for dead. [11]

I was at a local television station in South Burlington with State's Attorney Mark Keller when Keller got the call about the attack. Keller left for the crime site immediately. I did the show, which, as I remember, was about changes to Vermont's driving laws. Then I went to Essex myself.

Keller asked his chief deputy, Susan Via, and me to work full-time on the case. Susan was an expert in sex crimes and crimes against children in particular. She was the ideal choice to work with MO. At least one member of MO's family was with her 24-7. But Susan was with MO as her friend and protector during the difficult days that followed the attack as investigators from throughout Chittenden County joined with state police detectives to try to identify the killers.

Once doctors in the ICU authorized it, Susan began gently questioning this child about what had happened to her and her friend. I am amazed to this day—more than forty years later—at how brave, strong, and clear-headed this child was and at how sensitive and skillful Susan and the sketch artist, Vermont State Trooper Stan Strusinski, were in working with MO.

For my part, I worked directly with the detectives who were conducting the investigation out of the Essex Police Station. I worked in an office adjacent to the room where the detectives were working.

On a basic level, the work was similar to work I had done in the Army in Vietnam eleven years earlier. I went through all the information we had by going through 3x5 "lead cards"—summaries of interviews and lists of suspects that dozens of police officers had gathered. I made a chronological summary by date and time of what witnesses had seen and heard in the days before and after Melissa and MO were attacked. I made judgments on what was most relevant in figuring out who might have been the attackers.

For instance: How old were the killers? Were they local? What was the significance of the BBs? Were they likely to have criminal records? Were they mentally ill? I was continually refining my assessments or scrapping them outright after I discussed my ideas with investigators and got their thoughts on them.

I was also available on-site to work with police in drafting legal documents, such as search warrants and nontestimonial identification orders, after we had developed evidence to identify strong suspects.

I remember that I'd thought, at first, that based on an initial description MO had given Susan Via, one of the killers was a dark-haired man in his 40s and the other was a younger man in his 20s with lighter-colored hair. But the fact that the killers had shot the girls with BB guns ran counter to that description, at least as far as the age of the killers went. Vermont boys aged 10 to 14 might carry BB guns, but not men in their 20s and 40s.

On Saturday, the day after she had been raped, stabbed, and left for dead, MO worked off and on throughout the day with Stan Strusinski to come up with sketches. Strusinski marveled at her ability "to reach inside and bring up" a clear, detailed description of the attackers.

On Sunday morning, the *Burlington Free Press* published Strusinki's composite sketches of the two men MO had described to him on page 1. Both men looked younger than the original reports. The man with dark hair and a heavy beard looked to me to be in his late 20s or early 30s, and the man with lighter hair looked to be in his late teens or early 20s.[12] Two special phone lines had been installed to deal specifically with tips from citizens who had ideas about who the killers might be. Calls came in from all over Vermont and New England. Police estimated that at a minimum we were reviewing 10 times the calls they normally received.[13] But after the composites of the suspects were published, the flood of calls was even greater.

We had been working through, and eliminating, a stream of false leads on potential suspects for three days. But finally, on Monday, the composites brought about the first big break in the case. Ted White, the principal at H. O. Wheeler School in Burlington, phoned the tip line. He said that he thought he recognized the two men in the composites as former students. He thought the dark-haired man looked like Louie Hamlin and that the man with the lighter-colored hair was Jamie Savage. Hamlin, age 16, was a junior at Burlington High School. Savage, age 15, lived in Essex.

After I read the "lead card" identifying Hamlin as one of the men in the composite, I spoke to Mark Keller and suggested that Hamlin made sense as one of the killers. I described to Keller how just three or four months earlier, Hamlin had followed a UVM student at Rock Point, became enraged for no apparent reason, and held a knife to her throat. I told Keller that if the young woman, CH, had not been brave and cool-headed enough to calm him down, Hamlin might well have cut her.

The following day, Tuesday, May 19, eight officers were assigned to thoroughly investigate Hamlin's and Savage's backgrounds and track their movements in the weeks up to the time of the murder and in the days afterward.[14]

On Wednesday, May 20, five days after the attack, Keller and I met with Vermont State Police (VSP) Detective Sgt. Bob Horton, VSP Detective Nick Ruggerio, and Essex Detective Lt. Robbie Yandow to review what we had. We had eliminated most possible suspects except for Hamlin and Savage, who, we learned, were constant companions.

By late Wednesday evening, the investigators who were assigned to focus on Hamlin and Savage were able to develop evidence that showed there was "probable cause" (a "fair probability") that Hamlin and Savage were the killers. For instance, both Ted White and Joyce Hoffman, Hamlin's aunt, thought it was likely the dark-haired man in the composite was Louie Hamlin. Joyce Hoffman also told police that Hamlin was subject to fits of uncontrollable rage. As for Jamie Savage, his brother Rene confirmed that Hamlin and his brother often hung out together and that Jamie looked like the younger-looking man in the composite. In addition, Hamlin had shaved his beard once the composites appeared in the paper, and he and Savage each liked BB guns and had access to them.

While we may have had probable cause to arrest Hamlin and Savage, we did not have the evidence to convict them at trial by proving their guilt beyond a reasonable doubt. So rather than making an arrest that would put us "on the speedy trial clock" for a jury trial, we decided to apply to a judge for a "nontestimonial identification order (NTO)."[15] If a judge approved the proposed order, we would be able to take each young man into custody for the purpose of obtaining "nontestimonial" evidence—photographs, fingerprints, and blood samples.

Judge Edward Costello approved the NTO late Wednesday evening. It ordered Hamlin and Savage to appear at the Vermont State Police Barracks in Colchester at midnight, where their photos, fingerprints, and a blood sample would be taken.

Hamlin and Savage were each served with an NTO not long after midnight on Thursday, May 21, 1981. Hamlin was served at his home on Elmwood Avenue in Burlington and Savage at his home at 5 Gaines Court in Essex.

Savage's home was only two and a half miles from the Colchester Barracks where he was supposed to appear. The two Essex police officers who served the NTO on Savage also drove him there. Hamlin's home was roughly four and a half miles from the Barracks. The two South Burlington police officers who served Hamlin with his NTO drove Hamlin to the Barracks as well.

The Colchester Barracks were no more than four miles from the park in Essex where the two girls had been attacked six days earlier. I was waiting at the Barracks with four detectives: Bob Horton and Nick Ruggerio from the Vermont State Police, Lee Graham of the South Burlington Police, and Robbie Yandow of the Essex Police. We were there in case either or both of the men consented to be questioned.[16]

The four detectives were experienced at conducting interviews. I was not. Although I had a good grasp of what we knew and what we didn't know about the attack on the girls, and a good sense of what facts had to be proven beyond a reasonable doubt in a murder or attempted murder trial, the area in which I could be most helpful to investigators was drafting search warrants and affidavits in support of applications for search warrants and arrest warrants.

Hamlin and Savage arrived at the Colchester Barracks around the same time and began providing blood, fingerprints, etc. But an event that would prove to be the most important development in the entire investigation was unfolding three and a half miles away at the Medical Center Hospital in Burlington.

It was around 1:30 a.m., and Susan Via and South Burlington Detectives

Jay Fish and Steve Burke were showing MO two "books" of photographs.

One book contained twelve photos of dark-haired teenage men. One of those photos was a photo of Louie Hamlin. The second book contained twelve photos of teenaged men with lighter-colored hair. One of those photos was a photo of Jamie Savage.

Detective Sgt. Jay Fish went through the process of showing the photos to MO. He could not indicate in any way that the books contained photos of people police suspected of committing the assault on MO and her friend Melissa. He told her the books *might* contain photos of the men who attacked her and they *might not*.

Fish asked her to go through all the photos in one book and look at each photo carefully. When MO was finished, Fish said he would ask her if she recognized any of the photos as a photo of one of the men who had attacked her.

Fish gave the first book of photos to MO. She went through them one by one as Fish had asked. When she was finished, he asked her if she recognized any of the photos as one of her attackers. She said, "Yes." Fish turned the pages in the book and, when he got to photo #6, she said, "That's him." Photo #6 was the photo of Louie Hamlin.

Detective Fish showed no reaction when MO picked Hamlin's photo. He simply asked her to go through the same process with the second book of photos. Again, after reviewing all the photos, she said that she recognized one of her attackers. This time she pointed to photo #3—the photo of Jamie Savage.

Fish, Burke, and Via didn't tell MO that she had identified our prime suspects. They thanked her, wished her a good night's sleep, and left. Once they left her room, Fish hurried to a phone and called the Colchester State Police Barracks. VSP Detective Nick Ruggeiro answered. "We got 'em!" Fish yelled. "Perfect ID! Both guys!"[17]

Hamlin and Savage were at the Barracks waiting in separate rooms—Hamlin's mother Mary was with her son in one room. Both of Savage's parents were with him.

Ruggeiro and Detective Lt. Yandow read Savage his Miranda warnings. He had a right to refuse to answer questions. But Savage waived his rights and agreed to answer questions about the attack on the girls. Because Savage was 15 years old, his parents could have invoked his right to remain silent on their son's behalf. But they didn't. They signed the waiver of Jamie's rights, and their son did, too.

Savage said he and Hamlin were shooting squirrels with BB pistols at the park in Essex sometime after 3:30 on Friday afternoon. He said it was raining, and he wanted to go home. But Louie Hamlin wanted to "do some girls."

No surprise. Savage blamed everything on Hamlin. Savage said that he held one of the girls while Hamlin tore the clothes of the other girl and beat, raped, and stabbed her. Once Hamlin was finished with that girl, according to Savage, Hamlin turned to the girl Savage had been holding and beat, raped, and stabbed her. Savage did admit that he helped Hamlin hide the girls' clothes after Hamlin had finished.[18]

The detectives knew, of course, that Savage was lying to minimize his role in the rape, murder, and attempted murder. MO had been clear that both men had participated in the attack on her and her friend Melissa.

Detectives Bob Horton and Lee Graham interviewed Louie Hamlin at the Colchester Barracks. I recall that I was present but did not take part in the questioning. Hamlin's mother, Mary, was present for the interview. She had informed investigators who'd served Louie with the NTO that her husband, who was at work at the Koffee Kup Bakery in Burlington, had called and told her that he did not want Louie questioned without a lawyer present to advise him.

To our surprise, though, Hamlin and his mother both agreed to waive his rights, including his right to a lawyer. But we weren't surprised when he lied.

Hamlin admitted he was familiar with Maple Street Park but said he hadn't been there on the Friday the girls were attacked. He admitted he'd had a BB gun, but he said he'd sold it a couple of days before the girls were attacked. He continued to deny any role in the attack, even after Horton told him that Jamie Savage had confessed to being at the park with Louie and that Louie had been the one who'd attacked the girls. When Hamlin's mother heard that, she asked for a lawyer for her son.

The detectives stopped the questioning as they were required to under the law.[19]

I recall that Mary Hamlin broke down after she asked for a lawyer for her son. She was sobbing and moaning and saying something like: "Oh God, Oh God" and "God help you."

I also remember watching Louie sitting there as his mother wept and moaned. By that time, he had been arrested, and his hands and wrists were cuffed behind his back. I remember him lifting his head and snarling, "Fuck God" and then said something to the effect of, "What has God ever done for me?"

As soon as it was light, Savage led investigators to the spot in the woods where he and Hamlin had hidden the girls' clothes.[20]

Louie Hamlin and Jamie Savage were arrested on first-degree murder and sexual assault charges on Thursday morning, May 21, 1981—just six days after the vicious attack on the two girls walking home from school. But Savage, who was 15 years old, could not be charged and arraigned as an adult. He was transferred immediately to the Juvenile Detention Facility in Waterbury.

It had been less than 12 hours since MO had first picked Hamlin and Savage out of the photo lineups.

While Hamlin was being arraigned, investigators were less than a mile away searching his home on Elmwood Avenue. I had worked with investigators to prepare a search warrant application, a proposed warrant, and a supporting affidavit after MO identified Hamlin, and Savage implicated him in the attack. Seven investigators executed the warrant starting around 7 a.m.

During the course of executing the warrant, investigators came across photos of Louie Hamlin's father, "Butch," having sex with his 15-year-old daughter before she was 10. Hamlin's father was arrested two weeks later. Butch Hamlin pled guilty to sexual assault and was sentenced to 6 to 15 years in prison in December 1981.[21] Mary Hamlin assisted investigators in building the case against her husband.[22]

On May 22, 1981, the front page of the *Burlington Free Press* carried two stories announcing the arrests of Hamlin and Savage for first-degree murder and sexual assault stemming from the attack on Melissa and MO.

There was a third story on the front page, however, that prompted outrage throughout the state. Its headline said: "Under State's Law Convicted Juveniles Are Free at 18." This meant that Hamlin, who was 16, could be tried and convicted of murder as an adult in criminal court and sentenced up to life in prison. But under the law, Savage would have to be "adjudicated" as a "juvenile delinquent" through the juvenile court system. He would not be tried for murder as Hamlin would.

Instead, the juvenile court judge would determine whether Savage had committed "delinquent acts." The proceedings would be secret. The only thing the public would know for certain was that even if the juvenile court did find that Savage was guilty along with Hamlin, he would be released from custody at age 18. The record of the proceeding would be sealed, but there would be no doubt that Savage would be free.

There was shock and anger at this news. There was also sanctimonious hogwash. For example, the *Burlington Free Press* editorialized the day after the arrest that Hamlin and Savage were victims—"victims of a society that failed to meet their needs." The editorial went on to say that "somehow we must wonder whether each of us is not partly to blame for the crime." According to the editorial, "we" did not heed Hamlin and Savage's "desperate cries for help."[23]

Two women who had children in Melissa and MO's class at the Lawton School actually did something helpful following the crime.

Hope Spencer and Carol Hathaway started a petition drive to change the law, which then guaranteed that Savage would be tried in a secret proceeding and freed by the time he was 18, regardless of whether he still posed a danger to the public.

They circulated a petition that called on Governor Richard Snelling to take immediate action and call an emergency session of the Vermont Legislature to amend the law and protect the public:

> We are appalled to think that in less than three years a young
> girl will again have to fear for her life because her assailant will
> be set free with no record whatsoever. Not only one girl will
> be fearing for her life when he is set free, but any one of our
> daughters or wives could be the next victim.[24]

Governor Snelling and Vermont legislative leaders opposed calling an Emergency Session at first. But the mothers of Melissa and MO's classmates got immediate support from the general public. By June 10, just two and a half weeks after the attack in Maple Street Park, they were able to present petitions with 30,000 signatures to Governor Snelling.[25]

Snelling and Legislative leaders relented.

On July 15, 1981, just two months after Savage joined Hamlin in raping, stabbing, and torturing two 12-year-old girls, the Vermont legislators met in a rare special session. They were to consider legislation that would amend Vermont law to provide that any child age 10 and up who committed one of twelve "serious crimes," ranging from murder and aggravated assault to kidnapping, could be tried as an adult in criminal court.

Some members of the Vermont Senate grumbled about the special session, and one leading senator referred to the proposed legislation as "legal hocus pocus" that would "not prevent juvenile crime."

This argument was misleading and a cynical distraction. Supporters of the call for a special session, including me, were not asking for a rewrite of juvenile law aimed at preventing juvenile crime. It was clear from their petition that Hope Spencer and Carol Hathaway were demanding a Special Session to eliminate a specific loophole in the juvenile law—a loophole that had made it possible for Jamie Savage to be free in less than three years after his vicious crime.

The Legislature had an opportunity to close this loophole. The amendment would make certain that in the future, juveniles aged 15 and under who committed violent crimes could be prosecuted in a public proceeding and subject to sentences of up to life in prison.

A conference committee of House and Senate leaders resolved differences between the two bodies, and a compromise passed by an "overwhelming" margin on July 17. Under the new law, juveniles from age 10 up to 15 who were charged with 12 serious crimes, including murder, could have their cases transferred from juvenile court to criminal court if the county prosecutor convinced the judge that the transfer was necessary to protect the public.

The law would *not apply* to Jamie Savage. Most lawyers, including me, believed a law that would apply retroactively to Savage would be unconstitutional, and a proposal to make the law retroactive was rejected by the Conference Committee.[26]

The new law went into effect in July 1981. I know of two murder cases where juveniles aged 15 and under were prosecuted in criminal court after that. And I know that, following passage of the new law, there were many more cases where the public was protected because juveniles 15 and under were prosecuted in criminal court[27] and convicted of violent felonies like aggravated assault, sexual assault, and kidnapping.

In late September 1981, I left the State's Attorney's after I was offered a job with an excellent law firm in Burlington—Latham Eastman Schweyer & Tetzlaff ("Latham and Eastman").

I had gotten to know and like one of the members of the firm, Bob

Eastman, when I tried a DWI case against him in my first year at the State's Attorney's Office. Bob helped and encouraged me for several years even after I left the firm.

Another member of the firm, Matthew Katz, was particularly helpful to me. He was a former legal aid attorney who was respected by members of the local bar. Matt Katz went on to serve as an outstanding Vermont Superior Court judge for roughly thirty years.

I did relatively little criminal defense work for Latham and Eastman. But I do remember getting advice on one of my criminal defense cases from Charlie Tetzlaff, another partner who was considered one of the best criminal lawyers in the state.

In 1993, after more than 20 years in private practice, Charlie Tetzlaff accepted President Clinton's nomination to serve as US Attorney in Vermont. He served from 1993 to 2000.

Most of the work I did at Latham and Eastman was real estate work—property title searches, real estate closings, and commercial mortgage foreclosures. This work was generated by Ben Schweyer. Ben was quiet, smart, and an exceptionally good lawyer.

Ben didn't tell any "war stories." But I learned that he had entered the US Army in 1944 as a private when he was just 18 years old. He turned 19 fighting in the desperate "Battle of the Bulge" in Belgium in December 1944 as the Germans made one last unsuccessful effort to block the Allied advance into Germany.

Ben returned to Burlington after the war. He graduated from the University of Vermont, and later the University of Pennsylvania Law School in 1951.[28] He practiced law in Burlington for 40 years. During that time, his firm represented the University of Vermont, Merchants Bank, major land developers, and regular people who wanted to buy a home or start a business in Burlington.

Although I liked and respected everyone I worked with at Latham and Eastman, I missed trying jury cases as a prosecutor. In late summer of 1982, I was hired as an assistant attorney general in the Vermont Attorney General's criminal division.

Before that, though, I was called as a late potential backup to try Louie Hamlin.

I had played no further role in either the Hamlin or the Savage case after the pair were arrested on murder and aggravated sexual assault charges on May 21, 1981—but I almost tried the case.

In late 1981 or early 1982, while I was still working for Latham and Eastman, Mark Keller called and asked me if I would try the Hamlin case with him if the Supreme Court upheld Susan Via's disqualification. I had known that Susan had been barred from trying the Hamlin case. I told Keller, "Yes," I would try the case with him as long as I got permission from my bosses at Latham and Eastman. They quickly gave me permission.

The case had been transferred from Burlington in Chittenden County, where feeling was running high against Hamlin, to the Windsor Superior Court in Woodstock, some 90 miles to the south.

The presiding judge in Woodstock was Thomas Hayes, an important figure in the Vermont Judiciary at the time. Hayes had been a longtime political staffer and politician who had worked in Washington DC for Vermont Republican US Representative and US Senator Winston Prouty for 15 years (1950–65). Hayes ran for Lt. Governor as a Republican. He won and served one term (1969–1971).

An outspoken critic of the Vietnam War, Hayes switched to the Democratic Party in the early 1970s. Democratic Governor Tom Salmon appointed Hayes—who had graduated from Georgetown Law School while he was in DC—as his legal counsel in 1974. Before he left office in 1977, Salmon appointed Hayes to the Superior Court bench.

Judge Hayes had disqualified Susan Via from prosecuting Hamlin's case at trial on the grounds that she was likely to be a defense witness at the trial! The Vermont Supreme Court summarized Hayes reasoning: (1) "because of a probability that her testimony would be relevant on the issue of defendant's guilt" and (2) "because of the further probability that she would be called to testify on behalf of the defendant when he is tried for first-degree murder and aggravated sexual assault."

Hamlin's court-appointed defense attorneys, Christopher "Chris" Davis and Oreste "Rusty" Valsangiacomo, had argued in essence that MO no longer remembered details of what had happened during the attack. They said that Via had conducted a series of interviews of MO and that Via alone knew the details of what she had said in the earlier interviews.[29]

Fortunately, the Supreme Court reversed Hayes' order disqualifying Via in a brusque, two-page order. The Supreme Court said that Hayes had "struck too soon." The judge should have waited for the trial to see

(1) whether the defense actually did try to call Via as a witness and if it did, (2) whether the defense "showed a compelling reason to call the prosecutor."[30]

If Judge Hayes' order had stood, it would have made a difficult situation for MO—Hamlin's now 13-year-old victim—even more difficult. Susan Via was an expert in dealing with child witnesses in sex cases and an expert in helping them to try to get through their discomfort in describing the strange, confusing things that had happened to them. Beyond that, Susan had developed a rapport with MO and her family. They trusted her. To replace Susan Via would have made the experience of testifying at trial more confusing and difficult for MO.

As things turned out, Judge Hayes had, indeed, "struck too soon." The defense never called Susan Via as a witness.

It is an understatement to say that the Hamlin case was a difficult case for Valsangiacomo and Davis—two skilled, experienced trial lawyers—to defend when the case went to trial in the Woodstock Superior Courthouse in early May 1982.[31]

First, there was no question that MO and her friend, Melissa, had been raped, stabbed, and left for dead. Aside from expert medical testimony of doctors who had treated MO and conducted the autopsy on Melissa, there was the testimony of the railroad men who had carried 12-year-old MO, bleeding and naked, to an ambulance the day of the attack.

It wasn't a "whodunnit" either. There was no question that Hamlin was one of the men who'd attacked MO and Melissa. First, there was the fact that MO had picked Hamlin out of a photo lineup. Second, there were witnesses who would testify that Hamlin had admitted to the attack on three separate occasions—once while speaking with two friends a week after the attack, and two other times while he was speaking with fellow inmates when he was in prison awaiting trial.[32]

MO was, of course, the prosecution's key witness. Defense counsel always has an exceptionally difficult job in cross-examining a child witness. Children are innocent and vulnerable, and if jurors perceive that defense questioners fail to recognize the child's difficult position, some jurors may tighten up, ignore the point of the questions, and glare at the lawyer. I have seen it happen on more than one occasion.[33] Davis and Valsangiacomo had to tread particularly carefully in questioning MO.

Jamie Savage had at first told investigators that Hamlin alone had raped and stabbed MO and Melissa. But later, after he learned that he could not be prosecuted for murder because he was 15 at the time of the crimes, Savage testified at a deposition that he had stabbed both girls.

Davis and Valsangiacomo built their defense around Savage's confession that he, not Hamlin, was the killer. They argued that Hamlin had raped the girls, but he hadn't stabbed either girl and had no intent to murder either girl.[34] But this defense was directly undercut by MO's testimony. She testified that Hamlin had been the leader of the attack and that he had stabbed her in the back.

The prosecution argued that Savage was lying—but even if Savage had done most of the stabbing, it did not matter under the law. That is, because Savage was acting as Hamlin's accomplice and under the law of "accomplice liability," Hamlin was criminally responsible for Savage's action.

In other words, even if Savage was telling the truth, under the law, Hamlin was responsible for the murder as though he had done the stabbing himself. Vermont law is clear on this issue:

> Where several persons combine under a common under-standing and with a common purpose to do an illegal act, each one is criminally responsible for the acts of each and all who participate with him in the execution of the unlawful design.[35]

It took the lawyers, prosecution, and defense nine days to try the case.[36] It took jurors just four hours to find Hamlin guilty of first-degree murder and aggravated sexual assault. As the *Burlington Free Press* noted, the verdict came at 10:23 p.m. on May 14, 1982—"the eve of the first anniversary of the brutal attack on Melissa and MO, two twelve-year-old Essex Junction girls."[37]

On July 15, 1982, two months after the jury convicted him, Louie Hamlin was sentenced.

Hamlin was asked if he had anything to say before he was sentenced. He said he knew he had to be punished for what he had done. Hamlin told the Court that his father had started raping him when he was 6 years old, and it had affected him "more than anyone will ever know." He said he was not a "hardened criminal" and that "three weeks ago" he had given "his life to God" and was now "a born-again Christian."

When Hamlin and members of the victims' families finished speaking,

Hamlin was sentenced to serve 45 years to life in prison. Judge Hayes had called for a somewhat lesser sentence—35 years to life, citing Hamlin's "youth." But the two elected non-lawyer "side judges" (assistant judges) who sat with Hayes throughout the trial had overruled him. Defense attorneys Valsangiacomo and Davis said it was the first time in Vermont history that a presiding judge had been overruled by side judges on a felony sentence.[38] (It was to happen again a year later when "side judges" overruled a presiding judge in the Gordon Hunt murder case, which will be discussed below.)

The "traditional goals" of sentencing are "retribution," "incapacitation," "deterrence," and "rehabilitation." To me, "retribution" and "incapacitation" are the most relevant in murder cases. Judging from Hamlin's actions before and after his torture and murder of Melissa, he needed to be imprisoned ("incapacitated") to protect the general public. Hamlin was angry, defiant, and showed no remorse for his actions until it was time for him to be sentenced.

If Jamie Savage had been 16, rather than 15, at the time he and Hamlin raped, stabbed, and tortured Melissa and MO, Savage would likely have been sentenced to decades in prison just as Hamlin was. But because he was 15 at the time of the attack, he was released from state custody in September 1983, on his 18th birthday. He had spent just 30 months in state custody.

After his release from a treatment facility in Brownsville, Texas, Savage moved to Mesa, Arizona. An official at the Superior Court in Maricopa County, Arizona told a reporter that Savage had filed a motion to have his name changed to "John W. Barber" in December 1983. His motion was granted in January 1984, after a hearing where Savage acknowledged that he had a juvenile record in Vermont. The official, Chris Tountas, said that Savage had not disclosed that the juvenile record involved rape and murder.

Tountas informed Vermont officials of the name change once he learned the nature of Savage's juvenile record. Greg Packan, Savage's former guardian, told a reporter that he knew nothing about Savage after he turned 18. Packan said that he had explicitly asked not to be told anything about Savage. "My job is over. We did all we could [to rehabilitate Savage]."[39]

This case was instrumental in changing the law in Vermont and showing how powerful the voice of the community can be in our judicial system. It was thanks to the concerned citizens who petitioned the Vermont Legislature that the law was changed. Because of them the public will be protected from young killers like Jamie Savage. They will now face prison rather than two years of "treatment."

ALONG THE BANK OF THE RIVER

On April 9, 1982, Timothy, age 23, was dumped in the Winooski River. His body was found at a point where the river serves as the boundary between the small former "mill town" of Winooski and the much larger city of Burlington.

By 1982, the textile mills that had driven Winooski's economy had been closed for more than 20 years. The Champlain Mill, which borders the Winooski River, had been converted into commercial space—shops and restaurants. There was a large parking lot that sloped down to the Champlain Mill from the north. A "disco bar" called Le Club was located on the eastern edge of the parking lot.

A service road ran from behind the Le Club down to the Champlain Mill. The road led further to a parking lot and the service entrances to the Waterworks restaurant and other businesses in "the Mill." There was a concrete abutment at the east end of the Champlain Mill. The abutment bordered the Winooski River. A hole in the abutment permitted access to the flat, rocky riverbank.

Investigators determined that Timothy, who had just cashed his paycheck, had gotten very drunk while celebrating at local bars. He had been robbed and beaten in the parking lot near the abutment and then dragged through the hole in the abutment and along the rocky shore of the river. Evidence showed that the dragging started at a spot just upstream from where diners at the resturant can look out across the river to a tall brick smokestack at an abandoned mill in Burlington on the other side of the river.

Timothy's body hung up about 75 yards downstream from the hole in the abutment. The evidence also showed that Timothy was still alive, though probably unconscious, when he was dumped into the river. The state medical examiner said that the cause of death was "asphyxia due to drowning."

Timothy had been choked and beaten four times in the head with a large rock. His skull was fractured in two places. Investigators found the rock near the hole in the abutment. The rock had Timothy's hair and blood on it. There was no money in Timothy's wallet, no overcoat on his back, and no shoes on his feet.

His body was discovered after travelers crossing the bridge saw what turned out to be Timothy's body hung up on a rock in the Winooski River. The body was near the middle of the river, about eight miles from where it empties into Lake Champlain.

The spring snowmelt was on, and the river was running high and fast. The Green Mountain Power Company quickly closed the spillway at its hydroelectric dam upstream to enable search and rescue workers to recover Timothy's body.

Timothy was the youngest in a family of four brothers and two sisters. He lived in Winooski with his mother, Dorothy. He had overcome back injuries he'd suffered in an auto accident and had enlisted in the Army National Guard after attending Winooski High School. He had trained as a paratrooper and had received an honorable discharge in 1978.

Timothy was buried with full military honors, which included the presentation of an American flag to his mother, Dorothy.[40]

On May 26, 1982, a month and a half after his body was found, Chittenden County State's Attorney Mark Keller charged Richard "Ricky" Sorrell, age 23, and Timothy "Pucky" Miller, age 23, both of Winooski, with the second-degree murder of Timothy.

Both men were slender and well-built. Sorrell was described in law enforcement records as a dark-skinned, dark-haired Caucasian male who was 5 feet, 10 inches and weighed 170 pounds. He had just recently been released from prison after serving a sentence for armed robbery.

Miller was sandy-haired and light-skinned with tattoos on both forearms. He, too, was described as 5 feet, 10 inches and weighing 170 pounds.[41] Although the jury would never know it, Miller had racked up nineteen criminal convictions—including several for assault—in the six years since he'd turned 17 years old. Like Sorrell, he had only recently been released from prison. Miller had served four and a half years for assault and robbery.

While Sorrell was quiet and sullen, Miller tended to be much more open, sociable, and talkative—traits that frustrated his defense attorneys.

Winooski Detective David Leach, age 22, joined the Winooski Police Department in February 1982, shortly before Timothy's murder. Leach had gone into the US Army after graduating from high school in St. Albans, Vermont. He had little prior experience as a police officer—just a thirteen-month stint with the Sierra Vista in Arizona, Police Department from November 1980 through December 1981. Despite this lack of experience, Winooski Police Chief Anthony Grassano put Leach in charge of the Timothy murder investigation in April 1982. This was just two months after he'd begun working at the Winooski Police Department.[42]

At first it looked like the Chief's confidence in Leach was paying off. By late May, just a month and half after he'd been assigned to lead the investigation, Leach and other officers working with him had put together enough evidence against Sorrell and Miller to convince State's Attorney Keller to charge them with second-degree murder in the death of Timothy. In fact, Leach wrote the probable cause affidavit supporting the murder charges that Keller filed on May 26, 1982. But things went downhill fast for Leach after that.

On June 17, 1982, just three weeks after he wrote the affidavit charging Sorrell and Miller with Timothy's murder, Leach himself was arrested on three perjury charges for lying on another affidavit that he had written.

Officers from adjoining towns in Chittenden County often worked together to invesigate drug cases and obtain search warrants in drug cases. Two officers from the Town of Essex Police Department—which borders Winooski—became suspicious of Leach. Essex officers Gary Taylor and Robert Bouffard had become concerned that Leach was making up evidence in drug cases he was investigating.

Bouffard and Taylor had taken their concerns to Chittenden County State's Attorney Keller in early June. Keller had, in turn, gotten help from Vermont State Police detectives who'd posed as drug dealers. Together they'd developed a "sting" operation.

Leach claimed to have arrested one of the "drug dealers," who was, in fact, a state police detective who worked out of Brattleboro in the southern part of Vermont—150 miles south of Burlington.

Leach reported that the "dealer" had provided information that gave him (Leach) probable cause to believe that there was a quantity of cocaine in a South Burlington motel room. The claim was false. The "dealer's" conversation with Leach had been recorded. Leach put the bogus cocaine information in an affidavit and swore to the truthfulness of the information when he went to the home of Judge Edward Cashman for a nighttime ("after hours") search warrant for the motel room. This resulted in Leach's arrest on a perjury charges. [43]

State's Attorney Keller reviewed all of the cases Leach had been involved with in the four months he had been working for the Winooski PD, and he dismissed at least four of them. However, Keller did not dismiss the charges against Sorrell and Miller for murdering Timothy—charges that Leach had played a key role in bringing.

In late September 1982, I had been working in the Criminal Division of the Vermont Attorney General's Office for less than a month when I violated what has been said to be the one basic rule of new Army-enlisted men—"never volunteer." I volunteered to take on the prosecution of the second-degree murder cases of Richard "Ricky" Sorrell and Timothy "Pucky" Miller.

Neither man wanted a plea bargain. Each man demanded a jury trial. Each man would be tried separately.

As Chittenden County state's attorney, Mark Keller would have ordinarily prosecuted Sorrell and Miller. But Keller was about to go into private practice. And since his term ran out in November 1982, Keller had asked the Vermont attorney general, John Easton, to take over responsibility for trying the cases.

Keller's deputy, Susan (Sue) Fowler, would try each case with me. She had experience as a prosecutor and liked to try cases. She also knew more about the Sorrell and Miller cases than I did because she had been on the case since Timothy's body was first found.[44]

To convict Sorrell of Timothy's murder, Sue Fowler and I knew we had to prove each of the "essential elements" of second-degree murder[45] "beyond a reasonable doubt." In other words, we had to prove:

1. Identity: that Sorrell was the person who committed the acts we alleged (he "dunnit")

2. Causation: that Sorrell caused Timothy's death (e.g., not a suicide, an accident, or death by natural causes)

3. Unlawful Killing: that Sorrell's acts in killing Timothy were unlawful in that there was no legal justification for them (e.g., not done in self-defense or defense of others)

4. Intentional Killing: that when he unlawfully killed Timothy, Sorrell acted with either an intent to kill, an intent to do great bodily harm, or with a "wanton disregard" for the "likelihood" that death or serious bodily harm would result from his actions.[46]

There was no question that we could prove elements 2, 3, and 4. That is, there was no doubt that we could prove that Timothy was murdered. The undisputed evidence showed that he had been beaten in the head with a rock and that he'd been dragged face down across the rocky riverbank and dumped into the river while he was still breathing. There was no question that whoever had dumped Timothy into the river while he was still alive but unconscious had intended to kill him.

The only issue at trial was whether we were going to be able to prove the first element—"identity," i.e., that Sorrell and Miller had acted together in the murder of Timothy.

Sorrell and Miller both denied any knowledge of how Timothy had ended up dead in the Winooski River. When they were interviewed by police two days after Timothy's body was found, Sorrell and Miller each said that they'd had brief contact with Timothy outside Le Club on the night he was murdered. But each man insisted that that was the last they'd seen of him. They each said that they had left Le Club to go and pick up Miller's brother, Anthony.

Sorrell's trial was set for December 1982 at Vermont Superior Court in Burlington. This meant the trial was set for just six months after he was charged. Few murder cases go from charge to trial in Vermont that quickly.

The court-appointed lawyers assigned to defend Sorrell—Art Andersen and Phil Saxer—were skillful, experienced trial lawyers. They knew that Leach, the chief investigator on the case, was on his way to jail for lying on an affidavit in another case and that this had left his work on Sorrell's case suspect and in need of reinvestigation.

This was something they could exploit at trial. So they pressed for the "speedy trial" that Sorrell, who had been held in prison without bail since his arrest in May, was entitled to under the US and Vermont constitutions.

Like the prosecutors in the Hamlin-Savage case, we were relying on the law of "accomplice liability."

That meant we did not have to prove that Sorrell played any specific role, such as delivering a blow with a rock—only that he and Miller had worked together with a common purpose to kill Timothy. The judge would instruct jurors that if they found the prosecution had proven beyond a reasonable doubt that Sorrell and Miller had acted together with a common purpose to rob and kill Timothy, then each man was responsible for acts of the other.

In other words, Sorrell was criminally responsible for the acts Miller had committed in robbing and murdering Timothy, and vice versa. If it was Miller who had beaten Timothy in the head with a rock, according to the law, it was as if Sorrell had done it, too.[47]

The trial lasted five days—Monday, December 6 through Saturday, December 11, 1982.

Sue Fowler gave the prosecution's opening statement at the start of the trial. She and I had agreed that she would give the opening statement and I would give the closing argument and the "rebuttal closing."

In her opening statement, Sue Fowler laid out for jurors the events leading up to the discovery of Timothy's body and the investigation that led to the murder charges against Sorrell and Miller.

She told jurors that Timothy had worked for a cleaning contractor in Essex. After work on Thursday, April 8, 1982, Timothy had cashed his $227 paycheck and had begun to hit the bars in Winooski, his hometown. He'd been very drunk by the time he got to Le Club. In fact, he'd been asked to leave the bar on four occasions. He'd left briefly—but he'd just kept returning.

When Timothy had left Le Club for the last time around midnight, Miller and Sorrell had told the manager/owner of Le Club, Russ Martel, that they would "take care of" Timothy. The truth was that Timothy had been seen arguing with Sorrell and Miller outside Le Club. That was the last time Timothy was seen alive.

Roughly an hour and a half later, Sorrell and Miller had returned to Le Club. They'd spent lavishly. They'd been buying drinks for others and leaving large tips. This was in sharp contrast to their spending before they'd left with Timothy, when they'd bought drinks only for themselves and left no tips.

The evidence showed that before he left Le Club with Sorrell and Miller, Timothy himself had been spending wildly at Le Club from the proceeds of his paycheck. When police recovered Timothy's body, they'd found his wallet, but there was no money in it.

We argued that the question this all raised, of course, was: How did Sorrell and Miller come up with the "new money" in the hour and a half they were gone, and why wasn't there any money in Timothy's wallet? We argued that the obvious answer was that Sorrell and Miller, who were seen arguing with Timothy, had tried to rob him. When Timothy fought back, they had beaten him into unconsciousness. They'd then stolen all the money in Timothy's wallet and had gotten rid of his body by dumping him into the river.

On April 12, three days after Timothy was murdered, State's Attorney Keller had conducted an "inquest"—a secret proceeding—where several witnesses gave testimony under oath concerning circumstances surrounding Timothy's disappearance. The testimony at the inquest implicated Sorrell and Miller in Timothy's murder.

At the inquest, Miller's sister, Dorothy, said her brother, "Pucky" Miller, and Sorrell had come to her apartment, where Miller stored his clothes. This wasn't long after midnight on the morning Timothy had been murdered. It was also around the time Timothy had been seen arguing with Miller and Sorrell around a bus stop near the Champlain Mill.

Miller's sister lived at 114 West Allen Street in Winooski, less than half a mile from the spot where Timothy's body had been found. She testified that "Pucky" had taken a new set of clothes without ever turning on the light. She had turned on the light when the two men had come into her home, but her brother had immediately turned the light back off.

Miller' brother, Anthony, said that when he'd seen his brother "Pucky" and Sorrell sometime after midnight, both men had blood on their pants and the blood "looked fresh." Anthony had returned to Le Club with his brother and Sorrell after the men had changed their pants.

Miller's girlfriend, Elaine Bissonette, lived at 33 Malletts Bay Avenue, not far from where Miller's sister lived. Elaine Bissonnette also testified at the inquest that Sorrell and Miller each had spots of blood on their pants when they'd come to her home "some time after midnight." Miller had been holding his shoulder. She testified that when she'd asked her boyfriend what had happened, Miller had told her that he "had gotten into a fight with two negroes."

According to Bissonette, both men had brought a change of pants with them when they'd come to her home that night, and they'd changed into the new pants. Before they'd left, the men had asked her to wash the blood-stained pants they had been wearing when they had arrived at her home. She testified that she'd washed them at a laundromat in Winooski the following day.

We argued that physical evidence at the scene showed that Timothy was bleeding when he'd been dumped in the river and that, under the circumstances, the most reasonable explanation for the blood on their pants that evening around the time of the murder was that it was Timothy's blood.

The night of the inquest, Miller's sister, Dorothy, packed bags for her brother and Sorrell. They left for Florida that night. This happened just before a judge had approved State's Attorney Keller's request for second-degree murder arrest warrants for both men.[48]

A month later, Sorrell and Miller turned themselves in to police in Naples, Florida.[49]

We argued that the two men had left abruptly for Florida because they knew they were guilty of Timothy's murder and had fled the state to avoid being caught. They'd only turned themselves in a month later because they were out of money and knew they would eventually be caught.

We called approximately 12 witnesses before we rested our case on Friday morning, December 10, 1982. The evidence came in pretty much as we expected during the four days we put on our case.

The one major exception was the testimony of Elaine Bissonette, Miller's girlfriend. Bissonette had testified at the inquest that *both* Miller and Sorrell had blood on their pants when they'd come to her home not long after midnight on the morning Timothy had been murdered. But, at trial, she insisted that Sorrell *did not* have blood on his pants that night. I showed her the transcript of her testimony at the inquest, but she was adamant that only Miller had had blood on his pants.

However, Miller's brother Anthony testified contrarily to Bissonette—he said that both men had had blood on their pants when they'd come to Bissonette's home that evening. He said his brother, "Pucky," explained the blood on his pants by saying that he'd gotten in a fight. Anthony also testified, with some reluctance, that Sorrell and Miller had bought him "six or seven beers" when he'd returned to Le Club with them after they had changed their pants.[50]

David Leach, the disgraced former lead investigator in the murder of Timothy, testified as a defense witness on Friday, December 10. His testimony came after Sue Fowler and I had "rested" the prosecution case.

The defense had managed to bring Leach's conduct before the jury earlier in the trial through cross-examination of "Pucky's" sister, Dorothy. She testified that "a lot" of what she had told police "got twisted by Leach." Miller's sister also testified in response to a question from Defense Attorney Art Andersen that Leach had told her before the inquest that he'd been out to "get" her brother for Timothy's murder.[51]

Leach had already pled "guilty" to perjury for lying to a judge by the time of Sorrell's trial. But he had not been sentenced yet.

Under Vermont law, a person who has been "convicted" of perjury is disqualified from testifying in any court proceeding. But since he had not been sentenced yet, he had technically not been "convicted."

Although Leach was less than a week from sentencing and disqualification as a witness, the fact that he had not yet been sentenced meant that the defense could still call him as a "defense witness" when they put on their case on December 10, 1982.

William Braun, a reporter for the *Burlington Free Press*, covered the Sorrell trial. In his story about the last day of the defense case, Braun described Leach as a "key defense witness."

Leach told jurors that Sorrell and Miller had not appeared "nervous, disheveled, or wet" when he had seen them the evening Timothy was murdered. This was at a time, which the defense maintained, that Timothy had already been beaten and dumped into the Winooski River.[52] The obvious implication was that Sorrell and Miller could not have killed Timohy because any person who was truly responsible for the killing would have been "nervous, disheveled, and wet."

We didn't want to have anything to do with Leach or his testimony. My only response on cross-examination was to get Leach to admit that he had already pled guilty to committing perjury for lying to a judge.

(I later addressed the substance of Leach's testimony in my closing argument by pointing out that testimony of other witnesses showed that, contrary to the defense claims, the incident that Leach described had taken place *before* Timothy was last seen alive.)

The defense called a second Winooski police officer, Kim Halburian, who had been at Le Club the night Timothy was murdered. He and another Winooski police officer, Barry Lawrence, had both been off duty and were having a few drinks at Le Club when they came across Miller and Sorrell. They'd spoken with both men, who they knew professionally. Halburian told jurors that during the course of the conversation, Miller had said: "The next time I go down, it will be for something big."

The defense used this statement to support its argument that even if jurors were inclined to believe that somehow Sorrell and Miller had been involved in Timothy's murder, this statement showed that it was highly likely that Miller had killed Timothy by himself.

"Pucky" Miller was a former amateur boxer who all agreed had a reputation as a "street fighter." Miller had admitted that he'd been in a fight that evening. The defense argued that even if jurors tended to believe that Miller and Sorrell were together when Timothy was killed, it was more than likely that Miller had killed the drunken Timothy on his own with no assistance from Sorrell.

Richard Sorrell exercised his Fifth Amendment right under the US Constitution and declined to testify at his trial.

The defense's theory was that only one person killed Timothy and that person was "Pucky" Miller, Sorrell's co-defendant. In his opening, Defense Attorney Phil Saxer said that the evidence they would hear would be consistent with Sorrell's "complete innocence."

He said the evidence would show that "Pucky" Miller was a "fighter" who had been in a fight the night of the killing and would not need any help in handling Timothy alone. On the other hand, Sorrell, according to his lawyer, was "the quiet type." In fact, according to Saxer, the evidence would show that Sorrell was "scared, scared" of Miller.

As for Sorrell's trip to Florida with Miller after the inquest, Saxer said it was "only natural" that Sorrell had "returned" to Florida because he had lived and worked there recently.[53] Sorrell's other court-appointed defense attorney, Art Anderson, hammered this argument in his closing argument.

The main defense argument was that even if the jurors felt that Sorrell and Miller were involved in the murder, the killer was Miller—and the former amateur boxer had acted alone. Anderson said that the blood evidence of how Timothy had been dragged—alternating "blotches and streaks"—showed that just one man had dragged Timothy's unconscious body (the streaks), rested (the blotches), then dragged the body again, leaving another streak.

The windows of the Waterworks restaurant look directly out toward the area where Timothy's body was found. The manager of Waterworks had testified that he had looked out the window sometime between midnight and 12:30 a.m. on the morning of the murder and had seen two men—one of whom appeared to be drunk—moving along the bank. They'd stopped at a place on the river that was roughly parallel to the spot where Timothy's body was found hung up on a rock the next day. He could not identify the people he had seen other than to say they were "young men."

This testimony of the manager of the Waterworks restaurant turned out to be critical in the outcome of Sorrell's trial.

Art Anderson argued in the defense closing that the two "young men" walking were "Timothy [redacted] and his lone assailant." The defense had argued earlier that the "lone assailant" was probably Miller and certainly not Sorrell, who was the "quiet type" and not a "fighter" like Miller.

Bottom line, according to Anderson, there was only one killer—and he was not Richard Sorrell.

I argued that Anderson's "loan assailant" argument made no sense.

First, all the evidence showed that Sorrell and Miller were together all evening. They were together when they were arguing with Timothy at the time Timothy was last seen alive. They were also together when they visited Elaine Bissonette's home with blood on their pants, and they were together when they returned to Le Club and began spending money they didn't have earlier. There was simply no evidence that the two men had separated at the time Timothy was killed.

Second, I argued that it made no sense to believe, as Anderson claimed, that the "two young men" the Waterworks manager had seen walking in the area parallel to where Timothy's body was eventually found were Timothy and his killer. To believe this, I argued, the jury would have to believe that the "lone killer" had walked with Timothy along the river bank as if to say, "This is where I am going to dump you." It was much more likely, I said, that the "two young men" the restaurant manager had seen were Sorrell and Miller, who were walking along the bank of the river to see what had happened to the body they'd just dumped into it.

Although I didn't say it, I thought the defense had made a big mistake by making such an absurd argument because it was bound to undercut their overall credibility with jurors.

Wrong.

The jury only deliberated for a little over five hours on Saturday, December 11, 1982, before finding Richard Sorrell "not guilty" of the murder of Timothy.[54]

Shortly before they announced their verdict, jurors had asked the court reporter/stenographer to read the transcript of the testimony of the manager of the restaurant.

Investigators from the attorney general's office interviewed some of the jurors after the verdict in hopes that they could find out what mistakes we'd made and how we could do a better job in the trial of Sorrell's co-defendant "Pucky" Miller, which was coming up soon.

The jurors were clear. We simply had not convinced them that Sorrell was involved in Timothy's murder.

"Pucky" Miller's Trial

There was little time to mope about losing Sorrell's trial. The murder trial of his co-defendant, "Pucky" Miller, began in March 1983—a little over three months after Sorrell's acquittal.

David Leach, a so-called "key witness" in the Sorrell trial, would not be available for "Pucky's" trial. On Monday, December 13, 1982,[55] just two days after the jury acquitted Sorrell, Leach was sentenced to one to three years for the perjury he had admitted to a month earlier.[56] Once Leach was sentenced, he was formally "convicted" of perjury, and under Vermont law, he could not testify as a witness at any trial.

There was no guarantee that it would affect the ultimate outcome of the trial, but Sue Fowler and I were definitely going to be able to present a stronger case against Miller than we had against Sorrell.

This was thanks in large part to the work of two veteran investigators from the Vermont Attorney General's office. I had begun work on the Sorrell-Miller murder cases in September 1982. This was not long after the Vermont attorney general (AG), John Easton, was asked to take over. As soon as that happened, the AG's two criminal investigators, A. J. Ravenna and Randall "Randy" Moran, were assigned to the case.

Ravenna, who had served as a Vermont State Police detective for many years before coming to the AG's office, and Moran, who was a US Army Veteran (Airborne) and a former Burlington Police Department detective, re-investigated the Sorrell-Miller case since it had been "tainted" by disgraced Winooski Police Detective David Leach.

Moran and Ravenna located and interviewed new witnesses and re-interviewed old ones. In the process of doing this, they developed new leads and followed up on them. Ultimately, this meant that Sue Fowler and I were able to introduce new evidence that we didn't have when we tried Sorrell.

The trial lasted from Wednesday, March 16, 1983, through verdict on March 24, 1983.

In her opening statement on Wednesday afternoon, March 16, Sue Fowler reviewed the evidence surrounding Timothy's death. She walked through what happened from the time he came into Le Club drunk and disoriented late Thursday evening, April 8, 1982, through the discovery of his body hung up on a rock in the Winooski River. Then she described Miller's "flight" (hitchhiking) to Florida with Richard Sorrell. This came after the testimonies of several witnesses at an inquest led to arrest warrants issued for Miller and Sorrell.

We called roughly 16 witnesses in the prosecution case.

As the trial began, the *Burlington Free Press* highlighted the fact that security at the trial was "tight." Judge Paul Hudson had ordered tightened security. We had already had one incident of attempted witness intimidation by supporters of Miller, which I'll break down below.

The *Burlington Free Press* had also predicted that we would rely on "essentially the same circumstantial evidence" that had resulted in Richard Sorrell's acquittal.[57] This was not correct. There were two basic pieces of evidence that made our case against Miller stronger than the one we had presented against Sorrell.

First, investigators Ravenna and Moran were able to locate and obtain a statement from a witness whose testimony filled an important hole in our case by putting Miller and Sorrell with the victim near the site where he was beaten and murdered. Second, unlike Sorrell, who said very little, Miller had made false and contradictory statements about the source of the blood on his pants when he'd visited his sister after midnight on the morning Timothy was killed.

No witness in the Sorrell trial put Miller and Sorrell on the service road near the concrete hole in the abutment where Timothy was dragged. The witness developed by Moran and Ravenna before the Miller trial did just that.

Miller and Sorrell had admitted to having brief contact with Timothy outside Le Club. But they had insisted that they had no further contact with him after that, instead heading for Miller's sister's house. Her house was in the opposite direction from the service road.

On March 3, 1983, less than two weeks before the Miller trial was to begin, I got a call from Russ Martel, the manager of Le Club. Martel said that Daniel Tobler, a part-time DJ at Le Club, had information on the Timothy murder. I contacted investigators Moran and Ravenna, who located Tobler and obtained a statement from him on the evening of March 3.[58]

Tobler told Moran and Ravenna that he had been in the DJ booth at Le Club with the "on duty" DJ on the evening of April 8, 1982. He said that around 8:30 p.m., he saw two men drinking with off-duty Winooski Police Officer Kim Halburian. He later identified these men through separate photo lineups as Richard Sorrell and Timothy "Pucky" Miller.

Tobler told investigators that sometime between 11:30 p.m. and midnight on April 8–9, he had gone behind Le Club to urinate before driving home. He said he could see well because of lights in the parking lot and the lights down at the Champlain Mill. While standing at the corner behind Le Club, Tobler said, "Three guys came around the corner from the front of Le Club." The "guy in the middle was really drunk," and the "other two guys," who were on either side of the man in the middle, "were sort of helping him walk." Tobler went on to identify the two men who were helping the drunken man walk as Sorrell and Miller, who he had seen drinking with Winooski Officer Halburian.

Tobler said the last time he'd seen the "three men," they were walking on the service road "down towards the river's edge."[59]

Tobler's testimony filled the hole in our case, putting Sorrell and Miller with Timothy walking down the service road toward where he was beaten sometime between 11:30 p.m. and midnight.

It looked very good for our case at that point. But things quickly went downhill.

On March 4, 1983, I notified Miller's attorneys, Robert Keiner and Michael Kupersmith, that we would be calling Tobler as a witness based on the statement he had given to Moran and Ravenna the night before.

Keiner and Kupersmith were experienced, capable defense attorneys. They quickly arranged to take Tobler's sworn deposition. At his deposition, Tobler said that he *could not* identify any of the men he had seen walking around from the front of Le Club.

That was the way things stood until Tuesday, March 15, while we were selecting the jury.

My recollection is that someone had notified police that Tobler's life had been threatened.

Moran and Ravenna interviewed Tobler again the next day. When he was re-interviewed, Tobler reverted to his original statement. He said once again that he could identify the three men he had seen walking down toward the spot where Timothy was killed as Miller, Sorrell, and Timothy.

Tobler explained that he had changed his testimony at the deposition because he'd been threatened. He had returned to his car at some point after giving his original statement, and he'd found that his windshield had been smashed and a note had been left that said, "You're next."

When Tobler finally testified on Friday, March 18, he described what he had seen between 11:30 p.m. and midnight on April 8, 1982—the night Timothy was murdered. Tobler told jurors he had seen two men helping a third drunken man come from the front of Le Club and walk down toward the spot where Timothy was beaten. But Tobler could not identify Miller as one of the men.

Fortunately for us, we still had the fact that Tobler had identified Miller and Sorrell as the two men when Ravenna and Moran had shown him photo lineups two weeks earlier. As I recall, it was Moran who testified later in the trial to the fact that Tobler had already identified photos of Sorrell and Miller.

The defense elected not to cross-examine Tobler. It was a smart move. The judge had barred us from asking Tobler about the broken windshield and threatening note in our direct examination of him. If they had cross-examined Tobler, they would have "opened the door" for us to ask Tobler on redirect examination about the threats against him after he gave the statement that implicated Miller in the murder.

As mentioned earlier, unlike Sorrell, who said little to anyone about what had happened during Timothy's murder, Miller had made many statements that were not only contradicted by other witnesses but also contradicted by Miller himself.

Miller's girlfriend, Elaine Bissonette, and Miller's brother, Anthony, both testified that they had seen blood that had appeared "fresh" on Miller's pants when he'd gone to Bissonette's home sometime after midnight on the morning Timothy was killed.

Two days after the murder, Miller was interviewed by a Vermont State Police detective, and he denied any contact with Timothy either inside or outside Le Club—other than to offer him a ride. Miller said Timothy was talking with "three Black men" outside Le Club when Miller offered him a ride. At that point, Miller said, one of the Black men told Miller to leave, so he did.

But Russ Martel, manager of Le Club, told jurors that Miller and Sorrell did have contact with Timothy and, in fact, had agreed to "take care of" Timothy after he'd been ejected from the club for the last time. According to Martel, he saw Miller a couple of hours later after he had agreed to take care of Timothy. He thanked Miller for taking care of Timothy and asked what had happened with him. According to Martel, Miller replied, "We lost him. . . He's pretty much a ding-a-ling—he was always threatening to commit suicide."[60]

Miller's brother, Anthony, testified that his brother, the defendant "Pucky," had explained the blood on his pants that night by saying he'd gotten into "a fight at the Mill Restaurant" earlier in the evening and that he "had beat some guy up."[61] At another time, Miller had said that the fight at the Mill Restaurant was with "two Black men." However, we produced evidence that the Mill Restaurant had been closed that night.[62]

We introduced these statements through the testimony of witnesses who spoke to Miller the morning Timothy was murdered and in the three days after that before he and Sorrell fled to Florida.

Sue Fowler and I argued that these statements showed that Miller had lied repeatedly about what had happened the morning Timothy was murdered. And, as prosecutors—including me—often tell jurors: "People only lie when they know the truth would hurt them." We argued the truth was that the blood on Miller's pants was Timothy's blood—blood that had gotten on Miller's pants when Miller and Sorrell were beating and robbing Timothy and dragging his unconscious body to the Winooski River.

The basic thrust of the defense case was that we, the prosecution, had failed to meet our burden to prove Miller's guilt beyond a reasonable doubt because the evidence we had asked the jury to rely on was at best ambiguous and in some cases unreliable. The defense called seven witnesses on Monday, March 21 and Tuesday, March 22.

If the defendant asks for it, the judge is required to give a jury instruction similar to the one I have copied below, which has been approved by the Federal 9th Circuit Court of Appeals:

> A defendant in a criminal case has a constitutional right not to testify. In arriving at your verdict, *the law prohibits you from considering in any manner that the defendant did not testify* [my emphasis].

In my experience, most defense attorneys do not ask for this jury charge because they fear it only highlights the defendant's decision not to testify.

In my first closing, I went through a detailed review of the circumstantial evidence that showed jurors there was "no doubt based on reason" that Miller and Sorrell had acted together in beating, robbing, and dumping Timothy in the Winooski River shortly after midnight on April 8–9, 1982.

I started with the fact that on the morning he was murdered, Timothy had been very drunk and very disruptive at Le Club. He was asked to leave the Le Club four times. The manager of Le Club, Martel, claimed that Miller had said he would "take care of" Timothy—whom Miller had known in high school—to ensure he stayed out of Le Club and didn't make any more trouble.

I reminded them that sometime between 11:30 p.m. and midnight, Daniel Tobler had seen two men he had identified as Sorrell and Miller come around from the front of Le Club, walking a drunken man down the service road toward the spot where the blood evidence showed that Timothy had been beaten. Jurors also heard from the manager of the restaurant, who told them that sometime between midnight and 12:30 a.m., he had seen "two young men" whom he could not identify walking along the banks of the Winooski River in an area parallel to the area in the river where Timothy's body had hung up on a rock. I said that the only reasonable conclusion was that the two men the manager had seen were Miller and Sorrell.

Then, sometime after midnight, Miller and Sorrell went to Miller's girlfriend's home with blood on his pants that looked "fresh," according to Miller's brother. His girlfriend's house was a half a mile or less from where Timothy had been beaten.

I asked jurors to remember that Miller had lied about his contact with Timothy that evening and about the source of the blood on his pants. He told state police Detective Ron Williamson two days after the murder that he'd had no contact with Timothy that night. He told Williamson that he had intended to offer Timothy a ride home when he saw him outside Le Club. But he told the state police detective that Timothy had been with "three Black men" and that one of those men had waved him away.

In fact, though, there was no question that Miller had had contact with Timothy that night. Witnesses had told jurors that Sorrell and Miller were with Timothy around midnight the morning Timothy had died.

I argued that when he volunteered this "always threatening suicide" comment, Miller knew that Timothy's body was in the Winooski River and was likely to be discovered at some point. Miller also knew that he and Sorrell were the last people to be seen with Timothy before his death. I said the "suicide comment" was Miller's clumsy attempt to provide a preemptive explanation for when Timothy's body was ultimately found in the river.

As for the blood on Miller's pants, I reminded jurors that Miller had lied about where it came from. At one point, he explained it by saying he had gotten in a fight and had broken the guy's nose. At another point, he claimed he had gotten into a fight with two Black men at the Mill Restaurant. But as we know, the restaurant was closed that night. Why did Miller lie? I said the answer was simple: He knew the blood was Timothy's.

Finally, there was the fact that Miller had decided to hitchhike to Florida with Sorrell on April 12, 1982, the day after several witnesses had given testimony at an inquest that implicated both men in Timothy's murder. It made no sense to think that Miller's decision to leave for Florida at that time was a mere coincidence.

Miller's lawyer, Michael Kupersmith, was an experienced defense attorney who would go on to become an outstanding trial court judge. He told jurors that we simply had not proven our case. He said we had presented circumstantial evidence that was "very suspicious" but that the jury could not convict Miller of murder on suspicion alone. We had to prove our case beyond a reasonable doubt, and we hadn't.

Kupersmith accused investigators of having "tunnel vision" in focusing on Sorrell and Miller. He said that "suspicious circumstances could have just as easily linked five other men to the murder." And he pointed out that the prosecution had not presented "a single shred of physical evidence" linking either Miller or Sorrell to the murder of Timothy.

According to the *Burlington Free Press* account of his closing, Kupersmith "likened the state's case to a 'grand house of cards.' You have to marvel at the skill with which it's put together, but let a breath of fresh air come in the door and the house of cards the state has built on circumstance and speculation will come tumbling down."[63]

My closing argument in rebuttal was relatively brief. I asked the jury to "try to think of a reasonable explanation for Miller's conduct." I said, "If you can, you should acquit him." But I told them that there was no way the evidence they had heard would allow them to come up with any reasonable explanation of Miller's conduct other than that he was guilty of murdering Timothy. I pointed at Miller—"That's the man who was going to take care of Timmy. He took a human life and dumped it in the Winooski River like it was a piece of garbage." I said it was their duty to "speak for the community" and find Miller guilty.[64]

My family and I didn't live far from the Chittenden Superior Court on Main Street where the trial took place. A clerk at the court called me at home when the jury sent a note to Judge Paul Hudson announcing they had a verdict. It took at least thirty minutes to get the attorneys together before the jury could announce its verdict.

Waiting for the jury's verdict is a notoriously nerve-racking time for all trial lawyers. It was particularly so for me and Sue Fowler since we had already lost the Sorrell trial. Oddly enough, an hour before the jury announced its verdict, it asked for a "readback" of the testimony of the manager of the restaurant—the man who had seen "two young men" walking along the bank of the river parallel to the spot where Timothy's body had hung up.

This, of course, was the same testimony that Richard Sorrell's jury had asked to hear again before they had found Sorrell "not guilty" four months earlier.

This time it was different. The jury announced its verdict around 2 p.m. on Thursday, March 24, 1983—Miller was "guilty" of murdering Timothy. Jurors had deliberated for eight hours after closing arguments on Wednesday and then four more hours on Thursday.

I think the difference this time was Daniel Tobler's testimony. Because he came forward about what he saw at midnight on the night of the murder, we won the case.

Miller's sentencing hearing was on June 2, 1983, roughly two months after the jury found him guilty of murdering Timothy.

I pointed out to Judge Paul Hudson that Miller was 23 years old at the time that he and Ricky Sorrell robbed Timothy, beat him with a rock, and then dumped his unconscious body into the Winooski River. His second-degree murder conviction for killing Timothy was his 20th conviction since he had turned 16 years old. His earlier convictions included six for assault and one for assault and robbery. I asked the judge to sentence Miller to a "long time" in prison for the protection of the public.

Dorothy, Timothy's mother, also testified. She, too, asked the judge to sentence Miller to a "long time" in prison. I met with her before the Sorrell trial and then again after losing it. She was a kind, thoughtful person who was heartbroken.

Dorothy worked as a waitress at Howard Johnson's Restaurant in Burlington. Her coworkers had gathered together and attended her son Timothy's funeral to support and console her.

Dorothy said she felt sorry for Miller's family. But they would get to visit Miller in prison. Her son was gone forever. She said she would have to live with the constant reminders of him as she went to work. "I have to travel that road, cross that bridge, see that hole he was shoved through, see that bus stop, and I wish I could pick him up there. He took a lot of me to the grave with him."[65]

Judge Hudson sentenced Miller—who continued to insist on his innocence—to serve 20 years to life in prison to protect the public. Hudson also told Miller that "whatever light you have is a light Timmy [redacted] does not have."[66]

Miller appealed his conviction to the Vermont Supreme Court. Bill Nelson, an experienced, highly regarded appellate attorney from the Vermont Office of the Defender General argued before the Court that Miller's conviction should be reversed.

I argued the case for affirming Miller's second-degree murder before five justices of the Vermont Supreme Court at the Supreme Court building on State Street in Montpelier in the same room where I had been admitted to the practice of law five years earlier.

Miller's conviction was affirmed by the Vermont Supreme Court on July 19, 1985[67]—a little over two years after his conviction and sentencing. It was a unanimous decision that stated clearly that the jury had lawfully convicted Miller of second-degree murder under the accomplice liability theory despite the fact that Sorrell, his alleged accomplice or "co-conspirator," had been acquitted.[68]

PREYING ON THE ELDERLY

On July 7, 1982, Cornelia "Nellie" Irish, age 87, and her sister, Clara Carlson, age 93, were enjoying the garden in front of the home they shared on a quiet side street in South Burlington, when two men approached them.

The taller of the two men, who was later identified as Ralph Bissonette, age 41, pointed out that there were several shingles missing from the roof of their house. He said the roof should be repaired immediately. Bissonette told the ladies that he and the man with him, later identified as Norman Bevins, age 40, would do the job right away for $1,800.

Bissonette then tricked Mrs. Irish and Mrs. Carlson into believing that Mrs. Carlson's financial advisor had approved the work. Bevins drove both women to a local bank, where Clara Carlson obtained a cashier's check for $1,800 that was made out to "James Blackmer," who was Bevins's brother-in-law. Bevins then drove the ladies home.

Blackmer cashed the check that afternoon in Essex Junction. That was around the same time that Bissonette and Bevins were replacing the six missing shingles on the sisters' home.

On April 23, 1983, around a month after the "Pucky" Miller murder trial, Assistant Attorney General Ted Hobson and I tried Norman Bevins before a jury in District/Criminal Court in Burlington.

Hobson, a lawyer in the Consumer Protection Division of the

Attorney General's Office, had already been working on the case with Armand "Bucky" LaCount, a smart, dogged investigator in the Consumer Protection Division. Lacount had been pursuing Bevins and Bissonette and people like them for years.

Ted Hobson had charged Bevins and Bissonette with the crime of obtaining money by false pretenses,[69] a felony punishable by up to 10 years in prison, for defrauding Mrs. Carlson out of $1,800.

This was not the first time these men had preyed on the elderly.

Bevins had been convicted of fraud in the 1970s for cheating an Addison County woman in a roof repair scam. His brother-in-law, James Blackmer, had pled guilty to petit larceny and was sentenced to serve 15 days in jail on March 23, 1982, for cheating the same elderly Addison County woman out of $300 in another phony roof repair job. This was just three months before Mrs. Carlson wrote Blackmer a check for $1,800 to replace six shingles.

Bissonette had pled no contest in early 1982 for obtaining $195 from a Colchester woman for insulation he'd never installed and for obtaining $500 from a South Burlington woman for roof repairs he'd never made. This was just a few months before he'd cheated Mrs. Carlson in a new roof repair fraud.

Bevins and Bissonette also stood accused of cheating a 75-year-old Burlington woman out of $2,460 the month before they'd cheated Mrs. Carlson. The Burlington woman told investigators that Bissonette and Bevins had come to her home and pointed out that several bricks needed to be replaced for $35. After they got on the roof, they'd told her that the chimney was in worse shape than they had first thought. They'd said that an "inspector" from the fire department would have to look at the chimney because it might pose a safety hazard.

A bogus "inspector" came to the house and said the entire chimney needed to be replaced. Bevins and Bissonette did the job for $2,460.[70]

Under the law, the juries in the April–May 1983 trials of Bevins and Bissonette would not be told anything about these "prior bad acts" by Bevins and Bissonette.[71]

Bevins's trial lasted four days. We picked the jury and called witnesses on Monday and Tuesday. We had closing arguments after the defense put on their witnesses on Wednesday. The jury reached its verdict on Thursday, April 27.

Ted Hobson did the opening. We took turns on the direct examination of witnesses. I did the closing argument.

On the face of it, the case was somewhat complicated. We had to prove that Bevins had "by false pretenses. . . with intent to defraud" obtained the $1,800 from Mrs. Carlson.[72] We could prove that Bevins had obtained the $1,800 cashier's check from Mrs. Carlson, but it was Bissonette who had lied to Mrs. Carlson to get her to agree to pay for the roof repair.

In fact, though, it wasn't complicated. We relied on the law of "accomplice liability," just as Susan Fowler and I had in the "Pucky" Miller murder trial a month earlier.[73]

We could prove that Bevins and Bissonette had gone to Mrs. Carlson's house with a common purpose—to cheat Mrs. Carlson, the owner, out of $1,800. Under the law, Bevins was criminally responsible for "Tinker" Bissonette's lie. In other words, Bissonette's lie was Bevins's lie.

Our first witness was William Bissonette (no relation to Ralph), who knew Norman Bevins because Bevins had stayed for a time at the motel he managed. He testified that on the evening of July 6, 1982, the day before Mrs. Carlson had written the $1,800 check, he'd seen Bevins walking up the Carlson-Irish driveway with two other men.

Other neighbors who kept an eye on the Carlson-Irish house out of concern for the elderly women had testified that there were no shingles missing on the Carlson-Irish house during the day of July 6. It had been later that day, after nightfall, that William Bissonette spotted Bevins and two other men walking up the elderly sisters' driveway.

There had definitely been shingles missing from the house the next day. We argued that it was reasonable to believe that Bevins was responsible for the missing shingles. We contended it was not a coincidence that the shingles went missing between the time he and two other men were walking down the sisters' driveway on the night of July 6 and the time he appeared the next day with Ralph Bissonette.

Bevins and Bissonette had lied to the ladies and told them that they had noticed the missing shingles while they were working on a house nearby.

Helen Lawrence of Essex Junction, a financial advisor to the 93-year-old Clara Carlson, laid out for jurors how the Bevins-Bissonette scheme played out. She had received a phone call on Wednesday, July

7, 1982, from "Nellie" Irish. Mrs. Irish had told her that two men had come to the house and wanted to be hired to fix shingles on the house she shared with her sister, Clara Carlson.

Mrs. Lawrence testified that she'd told Nellie Irish that she would not approve the repairs. "We would always get an estimate for a big job like that," she explained.[74] She testified that a short time later she'd gotten another call, but the line went dead when she'd picked up her phone. She never approved the job.

Clara Carlson, the 93-year-old victim, never testified. But her sister, Nellie Irish, did. Mrs. Irish, who was 88 years old at the time of the trial, told jurors that two men had come to the home on July 7, 1982, and pointed out the missing shingles. She said that the men had wanted the job of fixing the missing shingles but that Mrs. Lawrence had said not to hire them.

Mrs. Irish went on to testify that the two men would not take "no" for an answer. They had eventually gotten her to call Mrs. Lawrence again, and the taller of the two men (Bissonette) had appeared to be speaking with Mrs. Lawrence. After a while, he'd hung up the phone and announced to the sisters that Mrs. Lawrence had said to go ahead with the roof repair.

Mrs. Irish did not identify Bevins at trial. But she said that it was the shorter of the two men who came to their house on July 7th who later drove her and her older sister to the bank. Mrs. Irish told jurors that her 93-year-old sister had obtained the $1,800 check, which was payable to the man later identified as Bevins's brother-in-law, James Blackmer.

Investigator Armand LaCount testified that not long after the incident, Nellie Irish had identified photos of both Bevins and Bissonete as the two men who had come to their home. He also testified that Mrs. Irish had identified a photo of Bevins as the man who had driven her and her older sister to the bank.

James Blackmer, Bevins' brother-in-law, swore that he was the one— not Bissonette—who had negotiated the $1,800 deal with Mrs. Carlson. He said he was the one who'd driven Mrs. Carlson to the bank—not Bevins.

His story was a tough sell. He said Mrs. Irish was "mistaken" when she'd said two men had come to speak to her and her sister. Blackmer, age 38, said that he had picked up two men to do the repair to the sisters' roof, and they had waited outside while he'd spoken to the ladies, who'd readily agreed to do the work. He didn't remember their names or where he'd met them. He speculated that it might have been at a tavern.[75]

Blackmer swore that he and the two men had spent two hours replacing "six shingles" after getting the $1,800 "bank check" from Mrs. Carlson. He knew the law. It seems like it should be a crime to charge a 93-year-old woman $1,800 to replace six shingles, but it isn't. "Overcharging" is not a crime. So Blackmer wasn't admitting to anything other than being a nasty, cold-hearted man.

I remember saying to the jury that the defendant, Bevins, claimed he'd never met Mrs. Irish. "So to believe that, you would have to believe that Mrs. Irish decided to come to court for the first time in her eighty-eight years" in order to falsely implicate Norman Bevins, a man she had never met, in a crime. Beyond that, they would have to believe that Helen Lawrence had come to court and made up a story about a phone call from Mrs. Nellie Irish asking for $1,800 for repairs.

Norm Blais, who was Mark Keller's chief deputy for a while when I first started at the Chittenden County State's Attorney's Office in 1979, was Bevins's defense attorney. He tried to plant a "reasonable doubt" in jurors' minds about whether the neighbors' claims that they had seen Bevins the night before the shingles disappeared was accurate.

The jury deliberated for at least two or three hours before going home for the night. But not long after they reconvened the next morning, they announced their verdict—"Guilty."

On May 16, 1983, three weeks after Norman Bevins's trial, Ted Hobson and I tried Ralph Bissonette before a new jury in district court for his role in defrauding Mrs. Carlson.

It took us a day and a half to pick the jury. This was much longer than usual in non-homicide cases.[76] Many people had heard of the Bevins trial and said they had prejudged Bissionette. We went through all the potential jurors on the first day, and the court clerk had to call in more potential jurors on the next day—Tuesday.

We called most of the same witnesses we had called in the Bevins trial. There was at least one important difference. Mrs. Nellie Irish had been unable to pick out Norman Bevins in court at Bevins's trial. But she had no trouble picking out Ralph Bissonette as the man who had lied to her and told her that Mrs. Lawrence, the trusted financial advisor, had approved the roof repair job. In fact, I can still picture her frail hand shaking as she pointed toward Bissonette.

James Blackmer testified again that he and two other men whose names he could not remember had replaced six shingles for $1,800.

The jury had little patience for Blackmer, or Bissonette, for that matter. You wouldn't have needed a "jury consultant" to read the jurors' mood. When Blackmer testified in support of Bissonette's defense, several sat staring straight ahead with their teeth clenched and their arms folded across their chests.

Paul Jarvis, an experienced defense attorney who had been a deputy state's attorney under Patrick Leahy,[77] tried to convince jurors that Blackmer had lied to protect his brother-in-law Bevins and that, in fact, Bevins and Blackmer had been the two men who had cheated Mrs. Carlson. Mrs. Irish had simply been mistaken when she had identified Bissonette as the person who had lied to her.

Ted Hobson, who did the closing argument this time, asked jurors to remember the testimony of Mrs. Irish: "You just can't believe this eighty-eight-year-old lady would come in here and tell you anything but the truth."

The jury agreed. They announced their "guilty" verdict in an hour.[78]

On July 28, 1983, three months after the jury convicted him of defrauding Clara Carlson, trial judge Frank Mahady sentenced Bevins to a "split sentence"—three to six years to serve, with all but 18 months suspended.[79] As a practical matter, this meant that Bevins would serve 18 months or less in prison.

Two weeks later, Judge Arthur O'Dea sentenced Ralph Bissonette to three to six years to serve in prison in early August 1983.[80] He told Bissonette that his treatment of the elderly made him "an undesirable person to have among us" and that "a hallmark of civilized society is respect for the elderly."

The Vermont Supreme Court confirmed the Bissonette conviction in February 1985[81] and the Bevins convictions in July 1985.[82]

A Quarry Hole Killing

In late fall, 1983, Terry Trono, the Washington County state's attorney, asked me to assist him in the first-degree murder trial of Harold Norton.

The killing took place on Labor Day Weekend, 1983, at the Wells Lamson Granite Quarry in Barre—a small city with a population of 9,278 in Central Vermont.[83]

The victim, Robert, died from injuries he'd sustained after he'd fallen 260 feet and struck the water at the bottom of the Wells-Lamson Quarry hole at approximately 88 miles per hour. State police divers found Robert's body on a rock ledge about eight feet below water level.

Harold Norton, 29, was the man charged with killing Robert. He was, as they say, "not unknown to police." He had served prison time two years earlier for kicking a 50-year-old Barre man in the head until the man was unconscious.

The Barre police chief, Raymond Jacobs, told reporters that Norton's and Robert's families often feuded. According to the chief, it was "sort of a Hatfield and McCoy thing."

This was not an Agatha Christie murder—no poisonings, no fiendish plots, no deranged nobles. I recall telling jurors in my opening statement that Robert died during "a night of drinking, brutality, and lies." That summed it up pretty well.

Our evidence showed that it all started at a party at Quarry Hole No. 6—one of 70 inactive granite quarries in the Barre area.[84] Robert had arrived at the party on Saturday night, September 3, 1983, with a friend, Dwight. Norton had arrived with his friend David "Frenchy" Charette.

Charette and Norton left the party in Charette's pickup truck around 2 a.m. on Sunday morning. Dwight, Robert's friend, had argued with Norton earlier in the night. For some unknown reason, Dwight and Robert tried to jump into the bed of Charette's pickup. Dwight made it. Robert didn't. Charette stopped, and he and Norton dragged Dwight out of the truck and left him on the dirt road.

Robert and Dwight started walking down the road away from the party site. Charette turned around and tried to "scare or run over" Robert and Dwight by driving his truck at them.[85] This happened at least three more times. Finally, Charette stopped his truck near the entrance to the Wells-Lamson Quarry. This quarry was one of the few "active" or "working" granite quarries in Barre. It was only half a mile from the party site.

Norton got out of the truck with a hammer belonging to Charette and began chasing Robert and Dwight.

Dwight fell as he was running away. When he looked up, he saw Norton swinging the hammer at Robert. It was around 3 a.m. on Sunday morning, September 4, 1983. Dwight ran to a nearby house and called police.

Police came in contact with Norton around an hour later at 4 a.m. Norton told the officer he spoke to that he had gone first to his girlfriend's house after he'd left the party at Quarry Hole 6 and that his girlfriend had kicked him out. The officer asked Norton why his knuckles were bloody. He told the officer that he had become angry with Charette for leaving him at the party at Quarry Hole 6 and had punched a piece of granite.

A little later, Norton told another officer a different story. He told this officer that he had gone to his sister's house after he'd left the party and had become angry and punched a wall. Norton denied any knowledge of Robert or what had happened to him.

For his part, David "Frenchy" Charette told police that Norton had told him to leave as Norton was jumping out of Charette's truck with a hammer to go after Robert and Dwight. Charette said that he had gone to the home of a woman he had recently met, and that later that day, he had met Norton at the home of Norton's girlfriend. According to Charette, Norton had said: "You should have been there. I made sixty-five dollars. I pissed on [Robert's] head and his eyes curled."[86]

Police began the search for Robert that night, but it wasn't until Monday, September 5, 1983 (Labor Day), that Dwight found blood spots and some loose change near the edge of the Wells Lamson Quarry hole.

The blood spots were analyzed by the Vermont forensics lab and found to be consistent with Norton's blood type, which was relatively rare. Only 1.5 % of the general population had this blood type. The blood spots were inconsistent with the blood of Charette, Dwight, or Robert.[87] This was before the days of DNA, when we could get an exact match.

The Vermont medical examiner (ME) found, as mentioned earlier, that Robert had died of injuries he'd sustained when he'd hit a submerged rock after falling 260 feet from the quarry's edge. But the ME also made another significant finding. He found that Robert had suffered a fractured hyoid bone, which is a bone in the neck just below the jaw. The ME said that in his opinion, the injury was consistent with Robert being choked or strangled.

We also retained a "blood spatter expert." He told us that in his opinion, the blood spots were drops of blood consistent with someone standing or moving slowly near the edge of the quarry hole with blood dropping straight down from an injury that he had suffered.

This physical evidence supported our theory of the case.

Terry Trono and I believed the evidence showed that after Dwight ran for help, Norton had beaten and choked Robert into unconsciousness near the edge of the quarry hole. Norton had stood over Robert, went through his pockets to steal his money (hence the loose change), and then carried, or dragged, Robert—who was still breathing but unconscious—to the edge and dropped him to his certain death.

Terry Trono and the defense attorneys, Kim Cheney and Nancy Kaufman, were concerned that pre-trial publicity about the killing would probably make it difficult to pick an impartial jury in Washington County. But rather than have the case tried in another county ("change of venue"), they agreed to pick the jury from residents of Windsor County, roughly 50 miles to the south, and try the case in Barre, where all the witnesses lived. As I recall, the jurors were "sequestered" at a motel in Barre for the duration of the trial.

I got on the case shortly before we selected the jury in Windsor County. It took no more than two days.

Terry Trono, as the state's attorney, would be the "lead" at the trial, and I would be "second chair." That meant that I would do the prosecution's opening statement, and Terry would do the closing argument. We would split the witnesses we intended to call on direct testimony.

I believe that I did the direct testimony of the chemist who analyzed the blood near the edge of the quarry hole and the medical examiner who testified as to Robert's injuries and his cause of death. I also did the direct questioning of police who spoke to Norton an hour after Dwight had seen him chasing Robert with a hammer. And I did at least one of the witnesses who saw Norton a day or two after the murder.

Terry Trono did the rest of the witnesses, including "Frenchy" Charette, who was the most important (and difficult) of our witnesses.

The trial took place in Barre in late March 1984—roughly seven months after Robert was murdered. It took a little over a week to try the case.

Our case went pretty well until we got to Charette. His direct testimony was consistent with what he had told police. But Defense Attorney Kimberley Cheney, a former Vermont attorney general, did a good job dismantling Charette's story on cross-examination.

Cheney's questions were, of course, designed to show that it was Charette, not Norton, who had attacked Robert. For example: *You were driving your truck the night of the party, right? Isn't it true that Dwight and Robert tried to jump in the back of your truck? That made you angry, didn't it? You heard Dwight's testimony, didn't you? You were the one who tried to run over Dwight and Robert at least three times, weren't you? You stopped your truck at the entrance to the Wells Lamson Quarry hole as Dwight and Robert were approaching—right? You testified that at that point my client, Harold Norton, got out of the truck and told you to drive away. That doesn't make sense, does it? That would have left him alone with no way to get home, wouldn't it? In fact, you were the one who got out of the truck and chased Dwight and Robert—weren't you?*

Norton testified in his own defense. He denied that he was in any way involved in Robert's murder.[88] Norton told jurors that it was Charette, not Norton, who had gotten out of his truck and began chasing Dwight and Robert. Norton testified that he couldn't see what happened after that, but he'd heard Charette and Robert screaming at each other near the edge of the quarry. Norton said he went to investigate and had walked near the edge of the quarry (thereby explaining why his blood was found there). He went on to tell jurors that Charette had called out to him that they should go because the police were going to be coming, and then, according to Norton, they'd left in Charette's truck.

Norton, a construction worker, was tall, lean, and fit. Terry Trono's argument to the jury was that Norton had choked Robert into unconsciousness, dragged or carried him to the edge of the quarry, and intentionally dumped his body over the edge of the quarry.

Defense Attorney Kim Cheney argued that we had not even come close to meeting our burden of proof. We hadn't proven Norton's guilt beyond a reasonable doubt. In fact, the evidence showed that it was more likely that Charette was responsible for Robert's death.

We were not sure what the jury would decide. There was no question that Cheney had badly damaged Charette on cross-examination.

The jury found Norton was "not guilty" of first-degree murder, which had a maximum sentence of life in prison. However, the jury did find Norton "guilty" of involuntary manslaughter, which had a maximum sentence of 15 years.

What happened? Why did it happen? The jury's decision actually made good sense. To prove first-degree murder, we had to prove that Norton had intentionally killed Robert. But we simply hadn't proved that he'd acted intentionally.

Our argument that the blood evidence that showed that Norton had been standing over Robert's body going through his pockets while he lay there unconscious simply didn't survive Charette's cross-examination. Cheney's cross-examination showed that Charette had lied about his role in what happened, which cast doubt on everything Charette said. This including Charette's claim—which was central to our argument—that Norton had told him that he (Norton) had stood over Robert while he lay unconscious on the quarry edge.

But there was no doubt that Robert had been strangled before he went over the quarry edge—the fractured hyoid bone proved that. Norton's claim that his blood was at the edge of the quarry because he had gone out there to find out what had happened between Charette and Robert was at the very least suspect.

Bottom line—we had left jurors with a "hot mess." But Judge John Connarn had told jurors in his instructions to them that if they didn't find that the prosecution had proven Norton was guilty of murder, they could consider whether the prosecution had proven "involuntary manslaughter."

For that to happen, they would have to find beyond a reasonable doubt that the evidence showed that Norton had unlawfully but unintentionally caused Robert's death.[89] That is, he "consciously disregarded a substantial risk" that his conduct would cause death. Norton's conduct easily met that standard: He had attacked Robert and beaten and strangled him near the edge of the quarry hole. It was reasonable for the jurors to conclude that Robert had fallen into the hole while he was fighting with Norton or while he was trying to escape from Norton.

Judge Connarn sentenced Norton to serve 12 to 15 years on May 25, 1984. Trono had recommended a sentence of 14 to 15 years based on Norton's poor performance while he was on probation for the aggravated assault—the case mentioned earlier in which he kicked a much older man into unconsciousness.[90]

The Vermont Supreme Court affirmed Norton's conviction two years later on June 26, 1986.[91]

THE RAID AT ISLAND POND

On June 22, 1984, a little after dawn, approximately 140 Vermont state police and social workers seized 112 children living in the community of the Northeast Kingdom Community Church. The church, which came to be known as Twelve Tribes,[92] was located in Island Pond, a Vermont village of around 800 people near the border with the Province of Quebec. The officers and social workers were acting under the authority of a search warrant and juvenile petition that I had helped obtain from a Vermont judge a day earlier.

There was no dispute that what came to be known as the "Island Pond Raid" was a shocking use of the state's power. David Dillon, spokesman for Vermont Governor Richard Snelling, told reporters at the time that the decision to conduct the raid was "absolutely agonizing." Dillon said the State made the decision to conduct the raid "only after every other avenue to discover the welfare of the children had been explored."[93]

Criticism of the raid was quick and harsh. A *Burlington Free Press* editorial writer, for example, compared us to Nazi storm troopers:

> Troopers swooping down on a small Vermont village to round up families who subscribe to an unorthodox religious philosophy awaken visions of booted storm troopers invading Jewish ghettos in Europe to pick up people who did not share the religious beliefs of the majority.[94]

No one, including church leaders, disputed reports from dozens of former Twelve Tribes members that young children in the Twelve Tribes community from age 6 months through early adolescence were subject to being struck repeatedly with slender wooden rods called "balloon sticks"—sometimes until they bled. More importantly, there was also no dispute that it was a basic tenet of the Twelve Tribes' beliefs that this "discipline" should be routinely inflicted not only by a child's parents but also by any one of the roughly 100 adult members of the church community.

Church leaders insisted the State had no right to interfere with this conduct because it was protected by their First Amendment right to "free exercise of religion"—to practice religion as they saw fit. They said that the "community's children" were struck repeatedly with sticks "out of love." The beating was necessary, they said, to "drive out Satan" whenever a child, particularly a young child, had been "deceitful" or had engaged in "fantasizing" or "reasoning."

Vermont Social and Rehabilitative Services (SRS) social workers had tried for more than two years to investigate multiple reports that children in the Twelve Tribes community, particularly those under 10, were subjected to systematic abuse. But no adult member of the Twelve Tribes community had ever recognized the Vermont law that gave the State the right to investigate to protect children. They said children were the "community's children" and God's law trumped any Vermont law.

"God's law" was interpreted by Elbert Spriggs, that is, the church's founder, as well as the "elders" Spriggs had appointed. Their interpretation of God's law gave adult members of the Twelve Tribes community what they considered to be the "right" to engage in "righteous lies" when state social workers sought to speak to adults in the Twelve Tribes to investigate reports that "the community's children" were being abused.

What were these "righteous lies?" When social workers asked about a specific child who was reported to have been abused, church members either lied and said they did not know the child or lied and said that the child and the child's family had moved to another community run by Spriggs' church, such as the Twelve Tribes community in Nova Scotia.

One thing was clear. Unlike their parents, the children we sought to examine had not chosen to be members of the Twelve Tribes. They had not chosen to be part of a religious community where they were subject to random punishment by any of the adults in that community for "reasoning" or "fantasizing." These children had not chosen to be part of a religious community that prohibited them from attending public school. Nor had they chosen to be part of a religious community that would consistently leave their medical care to members of the Twelve Tribes who had little or no medical training.

The ultimate purpose of the "Island Pond Raid" was to take the children into temporary state custody for 72 hours to determine the extent of the continuing medical neglect or physical and psychological abuse at the hands of all adult members of the Twelve Tribes community.

Our effort to protect the children ultimately failed. In my opinion, it failed because several Vermont judges focused solely on the adults in the Twelve Tribes and their right to "free exercise of religion." These judges ignored the independent rights of the children to be free from what the European Court of Human Rights condemned some 30 years later as the "institutionalized violence"[95] that was a fundamental tenet of the Twelve Tribes' religious beliefs.

In 1984, there were about 400 people in the Twelve Tribes "community" in Island Pond.[96] This was one of several offshoots of a church that had been founded in the early 1970s in Chattanooga, Tennessee, by Elbert Eugene Spriggs, AKA "Yoneq," or the "anointed one." Spriggs' teachings have been described as "a sort of hybrid of Christian fundamentalism, Hebrew Roots, and Messianic Judaism." [97]

In 1978, Spriggs moved a large component of his church—Twelve Tribes—to Island Pond. The village of Island Pond is roughly 17 miles from the Quebec border in the heart of what is known as Vermont's "Northeast Kingdom."

Twelve Tribes members were encouraged to believe that Spriggs was the "prime instrument that God's going to use to set up his Kingdom on earth." Spriggs' church was expanding. By the time of the "raid" in late June 1984, Spriggs was not in Island Pond. He was splitting his time between the Twelve Tribes in Island Pond and church settlements in Europe and Nova Scotia.

Judge Joseph Wolchik approved the state's request to temporarily detain all children in 20 buildings "used or occupied by" Twelve Tribes members on June 21, 1984. The seizure of the children took place the following day on Friday, June 22.

Wolchik had actually signed a warrant to search Twelve Tribes buildings in Island Pond roughly two weeks earlier on June 9. The warrant had been obtained by Phil White, who was the state's attorney in Orleans County.

At the time, Essex County, where Island Pond is located, had a population of approximately 6,000. They had one part-time prosecutor who worked out of an office in St. Johnsbury, which was a 45-minute drive from Island Pond.[98] White was a full-time prosecutor in Orleans County (population 27,000), which bordered Essex County. White had learned of a building in Barton, a town in White's county, where children from the Twelve Tribes were taken by church elders to hide them when social workers were in Island Pond investigating reports of child abuse.

White had evidently become frustrated with the failure of high-level Vermont state officials in Montpelier to respond effectively to numerous complaints of child abuse at the Twelve Tribes community.

On June 8, he and the investigator assigned to his office, James Leene, filed a "warrant application," which included the proposed search warrant and three supporting affidavits. They did this with Judge Wolchik, who at the time was working in the Orleans County Courthouse in Newport, Vermont.

The documents supporting White's warrant request were voluminous. White had subpoenaed investigative materials held by Vermont State Police Detective Peter Johnson, who worked in the Northeast Kingdom and had been the lead police investigator in the Island Pond case.

There were three supporting affidavits—one by White himself, which specifically identified 11 children in the Twelve Tribes community who had been abused by specific Twelve Tribes members. There was a second by Christopher Braithwaite, editor of the *Barton Chronicle*, whose newspaper covered Orleans and Essex counties, and there was a third affidavit by Leene, White's investigator.

White also submitted transcripts of interviews of people who had left the church community as well as two reports from physicians who had examined children in the community and an investigative report from Detective Johnson. He and SRS social worker Conrad Grims had done much of the work in investigating allegations of abuse.

The search warrant that White submitted and Judge Wolchik signed specifically identified 20 buildings that were controlled by the church. According to the supporting affidavits, there was probable cause (reasonable grounds to believe) that the buildings contained evidence that the children in these buildings were at risk of abuse and medical neglect.

On June 12, three days after Wolchik had signed the first search warrant, White, Leene, and Braithwaite met with Vermont Governor Richard Snelling and asked him to assign Vermont law enforcement officers to assist in executing the warrant that Judge Wolchik had signed. Snelling said, "No." But he did ask White to meet with some of his top advisors to describe the situation in Island Pond to them.

Two days later, on June 14, White met with Deputy Attorney General Charles Bristow; Snelling's legal counsel, Dean Pineles; Public Safety commissioner Paul Philbrook; and Dr. John Burchard, Commissioner of Social and Rehabilitation Services (SRS). They, too, initially rejected White's request.[99]

Pineles, Snelling's legal counsel, at first told White that the State would not help execute the warrant Judge Wolchik had signed. But state leaders changed their minds on June 19 after another Vermont judge, F. Ray Keyser, reversed himself and freed seven Twelve Tribes leaders who he had originally ordered jailed for contempt for refusing to answer questions about allegations of child abuse.[100] Once that happened, Governor Snelling approved an action based on Wolchik's warrant.

Importantly, though, the action that Governor Snelling approved on June 19 was not to uncover evidence of a crime. The purpose of the proposed action was based on Vermont's juvenile law, which not only authorized but required[101] state social workers to take steps to investigate reports of child abuse.

Under the plan that the leaders developed, the Attorney General's office would submit a petition under Vermont's juvenile law that was supported by an affidavit of probable cause. Phil White would resubmit the documents he had submitted for a search warrant. This time, they would be submitted in support of a juvenile petition to Judge Wolchik.

The judge would be asked to authorize temporary seizure of children living in the Twelve Tribes community under Vermont's juvenile laws so that SRS workers and physicians could examine them for the evidence of physical and emotional abuse that more than twenty former church members had reported to SRS social workers and investigators.

Deputy Attorney General Charlie Bristow, who was himself a former Vermont District Court judge, came to me on June 20, the day after

Judge Keyser reversed himself. Bristow asked me to present the juvenile petition to Judge Wolchik the following day in Burlington.

Bristow asked me pointedly if I thought there was "probable cause" to believe the children in the Twelve Tribes were at persistent risk of abuse. I said, "Yes," there was probable cause. That is, I believed documents we would present to Judge Wolchik would show that there were "reasonable grounds to believe" that all children living in the Twelve Tribes community in Island Pond were at immediate and persistent risk of "abuse" and "neglect" as defined in Vermont statutes.

My focus at the time Bristow called on me to present the petition to Judge Wolchik was on reviewing and editing the affidavit I had put together from transcripts of interviews done by state police and social workers in 1982 and 1983 with adults and children who had left the Twelve Tribes.

I paid particular attention to the transcript of an interview I had done with Jeff Jenke, a young man who had left the church community in March 1984, just three months before Phil White obtained the warrant from Judge Wolchik. I spoke with Jenke at the Burlington airport as he was about to fly home to Texas.

Jenke had been in the church community in Island Pond since the summer of 1983. As it turned out, my interview with him was the last interview of a former Twelve Tribes member before Judge Wolchik signed the order to pick up the children three months later.

Jenke told me that church members' determination to "discipline" children with wooden rods to drive out sin and bring them closer to God was as strong when he left the community on March 16, 1984, as it was when he moved into the community in the summer of 1983. He told me—as all other "defectors" from the church community told us—that any adult member of the community could use the rod on any child in the community as they saw fit, regardless of whether the child's parents agreed.

Jenke had lived in a church building in Island Pond that was called "Timothy's House." He said that all of the children in Timothy's House were disciplined by the adults who lived in the house except him. He named the nine adults who had done the disciplining and the seven children who they had "disciplined."[102]

I had not been aware of what Phil White had until he presented Judge

Wolchik's order to Governor Snelling on June 12. But five or six months earlier, I had proposed getting a court order to examine all children in the Twelve Tribes community. My proposal had been rejected at that time by senior officials in the Snelling administration who were more familiar with the process in juvenile courts—the courts that would have to rule on any motion to examine the children.

I had been a lawyer for less than five years at the time I started working on the Island Pond cases and had no experience in the juvenile system. At that time, I had been an assistant attorney general in the criminal division of the Attorney General's Office for roughly a year. Most of my time had been spent doing jury trials. These were cases that local state's attorneys had asked for help on or cases that had been generated by the attorney general's investigators.

In the early fall of 1983, I was assigned to take an active role in the investigation of allegations of child abuse and neglect at the Twelve Tribes community. During that time, I probably spent half my time working on Island Pond cases. I traveled to Island Pond more than once and met with state police and social workers who were working on the investigation. I also conducted recorded interviews of people like Jenke who had left the church community.

However, my primary contribution to the investigation was to draft the affidavit that I mentioned earlier. That affidavit cited and summarized the work of investigators—Detective Cpl. Peter Johnson of the Vermont State Police, Conrad Grims of SRS, and Detective Randall (Randy) Moran of the Vermont Attorney General's Office.[103]

The affidavit, which was eventually signed by Detective Moran (Moran affidavit) was a "work in progress" from November 1983 to June 20, 1984, the day before Judge Wolchik approved the petition and authorized the seizure of the children.

Phil White and I presented the petition and request for the second search warrant to Judge Wolchik on June 21, 1984, at the Vermont District Court in Burlington. Even though I worked out of the AG's office in Montpelier, the court in Burlington was familiar to me. I knew many of the people at the court from my days working as a Chittenden County deputy state's attorney from 1979 to 81.

I got my first strong indication that Judge Wolchik's decision to grant the earlier warrant authorizing the seizure of the children in the church community was not favored by others in the judiciary when I saw Judge Edward Costello as I was going through the court clerk's office to meet with Judge Wolchik and present the petition and warrant package to him.

I had appeared before Judge Costello many times when I'd worked as a deputy state's attorney in Chittenden County. I liked and admired him. Judge Costello looked shocked and angry when he saw me. He said: "You're not part of this, are you?" He gave me a long hard stare as I walked past him and into the office where Judge Wolchik was waiting.

There was a court reporter in Judge Wolchik's office who created a verbatim record of what was said at the hearing we had before Wolchik. (She later provided all parties with a transcript.)

Phil White essentially resubmitted the same information that he had presented to Judge Wolchik roughly two weeks earlier—three affidavits (Leene, Braithwaite, and White) and the hundreds of pages of supporting documents generated by SRS social workers and investigators from the state police and the Vermont Attorney General's Office.

White's affidavit identified 11 children who were assault victims by name and cited specific documents that detailed the assaults. It also detailed the death of two children, ages 8 months and 15 months, in the Twelve Tribes community—deaths that likely would have been avoided if the children had received adequate medical care.

Altogether, Phil White and I presented Judge Wolchik with well over 200 pages of documents that were referenced in the three affidavits that we gave to Judge Wolchik.

The juvenile petition that I signed and presented to Judge Wolchik asked him to find that there was probable cause to believe that "the health and welfare of all children residing in the church community in Island Pond are endangered because of their surroundings, that they may leave or be removed from the jurisdiction of the Court or will not be brought before the court, notwithstanding the issuance of a summons."

The Vermont law that governed investigation of allegations of abused and neglected children was Chapter 12, of Title 33 of Vermont Statutes covering "Children in Need of Care and Supervision (CHINS)." A child in need of care and supervision is a child who is: abused by a parent, guardian or caretaker; or a child who is "neglected" because they are "without proper parental care or. . .education, medical or other care necessary for his well-being."[104]

The Moran affidavit (27 pages) that I had put together in support of the petition was divided into sections corresponding to definition of a child in need of care or supervision: "Physical Abuse"; "Psychological"/"Emotional Abuse"; "Medical Neglect"; and Neglect of the Child's Education as well a section on the Twelve Tribes' "Attitude Toward the Law."

The basic supporting documents for the Moran affidavit and the three affidavits filed by Phil White were:

1. Reports and transcripts of interviews and hearing testimony of 28 people who had left the Twelve Tribes community that state police and SRS workers had recorded.

2. Eighteen juvenile petitions that contained facts and circumstances supporting the allegation that each one of the 18 children was a "child in need of care or supervision"[105] due to "child abuse" resulting from "discipline" meted out by Twelve Tribes adult members.[106]

3. State officials had been unable to serve any of the petitions because members of the Twelve Tribes refused to cooperate in identifying the children and adults who were named in each petition and supporting affidavit. These Twelve Tribes adults had relied on the "righteous lies" described earlier to make it impossible for state officials to serve the summons on the children and their parents.

4. A report written by Dr. Joseph Hasazi, an expert in child psychology, which explained in detail why he "believed strongly that all children residing in the Island Pond Community are at risk of physical and emotional abuse."

Some of the key pieces of evidence submitted to Judge Wolchik and eventually to Judge Frank Mahady are described below.

Children born into the Twelve Tribes community in Island Pond were ultimately the children of the "community"—not necessarily their parents;

> They (the children) are expected to live with their birth parents but if the parent is having problems with the children they are expected to give that child up on the basis that because that is not their child it is God's child the community's child.

Every one of the 28 former members of the Twelve Tribes (children

81

and adults) referred to in the affidavits and supporting documents described incidents where children in the community (from infancy through adolescence) were "disciplined" with wooden rods by adult members.

Again, Twelve Tribes leaders did not deny this. They said that because it was a basic tenet of their religion, they had a First Amendment right to do so.

In February 1983, David Jones, a Twelve Tribes elder, testified at a pre-trial hearing in the criminal assault case against another elder, Charles Eddie Wiseman, that unless children are disciplined with wooden "rods," they will not find salvation: "According to the word of God, without discipline, a child left to itself will bring shame to its father. . . . If they are not trained to know within themselves the desperate need for salvation, there will be no last generation on earth that brings about the collapse of the reign of Satan."[107]

One man who had lived in the church in Chattanooga and then in Island Pond, told investigators that "disciplining" children born into the church community was, in fact, the most important tenet of the church.

> The primary goal of the church is to discipline the children. . . .
> It's not money or industries, the first prime concern is the discipline of the children.

> The strongest of these [revelations from God] was the revelation of discipline, and this discipline is required by every member of the church, and not in the sense of it, it's not a spoken thing, but if you don't you can believe there is going to be pressure on you to discipline your child in that fashion. With the rod in that way. *And you're also expected to discipline other people's children.*[108] [my emphasis]

The undisputed fact that all adult members of the Twelve Tribes could discipline was a key source of concern for many involved in the investigation, including child psychologist Dr. Joseph Hasazi.

Carey Taylor, who left the church community after being a member for five years, testified at the Gregoire custody hearing before Judge Frank Mahady in 1983 that he had disciplined approximately *65 different children* with a rod during his time with the church. He said he had disciplined some children for failing to obey an adult "on first command," others for interrupting adults at the table, and some were disciplined with the rod for "asking for seconds" at meals.[109]

In November 1982, Christopher Braithwaite covered a two-day hearing involving efforts by Juan Mattatall, a former church member, to obtain custody of five children ages 2 through 9 years old who were being held in the church community by Mattatall's wife, Cynthia. Throughout the hearing Judge Ernest Gibson heard three former church members describe how children in the Twelve Tribes community were "disciplined" for up to two hours. He ordered that custody of the four children be transferred from the Twelve Tribes community and be turned over to their father, Mattatal.[110]

David Robinson, another former church member, testified that he saw the wife of one of the church's elders discipline two boys between 2 and 3 years old who had "strayed away from the nursery." According to Robinson, "She whipped the children until blood came down their legs." Robinson complained about the whipping of the boys to Elbert Spriggs himself. But nothing came of his complaint.

Linda Kelly, who lived in the Twelve Tribes community in 1982, told investigators in August 1983 that a 5-year-old girl was "scourged"— beaten with a stick for half an hour on her neck and calves—for being "deceitful" about the number of strawberries she had eaten.

"Scourging" was a step up in severity from normal "discipline," which involved striking a child repeatedly with a balloon stick on bare skin for five to 10 minutes. According to Ira Sawyer, who left the church community in 1982, the average child was "disciplined 20 to 30 times per week."[111]

"Scourging," on the other hand, involved striking a child, who was lying face down, intermittently with the stick for a longer period of time—sometimes as long as three hours. During the periods when the child was not being beaten, they "received" oral "reproof," or reprimands to emphasize the seriousness of being "deceitful."

Kelly explained that church members kept the intervals between blows during scourging uneven so that the child would not know when the next blow was coming. She said this was to "terrorize" the child— again to emphasize the seriousness of being "deceitful." She told investigators that a 4-year-old boy was scourged by his parents in the summer of 1982 for lying about having permission to play with a toy truck.[112]

Another young boy, DF, age 11, testified at the Gregoire hearing that he was hit eight times on the bare buttocks with a "paddle made of a two by four" by Twelve Tribes member Timothy Pendergrass. DF's father testified that he was not told until after the beating had happened that his son had been "disciplined." DF's father said that he had, in fact, asked earlier that his children not be disciplined by other members of the community.[113]

Both Pendergrass and Charles "Eddie" Wiseman, a member charged with misdemeanor criminal assault for "scourging" 13-year-old DC, another child, had the same defense—their conduct was protected by the First Amendment's "free exercise of religion" clause.[114]

Judge Arthur O'Dea rejected Wiseman's "freedom of religion" defense in March 1984—roughly three months before Judge Wolchik, acting on information and affidavits provided by Phil White and Chris Braithwaite, signed the first order authorizing the "pickup" of all children in the Twelve Tribes community on June 8, 1984.

Judge O'Dea wrote: "Members of the [Twelve Tribes] have a religious belief in the use of corporal punishment in the discipline of their children. The beating described in the probable cause affidavit is not corporal punishment; it is criminal assault."[115]

The Twelve Tribes community in Island Pond did not rely on licensed physicians for most medical treatment. Instead, it relied on people with nursing skills, midwives, and one person with training as a medical corpsman. Members were told they could seek professional medical assistance if their faith was weak, but otherwise they should trust in God rather than "worldly" outsiders.[116]

There were instances where nearby physicians were contacted to treat children, but these calls came too late. Police and social workers identified three babies who had died in the church community who might have been saved if they had received proper medical treatment. Two of the babies were buried illegally without death certificates, and a third died after the child's mother rejected a doctor's recommendation and refused to bring the child to the hospital.

We were all concerned that other infants and babies might still be at risk and that still others may have died "unknown" given the Twelve Tribes' refusal to keep birth and death records.

In December 1980, Robert Chambers, a Twelve Tribes member, was convicted of the felony "unlawful burial"[117] following a jury trial in the Essex County Courthouse in Guildhall.

Bob Gagnon, who was head of the AG's criminal division, tried the case for the State of Vermont. Gagnon was an outstanding trial lawyer who later taught trial practice at Vermont Law School. He was also a former Washington County state's attorney and one of the lawyers I had admired most when I had a chance to cover jury trials as a reporter for the *Barre-Montpelier Times Argus* newspaper.

Chambers was represented by the Vermont Office of the Defender General. He claimed the prosecution and conviction violated his First Amendment Right to free exercise of religion. I filed a brief and argued in support of upholding the conviction on appeal. The Vermont Supreme Court upheld the conviction[118] in March 1984. Chambers's lawyers attempted to appeal the case to the US Supreme Court, but the Court declined to hear the case.

The facts of the Chambers case provide a good example of the type of "selective obedience" to Vermont law that Twelve Tribes members exhibited in the time leading up to June 1984.

A child had died stillborn at a home owned by the Twelve Tribes on June 18, 1980. A member of the church had contacted a local doctor to examine the child and sign a death certificate. The doctor examined the child but refused to sign a death certificate. Instead, he contacted Vermont's chief medical examiner, who ordered an autopsy. Robert Chambers, the father of the dead child, rejected the autopsy order. He said the child's death was "God's choice." While police were waiting at the funeral home to transport the body, other members of the Twelve Tribes took the body to a waiting car and drove it away.

The Chambers case also introduced state officials to two people who would become key players in the struggle between the Twelve Tribes and the State of Vermont—Charles "Eddie" Wiseman and Attorney Jean Swantko.

When questioned by police as to why the Chambers child's body had been removed before the autopsy, Wiseman, a church elder, told police that it was "a question of who owns the child."[119] The Twelve Tribes' insistence that it "owned" complete control over all children in their community was the consistent obstacle state officials faced when they tried to investigate reports of physical and mental abuse of those children.

Wiseman himself was charged with criminal assault two years later, in July 1983. He was charged for striking 13-year-old DC, the daughter of a Twelve Tribes member, with a wooden rod for being "deceitful." She was allegedly stripped to her underpants and beaten on her back and ankles intermittently over the course of several hours. In the intervals between the beatings, "she was forced to detail two incidents in which she was sexually molested by adult men in the community." One witness counted 89 welts on her back. Her father told investigators that his daughter's back looked like a "zebra." As I said above, the Twelve Tribes referred to this type of "discipline" as "scourging." [120]

Wiseman was represented in the case by Attorney Swantko, a Vermont public defender. Swantko later joined the Twelve Tribes and married Wiseman, and she was living in the Twelve Tribes community at the time of the raid. She represented the Twelve Tribes in several cases in Vermont in the 1980s and 1990s.

According to an article in *Burlington Free Press*[121] published a week after the raid, documents filed with Judge Wolchik in support of White's affidavit described the events surrounding the December 1980 death of the 15-month-old child of John Sargent, a Twelve Tribes member.

The child, who was treated by members of the Twelve Tribes community, had a fever on December 7, 1980. After recovering briefly the next morning, the child developed a fever of 105.6 degrees around noon. The child "appeared lifeless around 5 p.m." and then began to suffer seizures around 7 p.m.

Dr. Bolton was finally called on the phone at 10 p.m. His diagnosis was that the child had meningitis, and he "recommended immediate hospitalization." The child's mother refused to bring the child to the hospital.

The child went into "respiratory arrest" around 1 a.m. Dr. Chad Finer, who lived in Island Pond, came to the Sargent home around 2 a.m. and confirmed the child was dead. According to Dr. Eleanor McQuillen, the state medical examiner at the time, "prompt medical attention in all likelihood could have and would have saved the child."[122]

In a similar instance, the death of 8-month-old Xiomara Rodriguez in October 1981 "appears to have been as a result of a lengthy process of gradual physical deterioration," according to a July 1, 1984, *Burlington Free Press* story that reviewed documents attached in support of Phil White's affidavit. Vermont State Police (VSP) Trooper Kathleen Cunningham, the outpost trooper serving Island Pond at the time, had reported that the child had received some medical attention in Maine. But the child had not been treated by a physician while she was living with her parents in the church community.

As with the Chambers child in June 1980, the Rodriguez child was "unlawfully removed" and buried without a permit, and her parents "fled the jurisdiction." Trooper Cunningham reported the incident but "the case went nowhere."[123]

Richard Cantrell ("Gladheart") was the primary member of the Twelve Tribes community who provided medical services such as suturing, removal, and minor surgery. This was done in the Twelve Tribes clinic located above the restaurant the church operated in Island Pond. Cantrell was convicted of the crime of practicing medicine without a license in spring 1984, just a few months before Judge Wolchik's June 21 approval of the order to temporarily seize the children in the Island Pond community.

Braithwaite covered the trial for his paper. Cantrell was sentenced to 30 to 40 days—all suspended. The judge ordered Cantrell to "prepare a written plan to eliminate all further engagement by you of practicing nursing or medicine without a license." Cantrell responded, "It would be very difficult for me to say that I am not going to do this anymore. I don't think I am ready to dismantle what I have received."[124]

As with Wiseman and Pendergrass on the assault charges and Chambers on the "unlawful burial" charge, Cantrell had not denied the factual allegations. He defended his actions on the grounds that he was exercising his First Amendment right to "free exercise of religion."

Cantrell's conviction was eventually affirmed by the Vermont Supreme Court in 1989—five years after his conviction by the jury.[125]

There was no dispute that children born into the Twelve Tribes community were not permitted to attend public schools. Investigators interviewed two children, ages 13 and 15, who had attended school in the church community. They said that only younger children up to age 12 attended classes at the school in a building in the Island Pond community and that classes lasted three to four hours per day. The 13-year-old, Laurie, told investigators that there were no books in her classroom, that her teachers were members of the Twelve Tribes community, and that the emphasis was on religious instruction. Most of the teachers in the Twelve Tribes schools had no training.

This, in itself, was a basis for finding that these children were "Children in Need of Care and Supervision" under Vermont law. I brought truancy charges against two parents of Twelve Tribes children in 1984 before the raid.[126] The parents, who were represented by one of Vermont's most prestigious law firms, defended on the grounds that the charges violated their First Amendment right to "free exercise of religion." The trial judge denied their motion to dismiss. The parents filed an interlocutory appeal to the Vermont Supreme Court.

The Vermont Supreme Court, which was plagued by "docket backlog" in the 1980s, did not issue a decision on the motion until 1990—six years after the raid and long after I had left the Vermont AG's office in 1987. The Court affirmed the trial court's denial of the parents' motion to dismiss in a thirty-page opinion by Justice John Dooley.[127]

To me, the report by Dr. Joseph Hasazi, a University of Vermont professor and an expert in child psychology, was one of our most compelling pieces of evidence. Dr. Hasazi reviewed reports and transcripts of interviews conducted by SRS investigators before he actually met in early fall 1983 with parents and children who had left the Twelve Tribes.

The report he provided to SRS was detailed and thorough. Dr. Hasazi concluded that, as an expert in child psychology, he believed "strongly that all children living in the Twelve Tribes community in Island Pond can be considered at risk for physical and emotional abuse."[128]

Dr. Hasazi's report focused first on the manner in which adults in the Twelve Tribes punished, or "disciplined," the children in their community. He said that in his opinion the "disciplinary practices," which were a basic tenet at the core of Twelve Tribes doctrine, posed "a specific threat to children" who lived in the church community.

In his opinion, these practices were "excessive in terms of frequency, duration and intensity." The fact that discipline was "begun in infancy" was particularly troubling to Dr. Hasazi. He explained that infancy is a "period in which children are particularly vulnerable to physical and emotional harm." He went on to say that the Twelve Tribes' disciplinary practices "appear to be designed to humiliate as well as hurt without regard for the children's sense of modesty or dignity."[129]

In Dr. Hasazi's opinion, the problems with the Twelve Tribes' disciplinary practices that he had identified were "compounded by the fact that all adults in the community can punish any child, and under some circumstances are obligated to do so." He said that as a consequence, a "child is exposed to possible abuse by 100 or more adults and not simply to parental abuse."[130]

According to Dr. Hasazi, the children's psychological well-being was further threatened by the degree to which Twelve Tribes doctrine required parents to defer "parental judgment" and control of their children to church leaders. He found that Twelve Tribes doctrine, as interpreted by "elders" speaking for the church "community" at times required "one, or both parents to be separated from their children" and even denied all access to their children if "the community," speaking through the elders concludes it is "desirable."[131]

The planned examination of the children by state physicians, psychiatrists, and social workers never took place. Judge Frank Mahady, who replaced Judge Wolchik on the day of the "raid," denied the State's motion to temporarily detain the children and ordered that the children be returned to the community in Island Pond. Mahady had replaced Judge Wolchik—the judge who found there was "probable cause"—only a day earlier.

Vermont's first administrative judge Thomas Hayes had chosen Mahady to replace Wolchik. More than thirty years after the raid, one prominent Orleans County lawyer, Duncan Kilmartin, told a reporter for the *Caledonian-Record* that Hayes had told him on the day of the "raid" that Judge Hayes had replaced Wolchik with Mahady because Wolchik had become too involved.

Kilmartin said that Hayes had told him that Wolchik had, in fact, been "a party to the planning" of the raid and thus had a "conflict of interest" that should disqualify Wolchik from the case.

A fierce critic of the raid, Kilmartin told the reporter that without Hayes' intervention, and that of God, Judge Wolchik would not have been replaced and the State's effort to seize and examine the children would have succeeded: "In my opinion Tom Hayes was divinely appointed to be the administrative judge."[132]

In my opinion, Judge Hayes focused solely on adults in the Twelve Tribes, who he saw as soft-spoken, hardworking men and women with unpopular religious beliefs whose rights were being crushed by overzealous prosecutors.

He saw himself as a valiant crusader for justice who embraced, even reveled in, his perceived role as protector of what he saw as the adult Twelve Tribes members' First Amendment right to "religious liberty." But as far as I could tell, he had spent little or no time considering rights of the "children of the community" and the overwhelming evidence that these children were at constant risk of being abused.

The ultimate question in the juvenile petitions we filed with Judge Wolchik was whether the children in the Twelve Tribes community were in "Children in Need of Care or Supervision" (CHINS).[133]

In order to obtain legal authorization to temporarily examine the children for evidence of physical and emotional abuse as well as medical neglect, we needed to present enough evidence to get through a two-step process.

First, we needed sufficient evidence to convince a judge that there were "reasonable grounds" to believe that all children living in the 20 buildings in the Island Pond community were subject to daily ongoing risk of physical and mental abuse. This would authorize the judge to sign what was called a "pickup order"—an order authorizing police and social workers to seize the "at risk children" and bring them and their parents to court. Judge Wolchik, who had signed White's search warrant two weeks earlier, had granted the pickup order and renewed White's warrant on June 21, the day before the raid.

Once the children were "seized," the law required that they be brought before a judge for a "temporary detention hearing"—a hearing (step two) at which we would again have to convince a judge that the children should remain in SRS custody for up to 72 hours because they "may be harmed" by "continued residence in [their] present environment."[134]

At dawn on June 22, 1984, 90 Vermont State Police officers working with 50 SRS social workers executed the "pickup order" authorized by Judge Wolchik. They brought the children to Newport, where Judge Wolchik was sitting as the designated judge. The children and their parents were held at a gymnasium where they waited for the State to try to prove its case in temporary detention hearings to be conducted by Judge Wolchik. But Judge Mahady conducted the hearings—not Judge Wolchik.

I did not know Judge Frank Mahady. But I had tried the Norman Bevins trial before him a year earlier and had gotten along well with him then.

Christopher Braithwaite's affidavit had summarized and quoted from rulings that Judge Mahady had made in a ruling in a child "custody battle" between a father who had left the Twelve Tribes and his wife who had remained with the church in Island Pond.

Braithwaite described a May 23, 1983, custody hearing that Judge Frank Mahady presided over. It involved four children (ages 2, 5, 8, and

9) of Eileen and Tom Gregoire. Tom Gregoire had left the Twelve Tribes. His wife, Eileen, stayed with the church. She explained how she disciplined her children with a wooden rod "out of love." (By that time, Judge Mahady had already asked that a social worker from SRS be assigned to the Gregoire case and report to him.)

In his decision two days later, Judge Frank Mahady granted a 60-day custody order to the husband. According to Braithwaite's affidavit, Mahady had written that in Island Pond the Gregoire children "were subjected to frequent and methodical physical abuse by adult members of the [Twelve Tribes] community in the form of hours-long whipping with balloon sticks. If the children are returned to Island Pond it is reasonably probable that abuse will resume."[135]

Since Judge Mahady had transferred custody of the Gregoire children out of the Twelve Tribes community based on his finding that it was "reasonably probable" that they would be subject to "frequent methodical abuse by adult members of the community" if they were returned to their mother in Island Pond, it seemed likely that he would at least consider our evidence.

That did not happen.

Judge Mahady began conducting detention hearings in the Orleans County Courthouse in Newport, Vermont, on the morning of June 22, 1984, to determine whether there was enough evidence to keep the children in temporary SRS custody for 72 hours. It quickly became clear that he had already decided we had no case.

Judge Mahady had only been assigned to the case for less than a day. It was unlikely that he'd had the time to closely consider the 200 pages of affidavits and supporting documents that White and I had presented to Judge Wolchik. After all, Judge Wolchik had taken two days to review them when he'd granted White's first request for a warrant. But if Mahady did read any of our affidavits and supporting documents, it was clear that he had ignored them.

Using phrases like "guilt by association," he spent the day denying our requests for temporary detention orders and ordering that the children and their parents be returned to Island Pond.

In late June 1984, not long after Judge Mahady threw out our case and sent the children home to the Twelve Tribes community, Bill Gray, a highly-respected lawyer who had served as US attorney for Vermont and as an assistant US attorney in the Southern District of New York agreed to serve as a special prosecutor. Attorney General Easton had given him complete control over the case.

Attorney Gray, who was a partner in a private firm in Burlington, had agreed to take over the Island Pond case after Charlie Bristow, deputy attorney general, left for a long-planned trip to England shortly after the "raid." Bristow had already left his position as deputy attorney general and was scheduled to take over as Vermont's commissioner of public safety upon his return from England.

Bristow's departure and the fact that Attorney General John Easton, who had made little public comment on the failed Island Pond operation, was running for Governor meant we were particularly lucky to have a lawyer with Bill Gray's experience and well-earned reputation for good judgment take on the case.

Gray agreed to review the case and decide whether the Attorney General's Office should ask Judge Mahady to reconsider his decision. After reviewing it, he decided we should ask Mahady to reconsider. He worked with me and my boss, Bob Gagnon, as well as Steve McLeod and other lawyers in the Attorney General's Office to file a memorandum and motion to reconsider Mahady's decision. We completed the work and filed the memorandum in less than three weeks.

The hearing on our Motion to Reconsider was held on July 12, 1984, at the scenic Grand Isle County Courthouse in the town of North Hero, which is located on an island in Lake Champlain. Gray asked me to sit beside him in case any factual questions came up that he wasn't familiar with. But Gray, who was later nominated by Senator Patrick Leahy to serve on the prestigious US Second Circuit Court of Appeals,[136] argued our case before Judge Mahady skillfully and respectfully (without any help from me).

Bill Gray emphasized to Judge Mahady at the outset that this was not the typical "corporal punishment" case where a parent insists that they have the sole right to discipline their child. The situation in the Island Pond community was much more dangerous for a child, as Dr. Hasazi had said, because under the tenets of the church, any of the adults in the community could discipline any other parent's child.

We had filed a memorandum in support of our Motion to Reconsider, which had been reviewed and approved by Gray. The memo emphasized that more than 20 former members of the church had confirmed that any adult in the church community could discipline any child in the community when the adult perceived the child was being "deceitful" or was engaging in "reasoning" or "fantasizing." The memo pointed out that many of these adults had admitted to beating children of other parents. It noted that Judge Mahady himself had heard and credited sworn testimony from one former church member who had "disciplined" 65 different children.

More importantly, as I have said repeatedly, no one in the church, including Twelve Tribes "elders," denied these allegations. Church leaders explained that all adult members were entitled to discipline any child in the church community because the children were the "community's children" and the adults were exercising their First Amendment rights to practice their religion as they saw fit when they meted out "discipline."

The fact that any adult in the "community" could strike any child with a stick as vigorously and as often as the adult felt necessary was the most obvious threat to the well-being of the "community's children"— the one highlighted by Dr. Hasazi.

The memo went on to point out, though, that under Vermont law, there were other bases for finding a child is "in need of care and supervision" aside from abuse by a "parent guardian or caretaker." For instance, a child who is "neglected," or if they are "without. . .education, medical or other care necessary for [the child's] well-being."[137]

The memo pointed out that there was no dispute that the church did not allow the "community's children" to attend public schools and required them to attend a church-run school that had made no effort to obtain a Vermont "Homeschool Waiver." Nor was there any dispute that the church discouraged parents from having the "community's children" cared for by state-licensed medical professionals rather than members of the church community who had little medical training.

Gray argued, citing the memo, that he had presented overwhelming evidence that there were reasonable grounds to believe that any child in the "church community" was at risk of abuse and neglect and entitled to state protection. He said Judge Wolchik had been right when he'd approved the order for authorizing temporary detention of all children in the 20 buildings controlled by the church because the evidence showed the children were likely to be harmed by "continued residence in [their] present environment."[138]

Judge Mahady's decision denying our Motion to Reconsider was both erudite and dismissive. He cited the Bible, the Magna Carta, and the Talmud and Cicero—to name just a few. He devoted an entire page of his opinion to citing 17th Century English legal cases. But he never addressed the rights of the children of Twelve Tribes to be free from the "institutionalized violence" that was part of their daily lives.

He summarized what he saw as the basic legal deficiency in our case. We could not specifically identify a single child out of the 112 children who had been seized as a child who had suffered abuse.

> There is not a single piece of evidence in the material submitted that documents a single act of abuse or neglect with regard to any of the 112 children. The theory is there is some evidence of some abuse of some children at some time in the past against other children.[139]

Judge Mahady was right. We could not "match a name to a face." Our evidence had specifically identified by name well over 40 children who had been physically abused. But we could not point to a single child who had been seized on June 22, 1984, and say this is a child named in the evidence we'd filed with Judge Wolchik in support of our petition.

Normally, the State's juvenile petition must cite "specifics" to satisfy the Fourth Amendment bar against "unreasonable" searches and seizures. That is, name the child who is to be temporarily seized and cite the specific facts that show there is "probable cause" to believe that child is at risk of abuse or neglect.

But the reason we could not match a name to a face was legally significant.

Gray cited the 1967 US Supreme Court case of *Camara v. Municipal Court*,[140] which we had highlighted in our memo. This was because under the US Supreme Court's reasoning in *Camara*, the fact that church members had for two years successfully stymied efforts by social workers, who were legally required to investigate reports of child abuse, *in itself* provided the *"probable cause" necessary* to detain the children and conduct the evaluations authorized in the petition and warrant.

Roland Camara had refused to allow a city building inspector to enter his property to conduct routine building inspections without a search warrant. The relevant city ordinance authorized the inspector to enter the building without a warrant. Camara continued to refuse entry and was found in violation of the ordinance. He appealed to the US Supreme Court.

Camara's refusal to allow inspectors to enter the building meant, of course, that they had not been able to conduct the "routine periodic inspections" that were necessary to ensure the public was protected. It also meant it was impossible to view the conditions inside the building. This, in turn, made it nearly impossible to determine whether there were facts and circumstances that made it "fairly probable" that there were violations of public safety code regulations. This is the "probable cause" standard the City would have had to satisfy if it were to qualify for a criminal search warrant.

The Court held that in such situations public officials would not have to meet the more stringent probable cause standard law enforcement is required to get in criminal cases. Importantly for our case, the court specifically noted that in such situations, "The passage of a certain period without an inspection" could itself "justify the issuance of a warrant." [141]

The US Supreme Court found that when a duly authorized inspector is denied entry into a building subject to regulation and the refusal is coupled with a "valid public interest" for the entry, then these factors alone can constitute the "probable cause" necessary to issue a search warrant: "If a valid public interest justifies the intrusion contemplated, then there is probable cause to issue a suitably restricted warrant." [142]

The lower probable cause standard adopted in *Camara* had been applied in cases where the "valid public interest" at issue was the health and safety of workers, and the employer had refused entry for an unreasonable period of time, which then precluded an OSHA inspection. The Federal District concluded, relying on the reasoning in *Camara*, that those facts alone constituted the "probable cause" necessary for a judge to issue the warrant authorizing entry onto the employer's premises to conduct the inspection. [143]

We had argued that the principles set out and adopted by the US Supreme Court's decision in *Camara* were clearly applicable in our case.

At the time Judge Wolchik issued his order, Twelve Tribes leaders had been refusing to cooperate with SRS social workers investigating child abuse for more than two years. This refusal to cooperate had made it impossible for state investigators to identify a specific child—or put a name to a face—of any "child of the community" whose health and safety were in danger.

We had strong evidence of this refusal. For instance, the supporting documents for the Moran affidavit included 18 petitions identifying

18 specific children that state officials had been unable to serve because of the Twelve Tribes' refusal to cooperate with state social workers and investigators. The Moran and Braithwaite affidavits each cited multiple instances where church members told what they referred to as "righteous lies" about the whereabouts of children who former members had identified as victims of child abuse to prevent social services from conducting investigations into child abuse that they were legally required to make.

Gray argued, relying on *Camara*, that the State's actions at Island Pond were "reasonable" and complied with the Fourth Amendment, regardless of whether we could identify a specific child whose health and safety was endangered.

There were three elements to *Camara*. We argued that we met all three and that because of this, the State's actions had been " reasonable" under the Fourth Amendment.

First, there was no dispute that our effort to investigate multiple allegations of child abuse was a "valid public interest." Judge Mahady had acknowledged as much:

> The problem of child abuse is a grave one to which this Court has given substantial attention. It is one of our most serious societal problems. It is, therefore, entirely proper and, indeed, desirable for the State to attack it aggressively.[144]

Second, there was no evidence to dispute our evidence that church members had stymied efforts to conduct what would normally be routine, legally required investigations into allegations of child abuse for more than two years. Judge Mahady did not mention this evidence or even address this second element of *Camara*.

The third and final *Camara* element was that the State must "issue a suitably restricted warrant."

Judge Mahady said this was where we had failed. He said that the warrant and petition that Judge Wolchik had approved was "grossly illegal" and broader than the one that had been issued 2,000 years earlier by "Herod the Great," who ordered the rounding up and killing of all male children under the age of 2 in and around Bethlehem:

> A broader warrant can scarcely be imagined. It is for 20 separate buildings, most of which are residences. The authorization to seize 'any and all children under the age of 18 years old' is

broader in scope (although admittedly less in purpose) than that
of Herod the Great.

This flippant characterization of the search warrant as broader than
Herod's order ignored the whole point of the US Supreme Court's
decision in *Camara*.

The Supreme Court had held in *Camera* that when public officials have
been prevented for an extended period of time from conducting an investigation the law requires, e.g., an investigation into reports of child abuse,
then that delay in itself is sufficient "probable cause" to conduct the search.

We argued that where public officials (in this case, social workers) have
been prevented for an extended period of time (in this case, two years)
from conducting an investigation required by law to protect the public (in
this case, investigations into reports of child abuse), *Camara* permits those
state officials to search a building where those officials reasonably believe
that the children who are the subjects of that investigation are located.

There were reasonable grounds to believe that the "community's
children" would be found in the 20 church-controlled buildings specifically identified in the warrant presented to Judge Wolchik. Phil White
and his investigator had documented this in the affidavits supporting his
request for the search warrant. In fact, it was common knowledge in Island
Pond that the "community's children" lived in and visited these buildings.

Under the law established by the Supreme Court in *Camara*, there
was no need for social workers to "put a name to a face" before entering
these buildings to conduct their investigations. This was because
the elders and other adults in the Twelve Tribes had spent two years
preventing that from happening. Two years of "righteous lies," which
prohibited state social workers from doing their legal duty to investigate
child abuse, was enough to establish "probable cause."

Judge Mahady did not agree.

He ended his condemnation of our actions by repeating his accusation
that we had practiced "guilt by association."

> Here, the State can establish probable cause only by adopting
> a theory of guilt by association. Such a theory is unlawful.[145]

No. We had repeatedly pointed out that this was not a criminal case.
Our goal in filing our petition was not to prove the church parents
were "guilty" of anything. Our goal was to protect the children of
Twelve Tribes who were at constant risk of what might reasonably be

characterized as "abuse by association." These children had not chosen to join the church. They had no choice but to "associate with" a religion that taught that God wanted any adult in the "church community" to beat a child with a wooden stick whenever that adult felt that God was calling them to "drive Satan out."

Judge Mahady remained unmoved. He denied our Motion to Reconsider once and for all.

Attorney General John Easton, acting on advice from Bill Gray, announced that the State would not appeal. I agreed with Easton's decision. It seemed clear, based on the reactions of the judges, that we were not going to get an opportunity to examine the Twelve Tribes children unless the church elders agreed to it.

That never happened.

After the raid, many members of the Twelve Tribes gradually left Island Pond. But the Twelve Tribes continued to grow to the point that there were multiple "communities" in Australia and Europe as well as the US and Canada.

Elbert Spriggs died on January 11, 2021, at the age of 83. This was nearly 50 years after he founded Twelve Tribes. His church generated controversy before the "Raid at Island Pond" and it continued to generate controversy in the decades that followed.

There were persistent allegations of "child abuse" by people who had left the church—people who confirmed that physical and psychological abuse of "the community's children" had taken place before the raid and had continued after the raid.

Luke Wiseman was the first male born into the Twelve Tribes. In 1975, he moved with his father Charles "Eddie" Wiseman and his mother to Island Pond where that group of Twelve Tribes members adopted the name Northeast Kingdom Community Church. Wiseman was 9 years old when he was picked up by police and social workers during the "raid" on June 22, 1984.

Luke Wiseman spent the first 39 years of his life in the Twelve Tribes community. He left Twelve Tribes in 2013. He said that he was a victim of physical and psychological abuse at the hands of adult members of "the community" at the time of the raid. He told the *Burlington Free Press*[146] in 2020—more three decades after the raid—that although his parents did not physically abuse him, he was beaten with wooden rods by other adult Twelve Tribes members. "There were welts on my ankles, on my legs, on my back," Wiseman said. "I would say, yes, there was abuse."

Wiseman said there was also "psychological abuse." He gave *Free Press* reporter Alek Fleury an example. Wiseman was a musician. Twelve Tribes members used his love of music to "discipline" him: "I was on numerous one-year punishments where I couldn't play music." Wiseman told Fleury that the accusations against him were "always really vague and frustrating to a kid."

Wiseman also indicated that the raid had resulted in at least one benefit to the children of the Twelve Tribes. He said that after the raid, physical abuse became less harsh: "They started just hitting us with the balloon stick on the hand, and it was always emphasized that it should never be done out of anger."

When Fleury asked Wiseman whether he regretted being returned to the Twelve Tribes community after the raid, he said, in effect, "It's complicated."

> "Yes, there was harsh discipline," Wiseman said, "but there were also many beautiful memories that I wish I could recreate for my own children. . . . On one level, you have all this amazing beauty of people collaborating and playing. . . and this culture where people had time to talk to each other, and drink tea, and go horseback riding, and go sledding and skating," he said. "But on top of that, you have this really dark religion by this guy Gene Spriggs."

Kayam Mathias was born into the Twelve Tribes in 1994—ten years after the raid. Mathias told *Daily Beast* reporter Luke O'Neil[147] that he was beaten 20 to 30 times per day:

> I grew to be numb to it, to quell the rage within and just not feel anything. What I cared about was when my infant sister was beaten and there was nothing I could do about it. To hear her screams and be powerless... and that even if you tried to stop you couldn't, is a crushing thing to go through. It broke my spirit, man. I still remember her screams to this day.

In the same *Daily Beast* online article, Luke O'Neil reported that in August 2013, a German documentary uncovered video of children in a local branch of Twelve Tribes being beaten so terribly that the government led a raid and took the children away.

In the video, a Radio Television Luxembourg (RTL) journalist filmed 50 instances of beatings on camera. The article went on to say that "one former member who appears in the film recounts being regularly beaten for such trivial offenses as pretending to be an airplane. According to the group's teachings, children are not permitted to engage in any type of 'playing or fantasy.' "

On June 22, 2018, exactly 34 years after the "Raid at Island Pond," the European Court of Human Rights issued a final opinion that upheld the decisions of German Courts to permanently separate children of the Twelve Tribes community in Germany from their parents.[148] This had come after the Courts had heard evidence of the Twelve Tribes' "systematic" beating or "caning" of children.

A seven-judge panel of the Court rejected claims of religious persecution made by parents from two families in the Twelve Tribes who had been separated from their children. The parents/"applicants" alleged that the "Federal Republic of Germany" had violated their right to "religious freedom" guaranteed by Article 8 of the European Convention for the Protection of Human Rights and Fundamental Freedoms.[149]

More specifically, the parents claimed that they had been: (1) denied their right to raise their children "in compliance with their religious beliefs"; (2) that they had been unlawfully separated from their children because of their religious beliefs; and (3) that the court proceedings that resulted in their separation from their children "had led to the stigmatization" of the Twelve Tribes.[150]

The European Court of Human Rights, located in Strasbourg, France, was established to protect the human rights of 700 million people in the 46 countries in the European Council. The Court's opinion, which is non-appealable, held that the Twelve Tribes children had the "right to a non-violent upbringing under German law" and that the children of the applicants had been subjected to a "form of institutionalized violence,"[151] which was a fundamental "element" of the religious beliefs of their parents.

The process that culminated five years later in the opinion of the European Court of Human Rights that the children of a Twelve Tribes community in Germany were subjected to a "form of institutionalized violence" began in 2013—the same year that Luke Wiseman, the first male born into the church in Island Pond, left Twelve Tribes for good.

In many ways, the process used by German authorities in 2013 was similar to the process authorized by Judge Joseph Wolchik that led to the "Raid at Island Pond."

On August 16, 2013, the reporter who had videoed the beatings of the children mentioned in the *Daily Beast* article, delivered the footage to the German family court in Nördlingen, a town of 19,000 people in South Central, Germany.

According to the final European Court of Human Rights opinion, the German family court initiated a preliminary investigation into the treatment of children in two nearby Twelve Tribes communities where the reporter had videotaped the beatings. On August 21, five days after receiving the video footage of the "canings," the family court heard testimony[152] from six witnesses, all former members of Twelve Tribes. These witnesses testified that children in the Twelve Tribes community were beaten with a slender wooden rod from age 3 to age 12. The witnesses testified further that the "children were punished by whichever adult was supervising the children at the time and that parents were pressured by the [Twelve Tribes] community to conform to the rules of upbringing."

On September 1, 2013, a week and half after hearing the testimony of former Twelve Tribes members, the family court "withdrew" the parental rights of parents of "all children in Twelve Tribes Community" to the local child protection agency after finding that there was a "reasonable likelihood" that the children would be subject to "corporal punishment" if they remained with their parents in the Twelve Tribes community. More specifically, the German family court withdrew the Twelve Tribes parents "rights to decide where their children should live, and to take decisions regarding the children's health, schooling and professional training, and transferred those rights to the youth office."

The family court gave the child protection workers the authority to obtain "the support of police" in entering the "premises of Twelve Tribes community" to bring the children "into care" of the local child protection agency ("youth office").[153]

On September 4, 2013, child protection workers took all children in the Twelve Tribes community into their custody. They were supported by "around 100 police officers" who searched the "community's premises" under the authority of the local public prosecutor and found "seven wooden rods."

The Twelve Tribes parents whose claims were eventually rejected by the European Court of Human Rights first litigated their claims in German courts. The German appellate court reviewing the family court decision confirmed that there was no dispute that the children in question—children aged 3 to 12 years—had been "caned" and that children between 3 and 12 would be caned if they were returned to their families. The German court made a specific finding that "bringing up children in this way was not justified by the parents' freedom of religion."[154]

In January 2016, the parents, having exhausted their appeals in German courts, filed suit against the Federal Republic of Germany in the European Court of Human Rights. Again, they relied on Article 8 of the European Convention, which protects the right to the privacy of "family life."

As I said earlier, the final decision of the European Court of Human Rights held that the orders of the German courts in separating the parents from their children who were age 12 and under had not violated Article 8 of the Convention.

The Human Rights Court concluded that the proceedings in the German courts had been "fair" and that the German courts had "struck a balance between the interests of the children and those of their parents which was properly intended to protect the best interests of the children." The decisions of the German courts were affirmed. There had been no violation of the religious rights of the Twelve Tribes parents.[155]

In my opinion, "the Raid at Island Pond" was lawful. Unfortunately, unlike the judges on the European Court of Human Rights, Vermont judges made no effort to "strike a balance between the best interest of the children and the parents." They ignored the rights of the children, and the result was decades of misery for children in the Twelve Tribes "community."

The "Roving Litigator"

In January 1985, newly elected Vermont Attorney General Jeffrey Amestoy, a Republican, replaced John Easton. Easton had just lost his bid to become Vermont's governor to Madeleine Kunin, a Democrat, who became Vermont's first female governor.

Amestoy served as attorney general from 1985 to 1997 when he was appointed chief justice of the Vermont Supreme Court by Governor Howard Dean, a Democrat. He served as chief justice until he retired in 2004. After he retired, Amestoy worked at Harvard as a fellow at the Institute of Politics and at the Harvard Kennedy School's Center for Public Leadership.

I had played a major role in the Island Pond raid and felt responsible for letting both the church's children and the Attorney General's Office down. I did not know what to expect from Amestoy, who would be my new boss. In fact, I was treated very well.

Thanks to Amestoy and Deputy Attorney General Brian Burgess, who also eventually became a justice on the Vermont Supreme Court, I would continue to handle a few criminal cases. But mainly I would do court trials and hearings for other divisions in the AG's office as—what we jokingly referred to as—a "roving litigator."

During the period from 1985 through late 1987, I did cases enforcing Vermont laws that were meant to protect Vermont's natural resources—streams, lakes, and groundwater as well as wildlife habitat.

Several of the civil cases I litigated for the AG's Office were for the Vermont Department of Environmental Conservation. It was a time when the DEC was identifying and cleaning up hazardous waste sites in the state. This Vermont agency worked with the Federal Environmental Protection Agency (EPA), which was charged with implementing the massive cleanup of hazardous waste authorized by the Comprehensive Environmental Response, Compensation, and Liability Act (CERCLA) passed by Congress in December 1980.

The first "environmental case" I brought was in Barre, Vermont, in February 1985. I was seeking a court order to support the Vermont DEC's efforts to stop hazardous waste from seeping into the Stevens Branch, a stream that flowed north from Barre into the Winooski River near Montpelier.

The hazardous waste was "coal tar sludge," a byproduct of the coal gasification process used to generate heat and light in Barre in the late 19th and early 20th centuries. The coal gasification firm that operated in Barre had gone out of business in 1954, leaving roughly 180,000 gallons of coal tar sludge in storage tanks. These tanks were no more than 100 feet from the banks of the Stevens Branch, and they were badly rusted.

The owner of the land where the storage tanks were located was the Gas Company of Vermont. The company had already spent $100,000 getting rid of some of the coal tar by having it shipped to a hazardous waste disposal site in Ohio. The company had refused to pay for the DEC's efforts to prevent the coal tar that remained in the tanks from seeping into the Stevens Branch. The company claimed that there was no evidence that coal tar from its property was, in fact, seeping into the river.

In early February 1985, I filed suit on behalf of the Vermont DEC to force the company to pay for the cleanup and "remediation" work, which would prevent the coal tar from traveling off the site and into the stream.[156]

I recall that we had one expedited hearing at the Vermont District Court in Barre. Cedric Sanborn, a DEC engineer, testified that he had found coal tar, which is harmful to aquatic life as well as a potential carcinogen, seeping into the Stevens Branch from the Gas Company's property bordering the Stevens Branch. Shortly after that, the Gas Company's insurer agreed to pay up to the limits of the policy—which I recall was $1 million—to help finance the DEC effort to prevent further seepage of coal tar into the river.[157]

In the spring of 1986, I traveled to Stratton, a small town in south-western Vermont. Stratton is the home of the Stratton Mountain ski area.

At the time, it had 43 homes for its roughly 200 full-time residents and 703 vacation homes. I represented the Vermont Department of Fish and Wildlife Department, which had denied a development permit to a New York developer who proposed to add an additional 33 vacation homes.

The developer had refused to alter the site plan for his proposed 33 unit "Southview" development despite being told by the Fish and Wildlife Department biologists that the vacation home development, as planned, would endanger necessary "wildlife habitat."

My job was to defend the department's position before the District #2 Environmental commission, which effectively served as a "trial court" for environmental cases generated in towns in the southwestern portion of Vermont. The Commission had convened a hearing at the town office in Stratton to consider Southview's appeal of the denial of its development permit.

The developer had retained Raymond Perra, an experienced, highly regarded environmental lawyer, to represent Southview in its appeal.

I relied on the advice and testimony of two wildlife biologists from the department—Larry Garland and Jim DiStefano—to support their decision to deny Southview's application for a development permit.

The "critical wildlife habitat" in question was a 44-acre portion of the only "deeryard" in a more-than-10-square-mile area of Stratton and neighboring towns.[158] The wildlife biologists explained in their testimony before the commission what a deeryard was and why it was important.

The Federal Second Circuit Court of Appeals later relied on this explanation in deciding that the deeryard at issue in the Southview case was a critical wildlife habitat:

> Deer endure harsh winter conditions in large part by drawing energy from fat reserves accumulated in late summer and early fall. Browse provides only a secondary source of energy. The deer's capacity to conserve use of its energy reserves is the most critical factor in whether it will survive the winter. The Commission and the Board found that the shelter afforded by an ideal deeryard, like the one on the Southview property, enables deer to minimize the drain on their energy reserves. Protected concentrations of softwood cover provide the best shelter, by (1) blocking cold winds; (2) retaining solar heat and reducing nighttime heat radiation; (3) reducing snow depth

(because snow remains on the boughs), thereby reducing the energy deer must use to move around within the deeryard; and (4) shielding deer from human and canine activity, which, if nearby, will cause the deer to stand or move and thereby expend energy. If human activity in close proximity to the deeryard reaches a certain level, deer will abandon the deeryard.[159]

We tried the case over several days. The commission even had a site visit to the deeryard. My clearest recollection of these hearings was cross-examining the developer from Rye, New York. The developer was enraged and incredulous that what he called a "deer nesting area"—which he said contained only six deer—could sink his development plans.

The commission denied Southview's appeal on April 23, 1986.

The Department of Fish and Wildlife suggested a smaller scale development that still protected the habitat, but Southview rejected these alternatives. They appealed to the Vermont Environmental Board (Board) in Montpelier, which handled appeals from all of the District Environmental Commissions in the state.

Southview lost its appeal to the Vermont Environmental Board.[160] After that, it appealed to the Vermont Supreme Court.

The Vermont Supreme Court denied Southview's appeal in a unanimous decision written by Justice James Morse.[161] The Court held that the Board had acted reasonably when it concluded that:

> The environmental and recreational loss to the public from the destruction and imperilment of the habitat is not outweighed by the economic, social, cultural, recreational, or other benefit to the public from the project.

> The existence of the deer in this area provides an opportunity to the public to hunt and to observe deer and provides the more intangible benefit of knowing that the deer exist. The loss of the deer in this area would be significant to the public who benefit from their existence.[162]

Southview appealed to the federal courts. Its challenge to the "deeryard decision" finally ended six years after it began when the Second Circuit Court of Appeals upheld the decision of the Vermont Supreme Court in October 1992.[163]

"It's Always Been in My Head to Kill Someone"

The environmental cases that I did were not tried before juries. They were either tried before judges, as in the hearing on the coal tar case, or before panels of experts, as in the Environmental Board hearing on Southview. I did, however, try one more murder case during the time I was working as a "roving litigator"—the murder of Peter.

In April 1982, Peter was murdered in his apartment on Summer Street in Barre, Vermont. Peter was shot to death by Gordon Hunt, who lived in an upstairs apartment directly above Peter's apartment. Hunt, a slender 19-year-old with curly dark hair and a wisp of a mustache, worked as a janitor at a nearby Burger King. Hunt did not know Peter personally. There was no apparent motive for the killing beyond Hunt's bizarre, chilling explanation to police:

> I don't really know why I shot him. I had nothing against him. He seemed like a nice guy. I've always had it in my head to kill someone.[164]

The evidence showed that Peter, a chiropractor, had walked home after lunch to get a file. Hunt knocked on the door. As Peter opened the door, Hunt shot Peter in the face with his father's 30-30 hunting rifle. The young killer dragged Peter's body into the kitchen, padlocked the door to Peter's apartment, and hid the rifle in an upstairs storage area.

Peter's body was discovered at around 4:30 p.m. that afternoon by friends who became worried when he failed to return to work. The friends broke through the door and found Peter's dead body lying in a puddle of blood on the kitchen floor.[165]

Hunt lied to police at first, but he eventually agreed to go to the Barre Police Department. Not long after he arrived at the police station, he gave a detailed confession. He explained to police that he had left the upstairs apartment where he lived with his father and went downstairs to ensure that Peter was alone. Once he was sure Peter was alone, he'd gone back upstairs, loaded his father's rifle, and then went downstairs and shot Peter in the face shortly after Peter opened the door.

Hunt killed Peter on April 19—just a week and a half after Richard Sorrell and Timothy "Pucky" Miller murdered Timothy in Winooski. As described above, Sorrell and Miller were tried in December 1982 and March 1983. But for reasons described below, Gordon Hunt was not tried for his murder of Peter until two years later, in late February 1985.

Gregory McNaughten was the Washington County state's attorney at the time of the Peter murder in 1982. Washington County covers 19 towns in central Vermont, including Barre, where the Peter murder took place.

In August 1983, McNaughten proposed a plea agreement to resolve Hunt's murder case. Robert Gaston was the court-appointed attorney representing Hunt. Under the terms of the proposed deal, Hunt would plead guilty to a reduced charge of second-degree murder and receive a sentence of 10 years to serve in prison. Hunt, acting on his attorney's advice, accepted the deal.

Plea agreements do not go into effect unless the agreement is "approved" by the judge assigned the case. This is normally a formality. In my experience, the judge approves the sentence the parties have agreed to 99 percent of the time. But in Hunt's case, this meant that he would serve 10 years in prison on a reduced charge of second-degree murder for killing a man he did not know and had done him no wrong.

The victim's father had been critical of the plea agreement. Peter's family as a whole said that there was too much emphasis on Gordon Hunt and what was best for him and not enough emphasis on the victim, Peter, and what his loss meant to his friends and family.

McNaughten defended the plea agreement as the best he could do under the circumstances. He told reporters that he thought there was a "reasonable likelihood" that the Vermont Supreme Court would suppress some of the prosecution's evidence. McNaughten pointed to the fact that Dr. William Woodruff, a respected and experienced psychiatrist, had conducted a court-ordered psychiatric examination of Hunt and had concluded that at the time he shot Peter, Hunt "had little contact with reality as you and I know it." McNaughten told reporters that he was concerned that a jury would acquit Hunt based on Woodruff's testimony. That is, jurors were likely to find Hunt was "not criminally responsible," because he was "insane at the time of the offense."

In Vermont at that time, all murder cases were prosecuted in superior court, while all other criminal cases—from manslaughter down to motor vehicle violations—were handled in district court. Vermont superior courts are unusual in that three judges sit on murder cases—not one. In addition to the presiding judge—who is an experienced lawyer appointed by Vermont's governor—there are two assistant judges who are elected by the people in the county where the superior court resides.

Assistant judges, also known as "side judges," have served in Vermont courts since 1777, when Vermont was an independent republic. This was twelve years before Vermont joined the United States of America in 1789. The founders of Vermont were said to have had an "enormous distrust of lawyers." Many lawyers had "supported England in its fight with the colonies." Side judges sit on either side of the law-trained presiding judge and are expected to provide "popular input in decisions."[166]

The Hunt plea agreement was presented to the Chittenden County Superior Court in Burlington for approval on August 11, 1983. The case had been transferred from Washington County to the Chittenden Superior Court—which was roughly 45 miles northwest of Barre—because of concerns that the extensive publicity of the case in Washington County would make it difficult for Hunt to get a fair trial.

The presiding judge in Chittenden Superior Court on August 11, 1983 was James Morse, a respected attorney who had supervised Vermont's public defenders before being appointed to the bench. The two "side judges" were Jane Wheel and Charles Delaney.

After a 15-minute conference, Judge Morse announced that the Court had rejected the plea agreement. More specifically, the two assistant judges, Wheel and Delaney, had rejected the agreement and outvoted Morse, who would have accepted it.[167]

Morse said that he would have accepted the plea agreement because he believed the prosecution would have trouble proving two things: (1) that

Hunt was sane at the time of the murder and (2) that he had acted with the premeditation necessary to convict him of first-degree murder.[168] But he did not challenge the authority of the assistant judges to overrule him.

Vermont assistant judges had never completely overruled the presiding judge and rejected a plea agreement in a murder case before. Both the prosecutor, McNaughten, and Hunt's attorney, Gaston, quickly got permission to appeal to the Vermont Supreme Court on the issue of whether assistant judges had the authority to disapprove plea agreements in criminal cases.

The case was argued before the Vermont Supreme Court on May 11, 1984. The defense and the prosecution agreed that the side judges did not have legal authority to overrule the presiding judge. They were supported by the Vermont Bar Association and the Vermont Chapter of the American Civil Liberties Union. Both organizations filed amicus curiae briefs arguing that assistant judges did not have the authority to overrule the presiding judge.

The assistant judges, led by Jane Wheel, retained the law firm of former Governor Ray Keyser to argue that they had acted lawfully when they'd overruled presiding Judge James Morse. Wheel had asked my boss, Attorney General John Easton, to argue in defense of the assistant judges' position, but he had refused at first.

Assistant Judge Jane Wheel was a former high school physical education teacher who was a powerful member of the Democratic party in Burlington. She was 42 years old when she was elected to her first four-year term as one of two Chittenden County assistant judges in 1974. She won reelection in 1978 and 1982. By the time she and Assistant Judge Delaney rejected the Hunt plea agreement, Wheel had become president of the Vermont Association of Assistant Judges and was lobbying the Vermont Legislature to increase the power of Vermont's 28 assistant judges.

Wheel became close friends with William Hill—the presiding judge in the Chittenden Superior Court—not long after she was elected in 1974. That friendship continued after Hill was appointed to the Vermont Supreme Court in 1976.

On November 2, 1984, the Vermont Supreme Court held that Assistant Judges Wheel and Delaney had acted lawfully when they'd rejected the Hunt plea agreement. In a 4-1 decision, the majority ruled that the side judges had the right under Vermont law to exercise their "discretion" in rejecting the plea agreement.[169]

The decision meant the plea agreement was dead, and Hunt's first-degree murder case should be set for trial.

Terry Trono asked me to assist him in the Hunt trial, which was likely to take place in Burlington in January 1985. Trono had been bound to honor the plea agreement McNaughten had negotiated. Now that it was officially dead, he had to get ready for trial.

I was happy to get another chance to work with Terry Trono. We got along well, and I knew after trying the Norton case with him eight months earlier that he was an honest, no-nonsense man and a good trial lawyer.

Trono had worked as a deputy state's attorney under McNaughten. Trono had won an election to replace McNaughten in November 1982. Trono went on to serve as Washington County state's attorney for 22 years before dying of cancer in 2004. He was liked and respected by the police, defense attorneys, and judges who worked with him.

I didn't realize it at the time, but when I signed on to work with Trono in the Hunt case, it put me on the periphery of what later became known as "Wheelgate"—a scandal that arose out of the very close personal relationship between Vermont Supreme Court Justice William Hill and Assistant Judge Jane Wheel. The scandal, which rocked the Vermont Judiciary in the late 1980s, is the focus of the 2018 book by Burlington lawyer and author James Dunn, *Breach of Trust*.[170]

I was working for John Easton as an assistant attorney general when Trono asked me to work with him on the Hunt case. Easton had refused at first to support the position of the assistant judges—i.e., that Wheel and Delaney had acted lawfully in rejecting the Hunt plea agreement.

According to Dunn, Wheel had not taken Easton's refusal well. She told Easton's deputy, Charles Bristow, that failure to support the assistant judges might have "political ramifications" for Easton, who was running for Vermont governor.

On May 12, 1984, the day after the Vermont Supreme Court heard the argument on the legal authority of assistant judges to reject plea agreements, Easton sent a letter to the Supreme Court offering the assistance of lawyers in the Attorney General's Office to serve "as amicus curiae on behalf of the Assistant Judges." Dunn says in his book that it is "unclear what brought Easton to change his mind."[171]

This had all happened five or six months before Trono asked me to work on the Hunt case in November 1984. I didn't know anything about Wheel's discussion with Bristow or Easton's change of heart. Fortunately, it all happened above my pay grade.

Hunt's attorney, Robert Gaston, filed a motion to disqualify Assistant Judge Wheel from further participation in Hunt's case when he learned of Wheel's efforts to get Attorney General Easton's assistance on behalf of the assistant judges in their efforts to convince the Vermont Supreme Court to rule that she and Delaney had acted lawfully when they'd overruled Judge Morse and rejected the Hunt plea agreement.

Morse granted Gaston's motion in a 16-page opinion on December 27, 1984. According to Dunn, Morse later characterized his decision disqualifying Wheel as "lighting the fuse." By that time, I was fully involved in the Hunt case. I had appeared before Wheel, Delaney, and Morse in Burlington, and I can confirm that Dunn was right when he wrote that "the tension in and around the courthouse was palpable."

Wheel quickly filed an appeal of Judge Morse's ruling disqualifying her from the Hunt case in the Vermont Supreme Court. She also filed a motion to stay her disqualification with the court. A stay would enable her to stay on the Hunt case while her appeal of Morse's decision was being considered by the Supreme Court.

Normally motions filed in the Vermont Supreme Court are filed with the court clerk and then distributed to all five justices. Wheel took the unusual step of filing her motion directly with her close friend Supreme Court Justice William Hill—and no one else. Hill promptly granted Wheel's motion without consulting the other supreme court justices. Then he went to the superior court in Burlington and delivered the notice that he had granted the stay directly to the court clerk.[172]

Hunt's attorney, Gaston, filed an appeal asking the full court to reverse Hill's decision. He also asked that Hunt's trial, which was set to begin in Burlington in early January (less than two weeks away), be allowed to continue as scheduled.

James Dunn described what happened next in his book:

> What follows next remains one of the darkest moments in the long history of the Vermont Supreme Court. On January 3, 1985, just seven days after Morse's decision disqualifying

Wheel from the case, and without a request from or even notice to the State or to Hunt's attorneys, the Supreme Court ordered the Hunt case transferred from Chittenden to Lamoille County. Then the Court declared Wheel's disqualification from the Hunt case moot and dismissed the case, thereby erasing the stain of disqualification from her record.

I learned of the change of venue in the Hunt case from Kevin McLaughlin, who was chief deputy in the Chittenden County Sheriff's Office at the time. I had known him from the time I had worked at the Chittenden County State's Attorney's Office in 1979 to 1981. He phoned me at my office at the Attorney General's Office and arranged to have me served with notice that the Hunt trial was being moved from the Chittenden County Court in Burlington to the Lamoille County Court in the town of Hyde Park, Vermont, which is located some fifty miles east and north of Burlington.

That was my only brush with what came to be known as "Wheelgate."

Back to the Gordon Hunt murder case.

Gordon Hunt's first-degree murder trial began in Lamoille County Superior Court in Hyde Park on February 19, 1985. The only real issue in the trial was whether Hunt's insanity defense would be successful—i.e., could Hunt escape criminal responsibility for killing Peter because he was suffering from a "mental disease" that caused him to lack the "capacity" to either (1) "appreciate the criminality of his conduct" or (2) "conform his conduct to the requirements of the law."[173]

The law governing the insanity defense had changed in one significant respect in the nearly three years between the time Hunt had shot and killed Peter in April 1982 and the time he went to trial in February 1985. The burden of proof on the issue of whether a defendant was "not guilty by reason of insanity" had shifted from the prosecution to the defense.

Why the shift? In June 1982, John Hinckley was found not guilty by reason of insanity on 13 counts, including wounding President Ronald Reagan. The prosecution had been unable to prove beyond a reasonable doubt that Hinckley was *not insane* at the time of the shooting. The fact that Hinckley escaped criminal liability despite intentionally shooting President Reagan and two others prompted legislatures throughout the country, including Vermont's, to shift the burden of proof on the insanity defense.

In 1983, the year after Hunt shot and killed Peter, the Vermont Legislature amended the insanity statute to *require the defendant to prove by a "preponderance of the evidence" (51-49)* that he was not "criminally responsible" because he was "insane" at the time of the offense.[174]

That did not help us in Hunt's case, though. Since Hunt had committed the murder before the change in the law, Terry Trono and I were still required to prove beyond a reasonable doubt—the highest standard of proof in the law—that Hunt was *not insane,* and therefore "criminally responsible" at the time he shot and killed Peter.

It had taken the defense and prosecution three days to pick the jury in this highly publicized case. Opening statements and testimony began on Friday, February 22, 1985.

In my opening statement, I reviewed the evidence that the jury would hear over the next few days. I focused on Dr. Brodsky's testimony and the testimony of two experienced investigators: Washington County State's Attorney's Investigator Howard Fitzpatrick, a retired New York City Police detective, and Vermont State Police Detective Ronald DeVincenzi. The detectives' testimony would provide crucial support for Dr. Brodsky's opinion that when Hunt had shot Peter, he did indeed have the "capacity" to: (1) conform his conduct to what the law required and (2) understand that shooting Peter in the face was a crime.

In his opening, Hunt's attorney, Gaston, told jurors that Hunt had "lost control" of his behavior a few days before he shot Peter. Gaston said this loss of control had been caused by the fact that Hunt's 15-year-old girlfriend and their child had moved out a few days earlier. Gaston told the jury that Hunt, who he said had been abused by an alcoholic father, had lived in a "disturbed world."

The first two witnesses we called showed that far from being a "troubled youth" who simply could not control his behavior, Hunt was a cold-hearted killer. The witnesses were the friends who had found Peter's body. Wendy Curran had been filling in as a receptionist for Peter. She had become concerned when he did not return for a 1 p.m. appointment. She had walked the 10 minutes to Peter's apartment, where she'd encountered Hunt. Of course, Hunt had killed Peter a short time earlier and dragged his body into Peter's kitchen before padlocking the apartment door. But when he'd spoken to Curran, Hunt had calmly told her that Peter must not be home because his apartment door was padlocked from the outside.

Curran and another friend, Tony Garcia, had returned later in the afternoon around 4:30 p.m. and found Peter's body right where Hunt had left it—in a puddle of blood on the kitchen floor. They testified that Hunt had come downstairs ostensibly to console them after they'd found their friend's body. Hunt had put his arms around their shoulders. Garcia glared at Hunt as he told jurors, "I thought he saw my grief and felt sympathy for me. He seemed like someone who was concerned."

We also called a witness who had lived in an apartment across the hall from Hunt's apartment. She testified that Hunt had shown her the rifle he'd used to kill Peter two months before the killing. She said Hunt had told her at that time that "he had always wanted to know what it felt like to kill someone."[175]

Our expert, Dr. Stanley Brodsky, a forensic psychiatrist from New York City, testified the following day, Saturday, February 23. He told jurors that in his opinion as a forensic psychiatrist, Hunt was sane at the time he'd killed Peter. Dr. Brodsky based his opinion on two interviews of Hunt that he had conducted as well as Hunt's recorded confession and his review of police reports.

Dr. Brodsky told jurors that Hunt did have the capacity to: (1) appreciate that killing Peter was a crime and that (2) Hunt also "had the capacity to control his conduct and conform his conduct to the requirements of the law if he chose to do so."[176]

We knew that Dr. William Woodruff would testify later for the defense that, in his opinion, Hunt was insane at the time of the killing. But we had strong evidence that Dr. Brodsky was right. We would emphasize the testimony of the witnesses who'd interacted with Hunt the day of the murder to prove that Hunt clearly understood that what he was doing was a crime and that he was calculating rather than "out of control."

First, of course, there was the testimony of Peter's friends about how Hunt had calmly lied about Peter not being home and Hunt's feigned show of shared grief at Peter's death.

Trono's investigator, Howard Fitzpatrick, testified right after Dr. Brodsky. He provided even more compelling testimony that Hunt knew what he had done was wrong. Fitzpatrick told jurors how Hunt had tried a desperate cover-up. Fitzpatrick was immediately suspicious of Hunt because Hunt, who lived right above Peter's apartment, first claimed that he had been sleeping all day and had not heard any gunshots. A half hour later, according to Fitzpatrick, Hunt had altered his story and said he'd been playing his stereo and that was probably why hadn't heard the gunshot.

Fitzpatrick began to look for the murder weapon. Hunt tagged along, and when Fitzpatrick started to go up the stairs to the attic—where he later discovered that Hunt had hidden the rifle that was used to kill Peter—Hunt had told Fitzpatrick that he couldn't go into the attic because it was "private."

Fitzpatrick told Hunt to go back downstairs, and he'd continued to the attic and eventually found the rifle. He testified that Hunt was coherent at the time but seemed tired.

State Police Detective Ron DeVincenzi testified on Monday, February 25, 1985, the third day of testimony. He had questioned Hunt after he had agreed to come to the Barre Police Station. After waiving his Miranda rights, Hunt at first denied involvement in the murder then gave a 25-minute confession, which DeVincenzi recorded. DeVincenzi played that recording for the jury at trial three years later.[177]

Jurors heard Hunt explain to DeVincenzi that he had heard Peter come home. He had first made sure that Peter was alone, then knocked on the door and did not respond when Peter told him to come in. Then Hunt had knocked again. Peter had come to the door and opened it. Hunt said that he'd shot Peter once in the face as Peter opened the door.

Hunt told DeVincenzi: "I don't really know why I shot him. I had nothing against him. He seemed like a nice guy. I've always had it in my head to kill someone." This is, of course, a bizarre, chilling statement. We couldn't explain why it made sense to the jury because it didn't make sense to us. Quite often, there is no logical reason for killing someone. But, of course, that doesn't excuse them from being criminally responsible for their actions.

The defense case centered on the testimony of Dr. William Woodruff, a well-known forensic psychiatrist from Burlington who testified that in his opinion, Hunt was insane at the time he killed Peter.

Dr. Woodruff told jurors that Hunt, in his opinion, had suffered from a combination of "personality disorders" that caused him to feel "compelled" to kill Peter. He testified further that Hunt did not realize until after he'd killed Peter that what he was doing was wrong. According to Woodruff, the "psychological boil burst" the day before the killing when Hunt had learned for certain that his 15-year-old girlfriend was leaving him and taking their child with her.

Woodruff emphasized that Hunt had been affected by the fact that he had grown up in a "grossly disturbed" family environment. There was no dispute on this issue. Hunt's father told jurors that he was an alcoholic who had abused Hunt as a child. He also testified that he had been hospitalized at the Vermont State Mental Hospital for depression. Hunt's mother testified that she, too, had been hospitalized for depression.[178]

However, Dr. Woodruff admitted under cross-examination by Terry Trono that he had once reversed his opinion that a defendant was insane at the time of an alleged attempted murder in Montpelier after he'd learned that the defendant had lied to him. Woodruff conceded that Hunt had a history of "persistent lying" and that in his taped confession, Hunt had made no mention of being in a "dream-like state" or of the "blackout" he had spoken of when Woodruff had interviewed him.[179]

For its part, the defense underlined the danger of a forensic psychiatrist relying on the truthfulness of the defendant he was examining. We made the point by getting our psychiatrist, Dr. Brodsky, to admit that he had once "diagnosed a man as suffering from the so-called post-Vietnam stress syndrome," and then he later learned that the man had never been to Vietnam. [180]

Thus ended "the battle of the experts" and the trial.

In his closing argument, Terry Trono emphasized that we did not have to prove a killing "made sense" to overcome an insanity plea and prove that someone is "criminally responsible." We had to prove that when Hunt shot Peter, he could control what he was doing and he knew what he was doing was wrong. He told jurors that the evidence and their common sense told them that Hunt could control his conduct and that he did know what he was doing was wrong.[181]

I had tried several low-level jury trials (e.g., drunk driving, burglary) for Lamoille County State's Attorney Joel Page, who was just starting what turned out to be 32 years of service as State's Attorney.[182]

As I said earlier, it was traditional practice in the Attorney General's Office to have assistant AGs from the criminal division fill in to try jury trials for state's attorneys who requested help. My experience with Lamoille County jurors had been good in that they took their duty as jurors seriously, were generally "no-nonsense," and took relatively little time to reach a verdict.

I felt we had proven that Hunt was not insane at the time of the killing.

Hunt knew what he had done was wrong. That is why he'd dragged Peter's body back into the apartment and locked the door. That is why he'd lied to Wendy Curran, Peter's receptionist, and had tried to convince her Peter wasn't home. That is why he'd tried to keep Howard Fitzpatrick, Trono's investigator, from going into the attic where the murder weapon was.

Moreover, Hunt was definitely not "out of control." For instance, he had waited and checked to ensure Peter was alone before he'd gone down to Peter's apartment with the rifle. And he had not charged in when Peter had responded to Hunt's first knock by saying to come in. Instead, he had waited a few seconds and knocked again, causing Peter to come and open it. This made it easy for Hunt to surprise Peter and shoot him as he'd opened the door.

Still, I was concerned that jurors would conclude Hunt "must have been crazy" because of his statement that he didn't know why he had shot Peter other than that he had "always had it in [his] head to shoot someone."

I needn't have worried. The jury found Hunt guilty of first-degree murder after deliberating for less than two and a half hours.[183]

Ironically, at the same time the Hunt murder trial was going on in Hyde Park in Lamoille County, another murder trial had been going on in White River Junction some 85 miles to the south in Windsor County.

Roger Davis, a 42-year-old logger, was charged with first-degree murder for shooting his longtime girlfriend to death in her home in Chester, Vermont, after a "lover's quarrel."

The Davis case was similar to our trial in that Davis had confessed to the killing and had pled not guilty by reason of insanity, and the prosecution had the burden of proving the defendant was sane at the time of the murder. Unlike our trial, though, the defense was able to document 10 years of Davis' paranoid delusions—multiple unfounded claims that his girlfriend had been having affairs with other men. And, unlike Gordon Hunt, who had at first tried to cover up his crime, Roger Davis made an unsuccessful effort to kill himself after shooting his victim.

Defense counsel Harry Black and Gary Weiland took the highly unusual and very risky move of putting Davis on the stand to testify in his own defense. According to press reports, defense counsel felt that Davis's testimony was the "turning point in the trial" because jurors could watch and listen as Davis testified with conviction about his girlfriend's alleged affairs with "several Chester town officials and her own son." Again, there were no affairs, but, according to Defense Attorney Gary Wieland, Davis was so convinced of the victim's infidelity that "he could pass a lie detector test."

On February 27, 1985, the day we rested our case in the Hunt case, the jury found Roger Davis *not guilty by reason of insanity* after 10 hours of deliberation.[184]

Davis was committed to the Vermont State Hospital in Waterbury, Vermont, where he would be held pending a hearing on whether he should be committed to the hospital for involuntary mental health treatment. The Windsor County prosecutors would again have the burden of proof. This time, though, they would have to prove by "clear and convincing evidence" that Davis was *"suffering from a mental disease"* and that as a result of that disease, "he was a danger to himself or others."[185]

Gordon Hunt was sentenced to serve 30 years to life in prison by Superior Judge Alden Bryan and two assistant judges in Lamoille Superior Court in Hyde Park on April 26, 1985. This was twenty years more than he would have served under the plea agreement that had been rejected by Chittenden County assistant judges two years earlier. The case, which the *Burlington Free Press* described as "one of the longest and most controversial" in Vermont history, had gone up to the Vermont Supreme Court for review on various issues six times before it even went to trial.[186]

The thing that I remember most about the sentencing was Peter's grandfather. The victim's grandfather stood up, looked directly at Hunt, and asked, almost pleading for an answer, "Was my grandson smiling when he opened the door?" I can still say now, almost 40 years later, that this is one of the saddest, most deeply affecting moments I can remember in my life as a lawyer.

Hunt's conviction and sentence were affirmed more than three years later in October 1988 by the Vermont Supreme Court.[187]

INSANE OR NOT?

In 1986, a year after I tried the Gordon Hunt murder case with Washington County state's attorney, Terry Trono, Franklin County State's Attorney Howard VanBenthuysen asked me to work with him on another murder case that was going to trial. The defendant in this case, like Hunt, was relying on an insanity defense.

The killer, Kent Hanson, age 42, had pled not guilty by reason of insanity to the May 4, 1985, murder of Helena, a woman from Middlebury, Vermont, who Hanson had been dating.[188]

The killing had taken place at a camp in Georgia in Franklin County in northwestern Vermont. The camp was on Georgia Shore Road, which runs along the eastern shore of Lake Champlain.

Hanson had been living at the camp—which was owned by William Gonyeau—since his release from prison in mid-April 1985. Mr. Gonyeau and his wife had found Helena's body when they'd come back to their camp around 10:30 a.m. on Sunday morning, May 5, 1985. Vermont's chief medical examiner, Dr. Eleanor McQuillen said Helena died "quite rapidly" of a single shot to her "left chest."

A state police officer told a reporter that Helena had met Hanson in prison while she was visiting her brother. Hanson, who had an extensive criminal record, had killed Helena just three weeks after his release from prison and while he was on parole. Hanson's release had been ordered by the Vermont Parole Board despite the objections of Hanson's Department of Corrections caseworker.

Hanson was arrested the day after Helena's body was found.[189] He had fled to New York state in her car and had gotten involved in a minor accident in Dannemora, which is approximately 50 miles west of the site of the killing. The weapon used to kill Helena was found in the car. It was still loaded.

It was not the first time Hanson had killed someone. Hanson had escaped criminal liability for killing his young wife more than 20 years earlier. That first killing was in 1964. It had happened in Brattleboro, Vermont, which is about 170 miles southeast of the camp in Georgia where Hanson killed Helena.

In November 1964, Kent Hanson, who was then 21 years old, shot and killed his 22-year-old wife. He left her body on the basement floor of his parent's home in Brattleboro. An autopsy revealed that his wife, Joan, had died from "a number of gunshot wounds to her head and body." The couple, who had no children, had lived less than a mile away from where the body was found.[190]

Hanson was held without bail and pled not guilty on grounds that he was insane at the time he'd killed Joan.

Two months later, in January 1965, a Windham County grand jury meeting in Brattleboro refused to indict Hanson for the murder of his wife. The jurors had evidently relied on the testimony of Dr. Rupert Chittick, a psychiatrist who'd testified that Hanson had been insane at the time he had killed his wife. Dr. Chittick was superintendent of the Vermont State Hospital, the State's secure psychiatric facility in Waterbury, Vermont, where Hanson had been held following his arrest.

Dr. Chittick warned that Hanson was "dangerous" and should remain confined to the Waterbury State Hospital until he overcame the mental illness that had caused him to kill his young wife.[191]

Howard VanBenthuysen asked me to work on the Hanson case sometime in the fall of 1986. He was not elected Franklin County state's attorney until November 1986. The former state's attorney, Helen Torino, had hoped to get the case tried before she left office.

The site of the trial had been moved out of Franklin County to Hyde Park in Lamoille County due to pre-trial publicity. But Torino and VanBenthuysen had been unable to pick a jury in Hyde Park— again, because so many potential jurors had heard of the Hanson case. According to Torino, "Too many people knew something about him or his past, including the prior homicide."[192]

By the time I got involved in late 1986, the plan was to pick a jury in Burlington in Chittenden County in early February 1987.

My family and I were living in Barre, Vermont, when State's Attorney VanBenthuysen asked me to work on the Hanson murder trial. I remember spending the night at the Cadillac Motel in St. Albans, meeting with VanBenthuysen, then later driving to the camp that was the site of the killing, which was about five miles south of the motel.

VanBenthuysen was the lead. As I recall, I was to do the opening statement and focus on countering Hanson's insanity defense.

Hanson's insanity defense was not as strong as it had been 20 years earlier when he'd shot and killed his first wife. For one thing, in 1964, the prosecution had the burden of proof. That is, in 1964, the prosecution had to prove beyond a reasonable doubt that Hanson was not insane at the time he'd shot his wife.

It was going to be tough to sell the defense to jurors.

While it was undisputed that in 1963 Hanson had undergone a dramatic change in his personality after an operation following a brain aneurysm,[193] the fact that he had immediately fled Helena's murder scene with the murder weapon would make it difficult to prove that he didn't understand that shooting Helena was a crime.

It was also going to be hard for Hanson to prove that he couldn't control his conduct. Hanson had killed Ms. Warner in a secluded cabin with a single rifle shot to the "left upper chest" that had caused her to die "quite rapidly." It was clearly a shot that was intended to kill.

In the end, I didn't get to attack Hanson's insanity defense. VanBenthuysen and I had gone to the courthouse in Burlington on Tuesday, February 3, 1987, prepared to pick a jury and eventually try Hanson's case. But the public defender who was handling Hanson's case came to VanBenthuysen just as we were about to pick a jury to tell him that Hanson wanted to settle the case.

VanBenthuysen agreed to what I thought was a reasonable plea agreement: (1) Hanson would plead "no contest" to second-degree murder; (2) State's Attorney VanBenthuysen would argue for a sentence of 20 to 30 years in prison; and (3) there would be a contested sentencing hearing at which Hanson would argue for a sentence of 10 to 15 years in prison.[194]

On July 25, 1987, Hanson, who had picked up 16 criminal convictions since his first killing in 1964, was sentenced to the 20 to 30 years VanBenthuysen had requested.[195]

It was a lot harder to sell an "insanity defense" in 1987 than it had been 20 years earlier. The law had changed, and so had jurors' willingness to accept the defense. Hanson and his lawyer undoubtedly took this into consideration when they accepted the plea agreement.

From Private Practice to Utility Cases

I left the Attorney General's office in late 1987 to give private practice another try. I worked as an associate in two good firms from mid-1987 to 1990. This experience confirmed that private practice was "not my cup of tea."

From 1990 to early 1994, I worked as a lawyer for the Vermont Public Service Department, which is the state agency responsible for representing the public in public utility cases before the Vermont Public Service Board and the Vermont Supreme Court.

There was no doubt that working for the Department of Public Service would be challenging for me because I would have to evaluate and challenge the testimony of economists, engineers, and accountants—something that I had never done before. But I was happy to get a chance to take on the work. Most of the experts I worked with in the department were more than willing to take the time necessary to explain the issues they were working on to me. I remember, in particular, that engineers who gave crucial expert testimony were gracious (and dogged) in trying to drill the basics into my head.

I had two basic jobs at the department.

I spent most of my time representing the tens of thousands of people and businesses ("ratepayers") who paid electric bills to Green Mountain Power (GMP) and Central Vermont Public Service Corporation (CVPS) in "rate cases" before the Vermont Public Service Board. This meant that I worked with other lawyers in the Public Service Department in challenging proposed increases in the rates per kilowatt hour that companies like GMP wanted to charge their customers. This litigation involved presenting testimony and cross-examining experts over the course of weeks of hearings in an effort to convince the Board to cut millions of dollars from rate increases proposed by GMP or CVPS.

The case I remember best was one in 1992. I litigated the case with another department lawyer over 20 days of hearings. The public service board had rejected the public service department's request to make cuts amounting to roughly three million dollars from a portion of Green Mountain Power's budget. We appealed. I argued the appeal before the Vermont Supreme Court. The court reversed the public service board's decision. As a result, ratepayers saved three million dollars.[196]

I spent much less time on my second basic job, which was to write briefs and argue appeals before the Vermont Supreme Court. As things turned out, most of the work I did was briefing and arguing against appeals by an environmental group that had challenged the Public Service Board's decision to approve a long-term contract to purchase what was projected to be $17 billion dollars worth of hydroelectric power from Hydro Quebec, Canada's largest electric power producer and North America's largest producer of renewable energy.

The Vermont Supreme Court ultimately denied these appeals in three separate decisions.[197]

I learned a lot working for the Public Service Department and met a lot of smart, decent people. But I missed doing jury trials and working as a prosecutor.

With the support and encouragement of my wife, Toni, I took a job as an entry-level deputy state's attorney in Chittenden County—the same job I had 15 years earlier when I first became a lawyer. It meant a cut in pay of nearly 33 percent—$40,000 per year down to $27,000. Our two sons would soon be going to college, but Toni never wavered in her encouragement.

Soon, I was back on jury cases.

PART II
1994-2006

BACK TO TRYING CASES BEFORE JURIES

In late April 1994, I returned to work as a deputy state's attorney for Chittenden County State's Attorney Scot Kline.

The Chittenden County State's Attorney's Office had more than doubled in size since I'd left in 1981. In 1981, I was one of just four deputy state's attorney's. When I returned 13 years later in 1994, I was one of 12 deputies.

There had been a nearly 40 percent increase in violent crimes—murder, rape, robbery, and aggravated assault—in the 1980s. In the 1970s, the annual average of reported violent crimes was 551 per year. By the end of the 1980s, the annual average of reported violent crimes had risen to 758 per year.[198] This sharp increase in violent crime had prompted the Vermont Legislature to appropriate more money for Vermont law enforcement.

The additional deputies were needed to meet the increase in the violent crimes, but they were also needed to prosecute "new crimes," such as the sale of heroin, and crimes that had barely been prosecuted before, such as "domestic assaults."

When I worked in the State's Attorney's Office from 1979 to 1981, we each handled the appeals of any of the cases we tried. But when I returned in 1994, there was a deputy who handled all appeals. There were other specialities as well. There was a deputy who handled all juvenile cases and other deputies who specialized in sexual assault cases, drug cases, and domestic assault cases.

I worked for Scot Kline for less than three years. He left the job as state's attorney in 1997 to work in private practice and later became head of the Environmental Division at the Vermont Attorney General's Office. In 2018, he was appointed a superior court judge.

After I worked for Kline, I was chief deputy for the new State's Attorney Lauren Bowerman and later served as state's attorney of Chittenden County (2001–2006).

There was a definite change in the types of cases I tried when I returned to the Chittenden County State's Attorney's Office (CCSAO) in the 1990s. Although I had tried four murder cases in the 1980s, the vast majority of the cases I tried for the CCSAO in the early 1980s and the Attorney General's (AG) Office later in the 1980s were not violent crimes.

The overwhelming majority of cases that I'd tried for the CCSAO and other state's attorney's offices while working on loan to them during the 1980s were misdemeanor motor vehicle cases (such as DWI, negligent driving, leaving the scene of an accident) and nonviolent felonies (such as fraud, burglary, and unlawful trespass).

When I returned to the CCSAO from 1994 to 2006, however, nearly all the cases I prosecuted and tried were felonies, and the vast majority of those were violent felonies. The only exception was misdemeanor domestic assaults.

Drug Overdose Death

The first major case I volunteered to work on when I got back to the Chittenden County State's Attorney's Office was *State v. Angela Cianci*—an involuntary manslaughter case arising out of a heroin overdose death.

Sometime late in the evening of December 30, 1993, Michael, who was not long out of prison, wrapped a belt around his right arm to serve as a tourniquet and make his veins protrude so that his friend, Angela Cianci, age 30, could inject him with heroin. Before long, Michael, age 36, fell to his knees. He was suffering symptoms of a heroin overdose. Cianci did nothing to help him and even prevented another man from calling 911. Michael was found dead in the shower in Cianci's apartment roughly three hours later.

Deputy State's Attorney Phil Danielson,[199] who prosecuted most of the drug cases in the office at that time, had been handling the Cianci case alone when I returned to work at the Chittenden County State's Attorney's Office in April 1994. Later that summer, he asked me to work on the case. I was happy to get the chance.

Detective Corporal Don Lilja of the Burlington Police had been assigned as the chief investigating officer on the Cianci case. I recall that Lilja worked particularly hard on the case and that he did a good job putting the case together. He was also an important witness at trial.

In October 1994, roughly nine months after Michael's death, Angela Cianci, a self-described "junkie," was arraigned on two counts of involuntary manslaughter for causing Micheal's death. If she was convicted, she faced a sentence of up to 15 years in prison.

Our evidence showed that Michael and another man, RK, had come to Cianci's apartment at 14 North Winooski Avenue in Burlington in the afternoon or early evening of December 30, 1993. Michael had been a heavy heroin user before he'd gone to prison for a burglary. RK was a heroin user, too.

Michael had been paroled from prison just 10 days earlier. He knew Cianci was also a heroin addict. Michael had money, but he had lost touch with the local heroin scene while he was in prison. He gave Cianci money and asked her to buy heroin for him with the understanding that he would share it with her when she returned.

Cianci left to buy the heroin while Michael and RK waited in her apartment.

According to RK, when Cianci returned with the heroin, she injected Michael, RK, and herself with it. RK said that not long after being injected, Michael "fell to his knees and held onto the counter." He was suffering symptoms of a heroin overdose.

Cianci called a friend who told her to put Michael, who was unconscious but breathing, into the shower in her apartment. His condition worsened while he was in the shower. According to RK, he began coughing and wheezing. RK told Cianci to call 911. She refused. So RK dialed 911 himself. But Cianci hung up the phone before it could be answered.[200]

Cianci was eventually charged with two counts of involuntary manslaughter.

The first count alleged that Cianci "unlawfully" caused Michael's death by injecting him with heroin and in doing so recklessly created a grave risk that Michael would die or suffer serious bodily injury.[201]

The second count alleged that Cianci had unlawfully caused Michael's death, again by acting recklessly—this time by ignoring the fact that once she had created a grave risk that Michael would suffer death or serious bodily injury, she had a duty to come to Michael's aid when he showed symptoms that he was suffering from an overdose.

We felt we could prove that she had ignored that duty. Instead of coming to Michael's aid, she had stopped someone who was present from calling 911 and had then dragged his unconscious body into her shower and turned on the water. By then it was New Year's Eve, and Cianci busied herself with making eggnog and otherwise preparing for the holiday.

The evidence gathered by Lilja and other police investigators showed that when he was dragged into the shower, Michael's body had covered the shower drain, and the water from the shower overflowed into the apartment and began draining down the walls into the apartment below. Cianci told RK to move Michael's body so that it was not covering the drain. The overflow stopped, and Cianci went ahead preparing the apartment for the New Year's holiday.

Three hours passed before Cianci finally called 911. When police and rescue workers arrived at the scene at 2:55 a.m. on December 31, 1993, they found Michael's dead body in the shower.

Phil Danielson and I were concerned, however, that people in Chittenden County might not agree with our theory of Ms. Cianci's liability. This would be the first time our theory of manslaughter for failure to come to the aid of a drug overdose victim would be presented to a Vermont jury in a criminal trial.

No doubt Cianci had behaved badly. But was she guilty of a crime? Was she "criminally responsible" for Michael's death? After all, he was the one who had asked Cianci to buy the heroin for him, and he had asked her to inject him. We wanted to feel confident that members of the Chittenden County community who would eventually sit on the jury would not find that Michael had "assumed the risk" or "brought it all upon himself" when he'd given Cianci money to get him heroin and inject him with it. Members of the community might say: *Why should Cianci be held criminally responsible for doing something that Michael had asked her to do?*

This concern was what convinced us to put our evidence before a Chittenden County Grand Jury to see whether citizens of Chittenden County thought there was enough evidence to indict or charge Cianci with manslaughter.

Grand juries, which originated in English common law in the Middle Ages, are not like 12-person criminal trial juries where the prosecutor must meet the highest burden of proof in the US Justice System—"proof beyond a reasonable doubt"—in order to get a conviction. Grand juries are called upon to determine whether there is enough evidence to charge a person with a crime. The burden the prosecutors must meet to get a grand jury to indict/charge a person is much lower than the proof beyond a reasonable doubt. More specifically, the prosecution must prove there is "probable cause" to believe (a "fair probability") that a person has committed a crime.

There are other differences between a criminal trial jury and a grand jury.

For one thing, grand juries in Vermont are composed of between 18 and 23 men and women who are drawn at random, usually from voting lists of the country where the crime took place. These are not the same as the 12-person jury that renders a verdict—guilty or not guilty—in criminal trials. For another, unlike a criminal trial jury verdict, which requires unanimity, a grand jury can charge if 12 of the 23 members vote to indict.

More differences. Unlike a criminal jury trial, the judge who convenes the grand jury is not present during proceedings and only reappears to preside when the grand jury announces its decision on whether to indict. And unlike criminal jury trials where the defendant and his attorney have a constitutional right to be present during the proceedings when evidence is presented, the "target" and his attorney have no right to be present during grand jury proceedings. Finally, in most cases, the rules of evidence that apply at trial (civil, as well as criminal) do not apply in grand jury proceedings.

In short, the prosecution "runs the whole show." This has given rise to the adage that prosecutors can get a "grand jury to indict a ham sandwich" because of their complete control over what evidence is presented and how it is presented.

As mentioned earlier, though, grand juries are used sparingly by state prosecutors in Vermont. In the federal system, the US Constitution requires a grand jury indictment if a person is to be charged with a felony in Federal Court. However, Vermont state court prosecutors have the discretion to charge crimes, including felonies, by presenting the proposed charge ("information") that is supported by a police officer's affidavit of probable cause to a judge. If the state court judge finds there is "probable cause"—i.e., there is a "fair probability" that the target committed the crime—then the person is "charged" and his case is scheduled for arraignment where he enters a plea of "guilty" or "not guilty."

The decision to put the Cianci evidence before a grand jury was not done on a whim. We wanted to charge Cianci with a homicide, but because the facts of the case were so unusual, we wanted to be sure that the people in the community shared our view. We didn't want to be "tilting at windmills."

We put our evidence before 23 grand jurors over the course of two days in early October 1994. As things turned out, the grand jury did not have any trouble indicting Ms. Cianci. I do recall, though, that one grand juror expressed some irritation that he and other grand jurors were being used to see whether they agreed with our view of the evidence. He was right, but I saw no reason to apologize. There was no need to put Cianci through a trial if members of the community like him did not agree with our theory that Cianci had a duty to get help for Michael once he'd collapsed following the heroin injection that Michael, himself, had asked Cianci to give him.

On October 6, 1994, the day after the grand jury indicted Angela Cianci, she was arraigned and pled not guilty to the two counts of involuntary manslaughter. Her court-appointed defense attorney was Bob Andres, an experienced trial lawyer.

Angela Cianci went on trial for Michael's death on Tuesday, April 11, 1995. Cianci's former apartment, where Michael had collapsed and died, was just four blocks from the Costello Courthouse in Burlington where Cianci was being tried for manslaughter.

Mike Donoghue, a veteran *Burlington Free Press* newspaper reporter,[202] wrote that the Cianci case was "precedent setting" because it was believed to be the first time a Vermont jury would be asked to find that a defendant was criminally liable "for failing to come to the aid of a victim of a fatal drug overdose."

The trial lasted a little over a week, from Tuesday, April 11, 1995 through the verdict on Wednesday, April 19, 1995. We called a dozen witnesses, including two experts.

Phil Danielson did the opening for the prosecution. He laid out the facts of the case, emphasizing Cianci's failure to help Michael or even permit others to get help for him after he'd collapsed from the heroin overdose she had administered. He went on to tell jurors that Cianci had told police conflicting stories about her role in Michael's death, including one that she had been asleep when Michael had collapsed and died.

Danielson told jurors that Cianci had prevented RK from calling 911. He said there was little doubt that Michael's life could have been saved if rescue workers had been called.

Bob Andres, Cianci's attorney, did not dispute the claim that Cianci had failed to come to Michael's aid. He told jurors she had no duty to do so under the circumstances. He said that Cianci had fallen asleep in her apartment and had not been aware that Michael was unconscious and not breathing until she'd woken up. When she'd realized Michael's condition, she'd called 911.

Andres also told jurors that "the State" (Danielson and me) had chosen not to charge our key witness and another man—the man who had sold the heroin that had eventually killed Michael. He said that by doing so we "had compromised the truth."

We called four witnesses on the first day of the trial.

A Burlington firefighter/rescue worker who was first on the scene reported that Cianci had not mentioned drugs or the fact that another man (RK) had been present. He said that when he came into the apartment, Cianci had pointed toward the shower and said: "He's in there, I don't think he is breathing." He'd quickly confirmed that Cianci was right. Michael was in her shower and there was no doubt he was dead.

A Burlington police officer, who was among the first to arrive at the scene, explained that he'd felt that Michael's death was "suspicious" in part because Michael was lying dead and "half-dressed" in the shower. But his shirt and coat were folded neatly under his boots next to the shower.

The State's expert chemist, Robert Middleberg, told jurors that tests revealed that Michael had morphine and a high amount of alcohol in his blood when he'd died. Middleberg explained to jurors that heroin is converted to morphine when it enters the body. The jurors also learned that there was a drug—Narcan—that reverses the effects of an opiate overdose if it is administered to a person who is alive but suffering from a heroin overdose.

Our key witness, RK, testified on Wednesday and Thursday. RK had moved to Nevada after Michael's death. The State of Vermont had paid to bring him back to Vermont for the trial.

RK's testimony was key because if the jurors believed him, then we had proven both counts of involuntary manslaughter. It was that simple. RK testified that sometime late on Thursday, December 30, 1993, he saw Cianci inject Micheal with heroin (Count 1) and that not long after that, he fell to his knees and began to show signs that he was suffering from an overdose. Cianci not only failed to come to Michael's aid, she'd prevented RK from calling 911 (Count 2).

But, of course, it was not that simple. RK was a heroin user himself. Bob Andres was able, during cross-examination, to pick away at his recollection in an effort to undermine his credibility before the jury.

I remember one particularly startling exchange between RK and Andres. I can't remember how Andres got him to do it, but RK testified that he had seen God one time while he was using heroin. Andres asked him what God looked like.

It was a long time ago, but my memory is that RK said God had "long blonde hair and blue eyes."

Phil Danielson brought RK's testimony back into focus on re-direct examination. RK eventually testified that Cianci had injected heroin into the arms of both men, RK and Michael. She had then injected herself. This had all happened not long before midnight on Thursday, December 30, according to RK.

RK told jurors that Michael had suffered a reaction to the heroin almost immediately. He'd fallen to his knees and grabbed the kitchen counter in Cianci's apartment. RK and Cianci had moved him onto the porch of Cianci's apartment in an effort to revive him. It didn't work.

According to RK, Cianci had balked at first when RK began to bring Michael back into her apartment from the porch, but eventually she'd relented. Then she'd called a friend, who had advised her to put Michael in her shower and turn on the water. After a while, they'd realized that Michael's body was covering the shower drain and the water was overflowing into the apartment. Cianci told RK to take the body off the drain but to leave it in the shower. He did.

RK told jurors that a short time after that, he, himself, had passed out. When RK woke up, Michael had been "purple and cold." RK had testified that he'd tried to call 911 to get assistance for Michael, but Cianci had grabbed the phone and hung it up. According to RK, she said she didn't want police in the apartment.

It was around 2:15 a.m. on Friday, December 31—New Year's Eve. RK said Cianci had ordered him out of her apartment but had allowed him time to call a cab. He'd called a cab and left.

Cianci's downstairs neighbor at the time Michael died was also an important witness. We claimed, based on RK's testimony, that Michael had suffered the severe reaction to the heroin Cianci had injected shortly before midnight on Thursday evening, December 30, and that Cianci had sabotaged RK's efforts to get help for Michael.

The defense, of course, had argued otherwise. Bob Andres told jurors in his opening statement that Cianci had been asleep when Michael had begun showing signs of distress and that she had called 911 as soon as she'd woken up and realized Michael's condition. That was around 3 a.m. on December 31. In other words, the defense argued that Cianci had learned of Michael's distress three hours later than RK said she did.

The testimony of the downstairs neighbor, Michael Bonnet,

supported our claim and our theory of the case. He told jurors that water had begun to leak into his apartment from Cianci's apartment above at 11:30 p.m. on Thursday, the 30th. Bonnet said that the water had stopped leaking into his apartment about a half hour later around midnight. This supported our claim that Cianci had waited at least three hours before calling for help for the victim.

We also introduced evidence, over Andres's objection, that Cianci had stolen money from Michael's wallet while he'd been dying in the shower.

Burlington Police Detective Peter Bottino testified that he had found Michael's wallet hidden in a hole in a cinder block just outside Cianci's apartment. There had been no money in it. However, RK had testified that Michael had approximately $160 in the wallet when Cianci had injected him. We called another witness, Stephen Duncan. He testified that Cianci had been broke when he, Cianci, and Michael had gone to the food shelf in Burlington on Thursday afternoon for free groceries. But according to Duncan, the next morning, about eight hours after Michael's body was found, Duncan said that Cianci had a "handful of money," and she had gone shopping at a local convenience store.[203]

On Friday, April 15, 1995, Detective Don Lilja, the lead investigator on the case, testified that Angela Cianci had told him at first she would not allow drugs in her apartment. She'd insisted that Michael had come to her apartment alone and intoxicated around 12:30 a.m. on Friday morning, December 31, 1993. Lilja told the jury that Cianci had told him that she'd fallen asleep after Michael's arrival and had not woken up until around 2:30 a.m. When she'd woken up, she'd found him dead in her shower and had called 911 right away.

Lilja said that she later admitted that she did use drugs. According to Detective Lilja, Angela Cianci also admitted that she had put the heroin in front of Michael on a counter in her apartment. But she insisted that he had injected himself with the heroin.[204]

Vermont's chief medical examiner, Dr. Paul Morrow, told jurors that in his expert opinion, Michael had died of a heroin overdose. Dr. Morrow also testified that marks on Michael's arms were "consistent with" him having been dragged. This supported RK's testimony that Cianci, acting on the advice of a friend she'd phoned, had ordered RK to drag Michael's unconscious body into her shower and turn on the water.

We rested our case following Dr. Morrow's testimony.

On the following Monday, the defense put on its case. Angela Cianci had exercised her Fifth Amendment right and declined to testify. As it turned out, the defense called two witnesses—John Lefebvre and Ed "Rocky" Campanelli. It is not clear why they were called. Both men testified that when Cianci had called after Michael's collapse, they had urged her to call 911 and get emergency help.

The defense rested its case on Monday, April 17, 1995.

The prosecution and defense made their closing arguments first thing Tuesday morning, April 18.

Phil Danielson asked me to do our closing argument.

In the prosecution's first closing, I went through key elements of the two counts of involuntary manslaughter and pointed to the evidence we relied on to prove them—evidence, that I said, required them to find Angela Cianci "guilty" on both counts. It was all very matter-of-fact and straightforward. It didn't take more than 15 minutes.

With respect to Count 1, I said we had proven the first element (the "identity" or "whodunit" element), through the testimony of RK, who had told jurors that he'd seen Angela Cianci inject Michael with heroin before she'd injected RK and herself.

As for the second element, there was no dispute that injecting someone with heroin, a dangerous, illegal drug, was a reckless act. We had proven the substance Cianci had injected into Michael was, in fact, heroin through the testimony of Robert Middleberg, an expert chemist, who had explained to jurors that tests revealed that Michael had morphine in his system and that the body converts heroin into morphine when the heroin enters the system. So, we had proven the second element.

We had proven the final element—that Cianci's reckless act in injecting heroin into Michael's arm—had "caused" Michael's death through the testimony of Dr. Paul Morrow, state medical examiner, who had testified that in his expert opinion Michael had died of a heroin overdose.

As for Count 2, I told jurors we had proven this count through the testimony of RK and the two experts. Much of the evidence we'd used to prove Count 1 also served to prove Count 2.

That is, RK testified that Cianci had injected Michael with heroin, a potentially deadly drug, shortly before midnight. RK had an adverse reaction almost immediately, and shortly after that he'd became unconscious. Since Cianci had given him the drug that had put Michael at risk of death, she had a duty to call 911 and get help for him. Help that would have saved his life. Instead, she'd not only ignored the advice of friends who'd told her to call 911, but she'd actually prevented RK from calling 911. She owed a duty to Michael, she ignored it for three hours, and she instead made eggnog and otherwise prepared for a New Year's celebration. When she'd finally called 911, Michael was already dead. Her reckless refusal to honor her duty to come to Michael's aid had cost him his life.

The defense closing was short. The defense attorney, Bob Andres, made the most of what he had in his closing argument. Not surprisingly, he went after RK, our key witness. He had done a good job in cross-examining RK. He portrayed RK as a drug-addled liar.

Andres reminded jurors that the prosecution had the burden of proof and that they simply could not find that we had met that burden by relying, as we had, on RK's testimony. He argued that it was more reasonable to believe that RK himself had injected Michael with heroin and that RK had made the false claim that Angela Cianci had done it to shift blame from himself.

My rebuttal to Andres's argument was also brief. I asked jurors to remember that Cianci had told Detective Lilja that Michael had come to her apartment alone. In her statement to Lilja, she'd never claimed that RK had injected Michael with heroin. In fact, she'd denied RK was in her apartment that night. Finally, I reminded them that after saying she would never allow drugs in her home, she had admitted to Detective Lilja that she had placed heroin on the counter in front of Michael.

I told jurors that if they were concerned that Michael had asked Cianci to commit what we were now labeling a "reckless act," they might be thinking: *Why should the defendant be found guilty for committing an act that Michael asked her to commit?* It's true, of course, that he did ask her to inject heroin into his system. He made a mistake, and he'd paid the ultimate price. He was dead. I asked them to please remember that this was not an errand of mercy on the defendant's part. She'd gotten something out of it, too. She'd used the heroin that she'd obtained for Michael with his money, and she'd injected herself with it after she'd injected him. That was part of the deal she made.

More importantly, I asked them to please remember that she'd waited at least three hours to come to his aid despite several people advising her to call 911. "The evidence has shown that she had a duty to come to his aid. He died because Ms. Cianci, the defendant, ignored that duty. You speak for the community. Here you are speaking as the conscience of the community."[205]

Judge Dean Pineles gave the jury his instructions on the law on Tuesday morning, April 18. He explained to the 12 jurors the law that they were to apply to the facts of the case. They were "judges of the facts," but they would have to apply those facts to the law that he was about to explain to them.

Charging two counts of manslaughter complicated the case. After all, Michael had only died once, and the fact that Cianci had injected him with heroin that eventually caused his death was alone legally sufficient to convict him. If Cianci was found "guilty" on both counts, it wouldn't change the maximum sentence under the law. The maximum would be 15 years whether she was found guilty of one or both counts.

However, if we did not charge the second count, the jury would not hear that Cianci had basically left Michael to die. If there had been such a thing as "aggravated involuntary manslaughter," Cianci would have qualified.

Judge Pineles made it clear in his instructions to the jury that there could be no "guilty" verdict unless jurors were unanimous. In other words, for instance, if only 11 jurors found that the State had proven that Cianci had caused Michael's death by injecting him with heroin (Count 1), Cianci could not be found "guilty." Even if the 12th juror who was unable to find the prosecution had proven Count 1 *did find* that the prosecution had proven that Cianci's failure to come to Michael's aid had caused his death (Count 2) Cianci could still not be found "guilty."

The jury deliberated for nine hours from 11:45 a.m. to 8:45 p.m. on Tuesday, April 18. It deliberated another hour on the morning of April 19 before announcing to Judge Pineles that they were unanimous in finding Ms. Cianci "guilty" on both counts.[206]

Judge Pineles sentenced Cianci to four to 12 years to serve in prison. He told Cianci: "The sympathy mat is not rolled out. Mr. [redacted] could have been saved with minimal effort."[207]

In the early 2000s, five to 10 years after the Cianci trial, the "heroin problem" subsided somewhat in Chittenden County. This was due to aggressive law enforcement and the creation of a "Drug Court," which had been developed by Judges James Crucitti and Dean Pineles. Both men had been shocked by the growth of the "heroin problem," and they set up a special court where people charged with crimes who were drug addicts were given an opportunity to get a "probationary sentence" (no prison) as long as they complied with a court-ordered drug treatment plan.

In late October 2002, Vermont's first medical treatment center for drug addicts opened in Burlington. It was named the Chittenden Center. The Chittenden treatment clinic treated heroin addicts with the drug methadone. The 100 slots available in the Chittenden Center were quickly filled, and by May 2003, there were 100 people on the waiting list.[208]

In 2003, the Vermont Legislature enacted a statute that made selling or "dispensing" an illegal drug that results in the death of person a crime punishable by up to 20 years in prison.[209]

In November 2003, Judge William Sessions, Federal District Judge in Burlington, sentenced Shawn Gibson to 25 years for injecting his girlfriend with heroin and leaving for Massachusetts. She died of an overdose in Gibson's bedroom.[210]

I was Chittenden County state's attorney from October 2001 through August 2006. My policy on overdoses was to charge these cases if the person who delivered the drugs left the scene when a person overdosed and "went down." If the person who overdosed died, the person who delivered the drugs and left the scene would be charged with manslaughter. If the person who overdosed recovered, the person who left the scene might still be charged with aggravated assault, which was a felony.

On the other hand, if the person who delivered the drug stayed at the scene and assisted the person who overdosed in getting medical attention, then there would be no charges for delivering the illegal drug.

This overall approach was later criticized in Vermont as too harsh. Whatever the approach was from 2005 to 2022, it failed miserably. In 2005, Vermont averaged 8.5 drug overdose deaths per 100,000, which put Vermont among the states with the lowest per capita overdose death rates in the country (37th). By 2022, drug overdose deaths in Vermont had more than quadrupled. Overdose deaths in Vermont in 2022 were 45.9 per 100,000, which left Vermont with the 9th highest per capita overdose rate in the US.[211]

FATHER KOVEOS

Emmanuel Koveos, a third-generation Greek Orthodox priest, came to the US in 1970. In January 1997, he was the resident priest at Dormition Mother of God Greek Orthodox Church in Burlington. The church, which had 100 members, was the only Greek Orthodox Church in Vermont and drew parishioners from as far away as St. Albans and Montpelier.

But on January 23, 1997, sex crime investigators for the Burlington Police Department received a complaint that Father Koveos had groped and fondled a 12-year-old girl (AM) at the church while he had ostensibly been giving the child a lesson in the Greek language. The incident had happened in the late afternoon the day before, Wednesday, January 22, 1997.

The complaint had come from the child's mother, who had been a devoted member of the church. She and her husband had considered themselves friends of Father Koveos. But that friendship had dissolved into shock and anger when their child had broken down in tears and told her mother that the priest had put his hands between her legs and rubbed her vaginal area. Some members of the church were so upset by the girl's complaint that they said that Koveos and his wife of 33 years should be evicted from their church-owned home.[212]

AM said that while they were sitting at a table in the church main hall/conference area, Koveos had placed her leg over his and begun to rub her leg. He'd eventually moved his hand up between her legs and rubbed her vaginal area. This had happened in the presence of two other girls who were also sitting at the table for Greek lessons. The child said that later, Koveos had led her into his office, where he'd slid his hand under her shirt, down under jeans, and down her leg.[213]

Father Koveos, age 62, was interviewed by sex crimes investigator Linda Carey and Detective Lt. Steve Wark of the Burlington Police Department. Wark persuaded Koveos to write a "letter of apology" to the young girl. Not long after that, Father Koveos was arrested and charged with engaging in "lewd and lascivious conduct with a child"—a felony punishable by up to five years in prison.

On Friday, January 24, 1997, Father Koveos, a short, slightly built man with a dark beard and glasses, pled not guilty. Father Koveos posted $15,000 bail and was released on the condition that he not have any contact with AM or her family. He promptly retained Karen Shingler, a capable, experienced criminal defense attorney to represent him.

Father Koveos was temporarily suspended from the priesthood pending the outcome of the case.

In February 1997, not long after Father Koveos was arraigned, State's Attorney Scot Kline asked me if I would handle this case.

Kline warned me before I agreed to take on the case that the "letter of apology" that the sex crime investigators at the Chittenden Unit for Special Investigations (CUSI) had gotten Koveos to write to AM was subject to a claim that it was "involuntary." That is, a judge could find that the "letter of apology" was inadmissible because the detectives had taken advantage of Father Koveos's unfamiliarity with the law and the English language. The defense argument would be that Koveos had essentially signed a confession that had been dictated by detectives.

I had little experience in prosecuting sex crimes involving child victims. But I was pleased to be asked to take on a case where a man had used his position of power and respect to take advantage of a child who'd trusted him.

Father Koveos had been in the United States for 28 years when he went to trial in criminal court in Burlington in February 1998. He had served at churches in Pennsylvania; Lowell and Quincy, Massachusettes; and Concord, New Hampshire, before coming to serve in the church in Burlington in 1993. While in Burlington, he had served as a Greek interpreter in Federal Court and as a substitute teacher in addition to serving his parish.[214]

In late January 1998, approximately a week before the trial, the trial judge, James Crucitti, had to rule on whether three important pieces of evidence would be admissible.

The first was the "letter of apology." Again, the defense argued that Koveos's "confession" was "involuntary." In other words, he claimed that detectives had confused him and tricked him into saying and writing something he did not believe and did not understand. He was sorry that AM was upset by his conduct, but he did not intend this to be considered an admission to the lewd acts AM had claimed he had done. In short, the police had taken advantage of him and had tricked him into saying something he didn't mean.

Judge Crucitti made a preliminary ruling that Koveos's "letter of apology" was not involuntary. This meant I could introduce the letter and Lt. Wark's testimony about it at trial. But, under the law, the jury would have the final say on the question. They would be asked specifically, after hearing the evidence, whether they had determined this statement was made voluntarily. If they determined it was not voluntary and that police had tricked Koveos, they could not consider the "letter of apology" in deciding whether the prosecution had proven its case beyond a reasonable doubt. (Stay tuned.)

The second was the testimony of the two younger girls who were present when Father Koveos had started molesting the victim.

I gave notice that I wanted the little girls who were at the table with Koveos as well as the victim to testify as to what they saw. The parents of the girls objected and hired a member of a prominent Burlington law firm to represent them. The girls' father even filed an affidavit in which he swore the girls had no first-hand knowledge that was material to either Koveos's defense or the prosecution's efforts to prove Koveos's guilt.

We—the parents' lawyer, Koveos's attorney, and me—all agreed that the older of the two girls would testify at a videotaped deposition, conducted in the presence of a judge. The videotape could be played at trial. The young girls would never have to go to court and testify before the jury.

But once the videotaped deposition was completed, Koveos's attorney, Shingler, objected to having the jury hear portions of the child's videotaped testimony. Judge Crucitti said that Defense Attorney Shingler had probably waived the right to object because she had not objected during the deposition. Despite this, Judge Crucitti agreed to redact portions of the child's videotaped testimony.[215]

The third piece of evidence had to do with a young woman who had been a parishioner of Father Koveos in 1988 when he was the priest at

Holy Trinity Church in Concord, New Hampshire. She came forward to say that she had gone to Koveos for counseling because her marriage was breaking up. The woman said that Father Koveos had "counseled" her by showing her hardcore pornographic movies, making her touch him improperly, kissing her on the lips, and trying to "fondle" her. [216]

Attorney Shingler had filed a motion in limine to exclude the woman's testimony at trial, citing evidentiary rule 404 (b)—the rule against admitting "prior bad acts."

I had argued that the woman's testimony should be admissible. At one point, Father Koveos had told officers that the child had misunderstood his actions—he had not touched her for sexual gratification, he saw her as his "grandchild." Testimony that Koveos had sexually abused a female parishioner a few years earlier showed that his *intent* in touching the 12-year-girl at his church in Burlington was for sexual gratification (i.e., "lewd and lascivious")—not the innocent hugs of a grandfather.

Attorney Shingler countered that Father Koveos would not testify that the child had misunderstood his actions. He would testify that she was not telling the truth; he had not committed the acts she alleged (e.g., he had not touched her vaginal area).

Judge Crucitti granted Shingler's motion to exclude the young woman's testimony based on her representation that Koveos would testify that he had not committed the acts the child had alleged—*not that she had misunderstood his intent in making them*. But, he warned, "Should the issue of Defendant's intent be raised during trial, the court will reconsider its ruling."[217]

This issue—whether the young woman who claimed that Koveos had sexually abused her would be permitted to testify—turned out to be crucially important as the trial unfolded.

We picked the jury on Monday, February 2, 1998. As the jury draw began, Koveos's wife and their three adult sons sat in the first row of seats, directly behind the defense table where the priest and his attorney were sitting.

Father Koveos also had the support of a former judge and several members of the local clergy. I remember a man in a clerical collar who had also been sitting in seats behind the defense table. This gentleman evidently felt it important to come up to me, the prosecutor. He gestured to four or five other men in clerical garb sitting nearby and told me: "We are all here to support 'Manny.'"

I remember thinking: *Okay, that's your right, but how do you think that makes the 12-year-old girl, "Manny's" accuser, and her parents feel? Maybe it would make sense as Men of God to hear her out.*

It was a difficult jury draw.

I was concerned that people would find it difficult to convict a priest who had undoubtedly done many good works for the people in his church and his community over the nearly 30 years he had been a priest in the US.

I recall putting the question to one woman who had a large cross around her neck. Judging from her facial expressions, she was unhappy with what was going on. I aked, "Are you going to be able to convict this man if the State meets its burden and proves beyond a reasonable doubt that this man, a priest, touched this young girl inappropriately for his sexual gratification?"

Her answer was "no," she wouldn't convict him. "I think he is innocent." At my request, she was excused from being a juror "for cause," because she said she had undoubtedly prejudged the case before hearing any evidence.

There were 24 people chosen to be questioned as potential jurors. In addition to the potential juror who said Koveos was innocent, three others were excused for cause because they said they had prejudged the case. Although, unlike the woman who had thought Koveos innocent, these jurors did not say anything more than that, having heard pre-trial publicity on the case, they "could not be fair." Four other potential jurors were excused because either they or someone related to them had been a victim of sexual abuse.[218]

We eventually selected a jury of eight women and six men.[219]

It was a brief trial—just two days of testimony. The testimony began on Tuesday morning, February 4, and ended the following day on Wednesday afternoon, February 5.

On day one, I called AM's mother early in the trial. She told jurors that she had dropped her 12-year-old daughter off at the Greek Orthodox Church in Burlington around 4 p.m. on January 22, 1997. Her daughter was to take a lesson in the Greek language from Father Koveos. There were two other young girls there. They were there to take the Greek lesson, too. When AM's mom left, the three children were all with Father Koveos at a table in the main hall, or the conference area.

When the mom came back, her 12-year-old daughter was sitting alone with Father Koveos in his office. The mom told jurors that the priest was on the phone with her husband, AM's father. Koveos was telling the father that he, Father Koveos, would take the child home—no need for dad to pick her up at the church.

Mom testified that she didn't think much of Koveos's call to her husband until later. At the time, she picked up her daughter and the two younger girls (ages 8 and 9), who the priest had left in the main hall/ conference area with an adult who was a volunteer at the church.

Not long after, they left the church and were on their way home. AM broke into tears and told her mom what her priest and friend of the family had done to her. Her mom reacted with disgust and rage at the betrayal by the family's priest and friend.

Shortly after the mom's testimony, the jury heard videotaped testimony of one of the younger girls who had been present at the table in the main hall/conference area. As mentioned earlier, Judge Crucitti had redacted portions of the videotaped testimony at the defense counsel's request.

Despite the redaction, however, the videotaped testimony the jury heard was still damaging to Koveos. The 9-year-old child said her 12-year-old friend appeared nervous, uncomfortable, and near tears as Koveos rubbed her friend's back for around 20 minutes. Her friend, AM, was still upset when the priest took the 12-year-old AM's hand and led her into his office.

The young child also confirmed the mom's testimony that AM had broken down on the drive home from the Greek lesson and told her mom how Koveos had touched her.[220]

Lt. Wark testified that Father Koveos had admitted three times to him and Investigator Linda Carey that he had fondled the 12-year-old child. He also told jurors that Koveos had gone on to demonstrate where and how he had touched the young girl and that Koveos had written a "letter of apology" to the child.

Attorney Shingler challenged Wark in cross-examination, saying that Wark had used threats and lies to get the admissions from Koveos.

For instance, she said that Wark had told the priest, who had emigrated to the US from Greece 28 years earlier, that the area "all over the legs" was the "crotch." Shingler also got Wark to acknowledge that he had Koveos write three drafts of the "letter of apology" before it had enough detail to satisfy Wark. The detective also acknowledged that he had made up a story that the young girl had been so upset about what the priest had done to her that she had written an account of it in her diary.[221]

Wark told jurors that police often used "deception" in questioning suspects and that he had made up the story about the girl's diary to get Koveos to admit certain facts.[222]

On the second day of trial, I called the 12-year-old victim as the prosecution's last witness. She spoke softly and clearly. It had to be a bewildering situation for her, but she did fine.

I had been told by prosecutors who had experience trying sex crimes cases that "conventional wisdom" had it that female jurors often tended to be tougher on and more suspicious of alleged female victims. That was definitely *not the case* with the 12-year-old victim of Father Koveos.

I can recall the look on the faces of the female jurors in the back row of the jury box as the young girl testified. It was a mixture of sorrow and anger. I remember thinking that there was no way they were going to find this child was lying or confused about what had happened to her.

The 12-year-old girl testified that the priest had taken her left leg and put it between his legs. He had then rubbed her upper leg and between her legs. She said she'd been confused by what the priest was doing and "looked at him weirdly." Koveos had just smiled and winked at her.

AM said that Father Koveos had explained that he had brought her into his office where they were alone because he did not want to be "distracted" by the other young girls. She went on to tell jurors that while she was in the office alone with the priest, he had put his hand under her shirt, rubbed her back, and squeezed the side of her chest and breast. AM said she had been scared while this was happening. She summed it up by telling jurors that she thought that what her priest had done to her was "pretty disgusting."[223]

After AM testified, I rested our case. Karen Shingler asked Judge Crucitti for permission to call another witness—a witness who was not on the defense witness list. She said the witness would testify that Koveos had put his hand on the witness' knee and there was nothing improper about it.

I objected for two reasons. First, the defense had been required to give me notice of its witnesses weeks earlier so that I could investigate and depose them before trial. Second, this witness was clearly being called to show what the defense had explicitly denied they would do—create a reasonable doubt about Koveos's intent by showing how the priest's actions could be misinterpreted.

The argument would be that Father Koveos was the kind of guy—a "Greek guy"—who did a lot of touching and hugging. That was his nature. It wasn't done for sexual gratification. But a person—particularly a young girl—could misinterpret his actions. I thought that was going to be the defense pitch.

I said the man should not be allowed to testify. But if he did, I should be allowed to call the young woman from Concord, New Hampshire, who the priest had sexually molested during a counseling session 10 years earlier. The woman had come to Burlington and was ready and eager to testify in support of 12-year-old AM.

Judge Crucitti ruled that the prospective witness could not testify, because in his opinion, the witness' proposed testimony was offered to show that Father Koveos lacked the intent to act in a "lewd and lascivious" manner. It was meant to show Koveos was a hugger and a "toucher." *It was a cultural thing. The touching was not done for sexual gratification.*

Judge Crucitti also warned Shingler that if Koveos testified to the effect that the touching was innocent—not with the intent of sexual gratification—then the judge would be inclined to permit me to call the woman who had been sexually abused by Father Koveos at his church in Concord in 1988.[224]

Father Koveos testified in the afternoon. He refused to say that AM had lied. Instead, he insisted that the child, who he said was like a grandchild to him, had not "remembered correctly." He categorically denied touching the child's crotch, rubbing her thigh, or touching her in any way for sexual gratification. He told jurors he had rubbed AM's hand while it was in her pocket only as a means of encouraging her.

Father Koveos said he had written the letter of apology because he was afraid the investigators would "punch or shoot" him. He said that Lt. Wark would not accept Koveos's letter of apology until he had written that he had touched the child's "crotch."

The priest was on the witness stand for most of the afternoon answering questions from his lawyer. My cross-examination of him took no more than 45 minutes. He admitted that most of what AM had told jurors was true—except, of course, for the part about him rubbing her leg and crotch and squeezing her chest and breast.

Father Koveos denied even realizing that AM was "upset" by what had happened at the Greek lesson. When I pressed him on the issue, he admitted that he had thought AM had been "upset," but he'd thought she was upset over a "family matter" and he did not want to interfere in family matters.

The jury never heard the testimony of the victim of Father Koveos's sexual abuse in 1988 because the priest testified that he had not touched AM in the way she had described ("she remembered incorrectly"). In other words, he said he didn't do the act—not that AM misunderstood his acts of innocent, grandfatherly affection.

I told jurors that the bottom line was this—Koveos had no explanation for why this child, a child he claimed to think of as his "grandchild," would make up the details of what she'd termed the "disgusting" way he had touched her. Everything about the way AM reacted made it clear that she wasn't making this up.

I challenged the jurors—"You saw that child testify. You know in your heart and your head that she told you the truth about what Father Koveos did to her."

Koveos's attorney, Shingler, who had done a good job discrediting the "letter of apology," argued that Koveos had told the truth. "You can stop Father Koveos's nightmare," she told jurors. "He didn't do it."[225]

My rebuttal was brief. *Attorney Shingler wants you to feel sorry for him. She is trying to make him the victim. Ladies and gentlemen, this man [gesturing toward Koveos] is not the victim here. The victim is the 12-year-old girl who trusted him. You heard her. Father Koveos abused that child, and he abused her trust.*

The jury announced its verdict—Koveos was "guilty"—at 9:30 p.m. on Friday, February 6, 1998. The jury had deliberated for approximately 17 hours—four hours on Thursday afternoon after closing and more than thirteen hours on Friday. This was a little longer than it took to put in all the evidence (prosecution and defense) during the trial itself.

Jurors obviously took their job seriously. They spent seven hours back in the courtroom on Friday with Judge Crucitti, listening to audiotape of the testimony of AM, Father Koveos, and Lt. Wark. Then they went back into the jury room and deliberated for another four hours before announcing their verdict.

I can still remember what happened when jurors announced their verdict. AM's mother screamed, "He's guilty!" and then began sobbing and hugging her daughter.

Father Koveos told reporters that he was "surprised" by the verdict. He said both Lt. Wark and the victim, AM, had not told the truth at trial.[226]

As mentioned earlier, Judge Crucitti had made a preliminary ruling that the letter was written "voluntarily" by Koveos. Based on that ruling, I introduced the letter and Lt. Wark's testimony about the letter and how it came to be written. But the jurors were going to have the final say on whether Koveos was acting voluntarily when he'd written the letter or whether his actions were involuntary in that he was tricked into writing it by the sex crime investigators.

Judge Crucitti did instruct jurors that they had the final word on whether Father Koveos had acted voluntarily when he'd written the "letter of apology" to AM and her family. The jurors' "final word" was "no." Father Koveos did not act voluntarily when he'd written the letter.

So, in addition to finding that Koveos was "guilty" of the felony of engaging in "lewd and lascivious conduct with a child (AM)," jurors made an additional finding that the "letter of apology" was "involuntary."

I had not heard of such a ruling/verdict from a Vermont jury before. As I recall, jurors did not go into detail as to why or how they reached their verdict on this issue. I think it is reasonable to believe, though, that jurors found that Shingler's argument made sense—investigators took advantage of Koveos's lack of knowledge of the law and his relative unfamiliarity with the English language and tricked him into writing a letter that supported AM's version of what had happened.

It might be reasonable to say, "so what?"—they still found him guilty. But this second finding/verdict was significant because it meant that the jury could not rely on Koveos admissions in the letter in reaching their verdict. They had to decide whether AM had told them the truth or whether Koveos had told them the truth—nothing else. They could not rely on Lt. Wark's testimony or the letter itself.

Their "guilty" verdict shows that the jurors believed AM and did not believe Father Koveos. There could be no claim on appeal that the verdict was tainted by police deceit in obtaining the Koveos's "admissions" in the "letter of apology." In fact, in a relatively rare move, the defense did not challenge the sufficiency of the evidence in support of the verdict at all on appeal.[227]

The press referred to the trial, quite accurately, as "emotionally charged."

A good example of this was the conduct of one of Father Koveos's sons, John. He was a computer consultant who lived in Boston, but he spent the entire week of the trial in Burlington attending the trial along with his mother and two brothers.

On Thursday, after the closings and as the jury began deliberations, John Koveos was frustrated with the trial testimony and the treatment of his father, and he "acted out" his frustration. As he left the courtroom, he deliberately slammed one of the heavy doors of the courtroom into John Borthwick, a court officer who was responsible for court security. Borthwick received minor injuries. John Koveos was charged with simple assault (a misdemeanor) and three months later he pled "no contest" to disorderly conduct, an even lesser charge, and paid a fine of just $67.50.

John Koveos was also very angry with AM's mother and father. Not long after the door-slamming incident, AM's father retained a lawyer and filed for a restraining order to keep John Koveos away from his family. AM's father claimed in an affidavit in support of his request for a restraining order that John Koveos had been harassing AM's mother and father throughout the trial in bizarre ways—e.g., following them around the courthouse taking pictures of them, bumping his shoulder into AM's father in the hallway, and following AM's mother to the bathroom.[228]

Emotions continued to run high at Father Koveos's sentencing, which took place about four months after the verdict.

AM's mother spoke directly to Father Koveos at the sentencing hearing: "You are no priest. You are no man. You are a vindictive coward." Father Koveos said he was innocent and asked Judge Crucitti to have mercy on him and "end this nightmare of mine."

I was quite surprised to see that the priest continued to have the support of many people, including powerful people, despite the jury's verdict.

George Costes, a state senator and former judge, joined dozens of other members of the clergy and former parishioners in writing letters to Judge Crucitti in support of Father Koveos. The Reverend C. Leland Udell, the former head chaplain of Vermont's largest hospital, joined them in supporting Koveos.[229]

The Pastor of the First Universalist Society of Burlington wrote in a letter to the editor of the *Burlington Free Press* that "we may never know what happened between Father Koveos and his accuser" because the "judicial process was tainted" by the "strong-arm, high pressure, deceptive tactics" of the investigators in getting the priest to write the "letter of apology." So, here was another Man of God who ignored the testimony of 12-year-old AM, the victim, and the 9-year-old child who was in the Greek lesson with her. He also evidently failed to make the effort to find out that jurors had said that they did not consider the letter of apology in reaching their verdict.[230]

For his part, Koveos told the judge that he had never had any "problems" during his nearly 30 years as a priest. This was not true. As I mentioned earlier, a young woman had complained that Koveos had made her touch him inappropriately and kissed her on the lips during a counseling session at Holy Trinity Church in Concord, New Hampshire, in 1988.

I told the judge that the priest was no longer entitled to the respect he demanded because he had lied about his criminal treatment of a 12-year-old child. I asked him to sentence Koveos to six months in prison as the Department of Probation and Parole had recommended.

Judge Crucitti told Koveos that he was sorry the priest was in "complete denial." He told Koveos: "I have no doubt about your guilt." Then he sentenced the priest to serve six months in prison. Koveos would also be required to cover the portion of AM's counseling and medical expenses that were not covered by insurance. Once Koveos was released from prison, a probation officer would have to approve where the priest could work and where he could live.[231]

Judge Crucitti rejected Koveos's attempts to have his jail sentence put on hold while the Vermont Supreme Court considered his appeal. Koveos continued to claim his innocence as he entered prison. As the priest was about to enter the Chittenden County Correctional Facility in South Burlington to serve his six-month sentence, he complained to a reporter that: "This is no way to treat a priest." He said he had been "framed."[232]

Father Koveos had retained Nathan Dershowitz, an experienced New York lawyer and the brother of famous Harvard Law Professor Alan Dershowitz, to handle the appeal of his conviction in the Vermont Supreme Court.

Chittenden County Deputy State's Attorney Pamela Johnson, an exceptionally capable lawyer, argued the Koveos case for the State. Attorney Johnson ultimately argued more than 100 cases before Vermont Supreme Court over her more than 30-year career.

The Vermont Supreme Court rejected Koveos's appeal and affirmed the conviction on February 5, 1999. This was a little less than a year after the guilty verdict and just five months after Dershowitz made his argument before the Vermont Supreme Court. This turnaround was "warp speed" for Vermont's high court, which in the 1980s had averaged three to four years between argument and decision.[233]

As mentioned earlier, Dershowitz did not make the standard argument that the prosecution did not present enough admissible evidence to prove the defendant's guilt beyond a reasonable doubt. Again, this was probably because of the jury's decision to ignore the "letter of apology" because the police put words in Koveos's mouth. This deprived Dershowitz of a key appellate issue. Instead, Dershowitz raised four fairly technical arguments that were rejected in a unanimous decision.

The jury's finding that the "letter of apology" was involuntary is a good example of jurors' willingness to signal that they did not approve of the conduct of the police. But it is not the only example.

When I was first starting out as a lawyer—nearly twenty years before the Koveos trial—I worked with a jury that made it clear that they thought the police had not acted lawfully when they'd searched a car following a traffic stop.

In 1981, I tried Robert "Bobby" Desjardins for assault on a police officer. The statute required the prosecutor to prove three essential elements: (1) "identity," showing that the person charged was the actor or the person who (2) caused "bodily injury" (3) to a police officer who was "performing a lawful duty."[234]

If the jury found that the officer was not "performing a lawful duty" when the person charged had injured him, then the person charged was guilty only of "simple assault" and was subject to a lesser penalty, which, unlike "assault on a police officer," would not result in a jail sentence.

A police officer had stopped Desjardins, who had been driving to pick up his pregnant wife at a bingo game. Desjardins had his infant daughter with him. The police officer had been informed, mistakenly as it turned out, that Desjardins was driving a car that was not registered to him. As the officer approached the driver-side window to check Desjardins' license and registration, he noticed the glove compartment was open and saw an empty holster and several bullets inside. The officer called for backup after he also noticed a rifle in the backseat that was partially covered by a coat.

By the time a sergeant and another officer arrived at the scene, the dispatcher had informed the first officer that there had been a mistake and that the car Desjardins was driving was, in fact, registered to him. But by that point, the sergeant was shining a flashlight into the back seat. That woke the baby, who started crying. Desjardins said that the sergeant had no right to search the car and pushed the flashlight away. The sergeant insisted he had the right to search the car and, as I recall it, started to open the door.

At that point, Desjardins "lost it" and attacked the sergeant. In the meantime, Desjardins's pregnant wife had left the Bingo Hall, walked across the street, and taken the baby out of the car. Wife and baby watched the ensuing melee, which resulted in two officers suffering slight injuries. The officers, in turn, sprayed Desjardins with mace, beat him with "leather and lead sap,"[235] and then forced him face down in the street before handcuffing him.[236]

I argued that the officers who were injured had been "performing a lawful duty." Given the open glove compartment and the empty holster, the sergeant was concerned that there was a deadly weapon in the car. But regardless of whether the sergeant had acted reasonably (it was not illegal to have a weapon in the car), Desjardins had no legal right to physically attack the sergeant. The officers who stepped in were performing a lawful duty while trying to protect the sergeant who was under attack.

I am sure I was right on the law—the officers were performing a lawful duty. But I was not surprised when the jury found Desjardins "not guilty" of "assault on a police officer" and instead found that he was only guilty of "simple assault." In other words, the jury found that Desjardins had no right to attack the sergeant, but the sergeant and the other officers were not "performing a lawful duty" when they'd responded to the attack on the sergeant.

The jury had reasonably concluded that officers had not been "performing a lawful duty" when the sergeant and two other officers had forced Desjardins to lie face down in the street in front of his pregnant wife and baby after macing and bludgeoning him.

The Vermont Supreme Court certainly agreed with the jury. In a unanimous decision written by Chief Justice Albert Barney, the Court upheld the jury's decision in finding Desjardins guilty of the lesser charge of "simple assault." But the Court's decision also vigorously supported the conclusion that the officers had not been performing a lawful duty when they were injured.

The chief justice's opinion used particularly harsh language. The first paragraph of the decision "condemned" the "aggressive actions of the Essex Police Department." The decision went on later to criticize what it termed the "antagonistic" and "immature actions" of the sergeant.

This was another example of a case where, as in the Koveos case, a jury made it clear that although they found the defendant had broken the law, jurors were concerned that police had not acted properly.

Dangerous Victim

In the early morning hours of November 26, 1999, an attempted murder took place at a two-story, four-apartment complex at 72 Hyde Street in Burlington's Old North End. After an evening of drinking and karaoke, Minh Nguyen (Minh), age 31, attacked his roommate, Duyen Nguyen (Duyen), age 30, with a meat cleaver following a heated argument. Minh then went after Dung Tran (Dung), age 28, when Dung tried to come to Duyen's defense.[237]

The gray clapboard apartment complex at 72 Hyde Street was less than a mile from the Criminal Court building at 32 Pearl Street in Burlington, where Minh Nguyen was tried just two months after the attack.

Dung was hospitalized in serious condition at the Fletcher Allen Health Care, formerly known as Medical Center Hospital of Vermont. He had a fractured skull, a fractured cheekbone, and a broken arm (fractured ulna). Duyen, who suffered a "substantial" cut to his forehead that exposed his skull, was treated and released.[238]

All three men were Vietnamese refugees who were born in Vietnam in between 1968 and 1971. Minh, the defendant, had come to Vermont after settling first in Mississippi at age 18 with the assistance of Catholic Charities. My records do not show whether the victims, Dung and Duyen, came to the US through California or Texas (as most Vietnamese refugees did), or whether they had been part of Vermont's Refugee Resettlement program.

The jury was not told about it during the trial, but Minh Nguyen had shot and killed a man in Mississippi seven years earlier.

The evidence of the Mississippi killing was inadmissible under the law because what little relevance it might have had to the meat cleaver attack was "substantially outweighed by the prejudicial impact it would have on the jury.[239] The concern was that jurors would let their knowledge that Minh had killed someone else influence their thinking on whether the prosecution in his case in Vermont had proven that he had committed attempted murder in Burlington.

Minh was convicted of manslaughter in Jackson, Mississippi, in 1992. He had gone to the home of another Vietnamese American who he'd suspected had stolen a VCR,[240] and then he shot and killed him. Minh claimed that the man posed a "direct threat" to him. This was questionable at best. In fact, based on the facts reported by Mississippi police, there was a good argument that he had murdered the alleged VCR thief.

Nevertheless, Mississippi prosecutors allowed Minh to plead guilty to the lesser charge of manslaughter and get a fully probationary sentence—no prison time.[241]

The national "record check" that Burlington Police conducted after Minh was arrested showed that not long after he had been placed on probation for the killing in Mississippi, Minh had been charged with a stabbing in New Orleans that prosecutors there ultimately dismissed. This too was inadmissible—again because any relevance it might have had to the case was outweighed by the prejudicial impact it would have on jurors.

It took four days to try Minh's case from the jury draw on Monday, January 24 through the jury's verdict on Thursday, January 27. Minh's case was a tough case to prepare and try. I was fortunate to get help from Craig Matanle, a smart, new lawyer in our office.

Bob Andres, the trial lawyer who had tried the Cianci case, was appointed to serve as Minh's defense counsel. Andres wisely pushed for a speedy trial. Andres knew that we would be scrambling to prepare the case because the three key witnesses would need help from interpreters. The interpreters would first have to translate detectives' questions from English to Vietnamese and then translate the Vietnamese response back into English.

It turned out to be the shortest interval between the charge and the trial of any major trial I have been involved in. It took roughly two months from Minh's arrest on November 26, 1999, to the jury's verdict on January 27, 2000.

Everyone involved in ensuring the case was ready for trial did a good job. The Burlington Police, led by Detectives Lieutenant Emmet Helrich, a Vietnam veteran, did an outstanding job collecting evidence, identifying key witnesses, and getting statements from them—basically organizing the case that we were going to try.

There were two interpreters at the trial. One interpreter (Phi Nguyen) translated the testimony of witnesses who testified in Vietnamese—Dung, Duyen, and Aly Tran—into English for the judge and jury. A second interpreter (Phi Doane) worked exclusively for Minh and his lawyer, Bob Andres.[242]

We called a total of eleven witnesses. First, the police officers who responded to the scene—Lt. Helrich and Detective Art Cyr—had collected evidence, including the meat cleaver, and taken statements from the witnesses. They were followed by testimony from the two victims, Duyen and Dung, and a third Vietnamese immigrant, Aly Tran (Aly) who was also present during the attack. The final witnesses were the technicians who'd identified the blood found at the scene as the blood of Duyen and Dung and two physicians who told the jurors the severity of the injuries that Duyen and Dung had suffered in the attack. [243]

According to the testimony of the witnesses who were present, there was nothing unusual about the way the evening had started. Minh was drinking beer with the two men he'd later attack (Duyen and Dung) and a third man (Aly).

As the evening and the drinking wore on, Duyen started an argument with Minh. Minh had been rooming with Duyen for a month but wasn't paying rent. This argument happened downstairs in the living room on the first floor of the house at 72 Hyde Street.

Dung, who was Duyen's brother-in-law, took Duyen's side. He grabbed Minh by the throat and pushed him into the kitchen. Aly, who appeared to have been a neutral witness, testified that Dung had grabbed Minh's throat so hard that it left an injury. At that point, both Duyen and Dung were fighting with Minh, who, according to Aly, was trying to avoid the fight.

Aly eventually broke up the fight and everyone went upstairs. Minh went into the room he shared with Duyen. Dung, Duyen, and Aly went into Aly's room. But according to Aly, Duyen was still angry. Minh had closed the door of the room that he was sharing with Duyen and was trying to sleep. Soon after, Duyen kicked in the door and continued to berate Minh.

Minh got up and went into Aly's room. Duyen wouldn't leave it alone. He followed Minh into Aly's room and continued to shout and swear at him. At this point, all four men—Aly, Dung, Duyen, and Minh—were in Aly's room on the second floor.

Aly, Dung, and Duyen all testified that none of them had a weapon.[244]

Minh left the room, went downstairs, and got a meat cleaver from the kitchen. Then he turned off the lights and ran back up the stairs with the meat cleaver in his hand.

Minh first attacked Duyen in the hall outside Aly's room. He went for Duyen's head with the meat cleaver. The blow took off a chunk of Duyen's scalp and hair.

Minh then went after Dung, who had attempted to come to Duyen's defense. Minh struck Dung 10 times with the meat cleaver. Again, Minh went for the head first. Dung was trying to protect his head with his hands and arms. Minh hit him in the left forearm, fracturing the ulna. His blows to the head fractured Dung's skull and cheekbone. As Dung slumped to the floor, Minh struck him in the chest, abdomen, and both ankles.[245]

Dung and Duyen fled to Dung's home at 305 North Winooski Avenue, less than half a mile away. Both men were bleeding heavily. They both sat down to, in Dung's words, "wait to die." Fortunately, a neighbor who had seen the men bleeding called 911. If the neighbor hadn't gotten involved, Dung and Duyen would have "bled out" and died. Police arrived at Dung's home around 4 a.m., and EMTs arrived shortly afterward. This was about an hour after the attack had ended.

The physician who treated both men later testified that both men would have bled to death if they hadn't been treated promptly.

At trial, Minh waived his Fifth Amendment right and testified. He told jurors through the interpreter that he had, indeed, gone downstairs, grabbed the meat cleaver from the kitchen, and gone back upstairs and attacked both men. But he insisted he'd acted in self-defense. He said Duyen had kicked in the door and choked him. Minh insisted that the men had knives when he'd attacked them after he'd gone back upstairs.

Minh had spoken to Lt. Helrich and Detective Cyr the morning after the attack. He'd told them a similar story to the one he told at trial: that Duyen had kicked in the door and choked him, and so Minh had acted in self-defense. He admitted he had responded by attacking both Duyen and Dung with the meat cleaver he had taken from the kitchen downstairs. He showed the detectives where he had tossed the meat cleaver in a nearby dumpster. But when he first told the detectives what had happened, he made no mention of either Duyen or Dung having a weapon.

When he testified at trial, however, he claimed they had knives.

The cross-examination was brief, although it must have seemed long to the jury. I realize that many prosecutors try cases all the time with interpreters—particularly those in states along the southwestern border. I had tried an aggravated assault trial with a Vietnamese interpreter and a domestic assault trial with a Serbo-Croatian interpreter before, but I never developed the knack of trying cases with an interpreter.

Looking back now at my cross-examination notes, one problem is obvious—my questions were too long.

Cross is supposed to be crisp. Short questions that call for a "yes" or "no" answer. For example: *"You heard the medical examiner's testimony, didn't you?" "She testified that Zeke was hit in the head with a blunt instrument, didn't she? "This is your baseball bat, isn't it?"* You get quick "yes" or "no" answers—then move on.

My questions were way too long. For instance: "Dung, Duyen, and Aly all stayed upstairs when you went down to the kitchen to get the meat cleaver. You didn't have to come back upstairs and attack Dung and Duyen to protect yourself from them, did you?"[246]

This is my best recollection of how Minh's response to that question unfolded: The interpreter gave Minh the question in Vietnamese. That took a while. Minh spoke to the interpreter. The interpreter spoke to Minh again. Minh spoke to the interpreter again. Then the interpreter spoke in English to me and the jury and said just a few words to the effect of: "No. Self-defense." The whole exchange, from my question to the interpreter's response, probably took at least two or three minutes. Not a good cross at all.

In closing, I went through the essential elements of attempted second-degree murder that we had to prove beyond a reasonable doubt. One, we had to prove that Minh had *attempted to kill* each man (Dung and Duyen). Two, we had to prove that he had *acted intentionally*. In other words, there was no accident. Three, we had to prove that Minh's actions *were not justified*—that he had not acted in self-defense.[247]

Minh was entitled to be angry with Duyen and Dung, but he had no right to try to kill him. There was, however, no question that when Minh chose to go downstairs and grab the meat cleaver, he intended to kill Duyen and Dung. Minh did not deny that he'd attacked both men. You don't hit someone in the head with a weapon like that unless you mean to kill them; there are no "warning shots" with a meat cleaver.

I argued that the only question for jurors was whether Minh's use of deadly force was legally justified. I told jurors that the judge would tell them that Minh was not entitled to rely on the doctrine of self-defense unless he "reasonably believed" he faced "imminent death or serious bodily injury." But, I argued, that just wasn't the case. Minh was alone when he went downstairs to get the cleaver. The others—Duyen, Dung, and Aly—were all upstairs. There was no threat of any kind. Minh could have left or called the police. Duyen and Dung posed no danger to him.

Bob Andres argued that Minh had reasonably believed that Duyen and Dung were going to kill him. He pointed out that Minh's entire life had been about self-preservation. Minh didn't know who his father was, and his mother was dead. He had immigrated to the US when he was 18 years old after living in a refugee camp in Thailand, where he had no one to count on for protection but himself. Minh had lived a life that made it reasonable for him not to trust police or anyone in authority. Given the life he had been forced to live, his attack on Duyen and Dung was reasonable.

Andres made a good argument. I was not sure about the verdict until the jurors came back into the courtroom and announced their verdict—"guilty" on both counts of attempted murder.

In December 2000, Judge Michael Kupersmith sentenced Minh Nguyen to serve 45 years to life in prison for two counts of attempted second-degree murder.[248] It was the sentence that I had argued for. I told Judge Kupersmith that I thought Minh was one of the most dangerous people I had ever prosecuted.

Under the law, those convicted of attempted murder face the same sentence they would have received if their attempt had been successful and they had been convicted of murder.[249] At that time, it also meant that the sentencing judge should consider "aggravating" and "mitigating" factors identified in Vermont statutes in determining whether the sentence imposed should vary the statutory minimum—which was 20 years to life in prison.[250]

I argued in my Sentencing Memo to the judge that three of the statutory aggravating factors and none of the mitigating factors applied in Minh's case. Here was part of what I laid out:

"(1) The defendant was previously convicted of a felony involving the use of violence to a person."

The fact that Minh had killed a man in Mississippi eight years earlier may not have been relevant in Minh's Vermont trial, but it was definitely relevant to his sentencing. The facts of the Mississippi killing were chilling:

On June 2, 1992, Minh was convicted of manslaughter for shooting and killing another Vietnamese American. The killing took place in Jackson, Mississippi, on November 12, 1991. The victim, Can Thanh Nguyen, was suspected of stealing a VCR from the apartment where Minh lived. Minh's response was to take a "borrowed" handgun to the place where the suspected thief was living and kill him.

Minh told the probation officer in Mississippi who completed the pre-sentence investigation that he shot Thanh because he "perceived him as a direct threat." But there was little evidence that Thanh, the alleged VCR thief, was a threat at all.

The evidence showed that Minh had made up his mind to kill Thanh. On November 12, 1991, he'd borrowed a handgun, left the safety of his own home, and went to where Thanh was living. Minh shot Thanh in the upper left chest. Thanh tried to flee to another room. Minh shot him twice in the back, finishing the job of killing him.

Minh then fled Mississippi. The prosecutor in Jackson, Mississippi, charged Minh with murder and obtained an out-of-state arrest warrant. Minh was arrested in Barstow, California, five weeks later on a murder warrant. It was never clear to me why the prosecutor gave Minh a plea agreement six months later that allowed Minh to plead to the lesser charge of manslaughter and escape a prison sentence altogether.

After Minh's trial up here in Vermont, I called the prosecutor in Mississippi to find out why a killer who had been charged with first-degree murder ended up with a fully suspended sentence. By then, it had been eight years since Minh had shot and killed Thanh. My notes say that the prosecutor, who had become a judge by that point, told me he did not remember the case. He insisted, though, that he would not have made such a soft plea agreement if there hadn't been a good defense.

I got the name of the investigator who had been the lead in the Thanh murder case and called him. The investigator said he did not remember anything about a good defense. But he did remember that Minh's change of plea hearing took "half a day" because of the "language problem."

(2) "The (attempted) murder was particularly severe, brutal, or cruel."

Minh's choice of weapon (a meat cleaver) and the spot on the first victim's body where he chose to deliver his first blows (the head) made it clear that his attacks were not only meant to kill—they were meant to kill brutally.

Minh's attack on his second victim—Dung, the man who came to Duyen's aid—was "particularly brutal." The evidence showed that Minh had struck Dung three times in the head. These blows came with such ferocity that they not only opened up wide gashes in Dung's head, they also fractured his skull and his cheekbone. Dung testified that the blows to his head had knocked him to the floor. Dr. Leffler's testimony corroborated Dung's statement. The doctor testified that the blows would have taken Dung off his feet and left him unable to fight back.

While Dung had been helpless and trying in vain to defend himself, Minh had continued to hack at him with the cleaver. He'd hacked Dung with such savagery that he'd fractured a major bone in Dung's forearm (ulna), and he'd continued to hack away at Dung's hand, back, stomach, chest, and both ankles.

Minh had left both victims bleeding on the floor. Dr. Leffler testified that Dung would have bled to death from his injuries if he had not received prompt medical attention.

(3) "The (attempted) murder involved multiple victims."

Minh was convicted of trying to kill two men—Duyen and Dung.

As I mentioned earlier, in addition to the aggravating factors, the law also listed six potential "mitigating factors" that a judge might consider in reducing a sentence below the statutory minimum of 20 years to life.[251] I argued that none of the mitigating factors (e.g., no prior criminal record) applied in Minh's case:

> The defense made much of the cruelty and hardship that (Minh) had suffered. It also suggested that this savage attack was somehow a "cultural thing" that was beyond the understanding of people who were born and raised in the U.S. That is not true. The cruelty and hardship that Minh has experienced in his life has been experienced by thousands of other Vietnamese Americans who have come to live in the United States and have made their way without committing acts of

savagery. In fact, the hardships Defendant has endured are probably no worse than those that were almost certainly endured by the man Defendant killed in Mississippi eight years ago and the two men he attempted to kill in Vermont one year ago.

It is an understatement to say that Minh, Duyen, Dung, and tens of thousands of other refugees from Vietnam were dealt a bad hand. They were all victims of the "Vietnam War."

After Saigon fell in 1975,[252] the US government evacuated approximately 125,000 Vietnamese men and their families from Vietnam.[253] Hundreds of thousands more South Vietnamese fled their country in the years following the North Vietnamese victory. These people had supported the US military and were likely to face reprisals if they'd stayed in the country they loved.

The CIA's brutal "Secret War" in the small country of Laos that neighbored North and South Viet Nam was carried out in the 1960s and 1970s. It created another 750,000 refugees, many of whom had supported the US against the North Vietnamese.

I had firsthand experience with both Vietnam and the events in Laos.

My Own War Story

I received a draft notice at my parents' home in Randolph Center, Vermont, the week after my graduation from Colgate University in May 1967. By that time, I was opposed to the Vietnam War. But I wasn't a "conscientious objector" to all wars, which would have meant "deferment" from the draft. Because I was just an objector to the Vietnam War, I was still "draft eligible."

The draft required two years of service. I eventually enlisted in the Army for four years after I found out that I qualified for "language school." I would receive a year of intensive training in a foreign language and then be assigned to a military facility overseas—most likely to work in military intelligence. I hoped to learn a language like Russian or Chinese (Mandarin) and find interesting work once I finished my tour and got back to civilian life.

I did eight weeks of "basic infantry training" at Fort Dix, New Jersey. Our Company (D) consisted of roughly 200 men—the vast majority of whom were draftees. I was named a squad leader and given some responsibility for approximately 12-15 other men. The primary goals seem to have been to make us physically fit and instill discipline—to follow orders without question. I was fine with that. I had learned from my father, a retired Marine Corps officer, that this kind of hierarchy is essential in an effective military.

We were issued M14 rifles. We learned how to break down the rifle into its component parts for cleaning. We also went through a well-organized, time-tested procedure in which we were taught how to shoot. We were given brief instructions on how to fire an M79 grenade launcher and an M60 machine gun.

In addition to weapons training, we had very basic instruction in hand-to-hand fighting. ("Don't try this when you get back on the block—you'll get your ass kicked.") I remember that we also had a short course on the history of the US Army and another on the use of the bayonet.

After completing basic training, I received orders to attend the Defense Language Institute (DLI) in Monterey, California, to study the Thai language. It was a 37-week intensive course. There were about 12 enlisted men in the class—Army, Navy, Air Force, and Marines. We spoke Thai all the time in class, from 8 a.m. to 4:30 or 5 p.m.

I met smart, decent men from all over the US at the DLI. This included men from Texas, Alabama, Louisiana, Arkansas, and other southern states. This turned out to be one of the advantages of my military service. It made it easy for me to reject stereotypes about people from the South during the awful MAGA wave.

At the time we were taking our class, the DLI gave the same class for officers (mainly Army Special Forces and Marines) and one or two men who were in the Foreign Service—or at least, that's what they told us. The DLI taught 37- and 47-week intensive courses in many of the languages of the world. I remember wondering what good it did for anyone to learn Arabic, Swahili, Hausa, Serbo-Croatian, etc. Now I know.

After I graduated from the DLI, I was sent to Fort Devens in Ayer, Massachusetts, to learn how to analyze intercepted enemy radio traffic—no mention of Thai.

I was in a branch of the Army called the Army Security Agency (ASA). Our job was "signals intelligence" (SIGINT)—basically using radio signals to try to track enemy activity.

In March 1969, I received orders to go to Nong Soong, Thailand, and report to the 7th Radio Research Field Station (7th RRFS). The 7th RRFS was in Northeast Thailand, about 12 miles south of the big US Air Base in Udorn. It was not more than 60 miles from Vientiane, Laos, and roughly 340 miles from Hue, South Vietnam.

I am not sure of the numbers, but I don't think there were more than 1,200 troops at Nong Soong. The duty was not tough. The 7th RRFS was protected by Thai soldiers. There were tennis courts and a swimming pool.

There were enlisted men from the Army and some Marines. I was aware of two basic "problems" that were analyzed and reported on from 7th RRFS.

One was the "Laotian Problem"—analyzing North Vietnamese troop movements into Laos in support of the Pathet Lao. These were Laotian guerillas who were fighting the Royal Laotian forces who were supported by the US, through the CIA.

The second was the "ChiCom Problem"—basically a study of Chinese (a communist country) troop movements in the southern Kunming Military Region in China. The Chinese were building a road into Northern Laos.

I worked on the "Chicom" problem, and I spent my time basically trying to use radio traffic to figure out where units were, who was commanding who, etc. I did not use my Thai except when I was off duty. The majority of the people there were Thai, but there were some Lao people as well.

After two months at Nong Soon, I was ordered to report to Phu Bai Combat Base in South Viet Nam, which is just about eight miles southwest of Hue. (Back then, it was called Viet Nam.) We came in through Saigon—now Ho Chi Minh City—and then flew up to Phu Bai in a C-130.

Phu Bai was a large supply base. Our compound, the 8th Radio Research Field Station (8th RRFS), was fenced off from the rest of the base and guarded by US Army Military Police. My best estimate is that there were approximately 1,200 US military personnel stationed there at the 8th RRFS. The station was commanded by an Army colonel, who, as far as I could tell, knew relatively little about what we were doing. The majority of the troops were Army—but there were quite a few Marines working in our outfit, too.

We lived in tents for awhile, but then we moved into trailers. We all took regular turns (roughly every three weeks) doing all-night guard-duty on the "perimeter" of the base—we were assigned a spot near an artillery unit. Our unit had M60 machine guns, grenade launchers, and M16 rifles. We took it very seriously, but we were *way behind* combat troops in skill and experience with these weapons.

Our outfit's real job was intercepting radio traffic, both Morse Code and tactical voice communications of Viet Cong and North Vietnamese units that were coming down through the DMZ that separated North and South Viet Nam. We were responsible for Northern I Corps— basically for all enemy activity from Da Nang in South Vietnam to just north of the DMZ. In addition, we were responsible for the portion of the Ho Chi Minh Trail in Laos that bordered our area in South Viet Nam.

Our primary function was to identify enemy units in the area and track their movements. The big units I remember specifically were the North Vietnamese infantry divisions—304th, 324B and 325C—although we were also able to track artillery battalions, infantry regiments, and some Viet Cong units.

The main US units in the area were the 101 Airborne Division of the Army and various Marine elements—e.g., at Khe Sanh in the West, and Dong Ha more to the north and east.

After I had been working for two or three months, I was promoted to head the "reporting" section. There was a warrant officer, not a bad guy, who was nominally our boss in the reporting section, but he did not do a lot except proofread what we wrote. We worked in a guarded building from mid-afternoon until our work was done—usually two or three in the morning. The main job was to: (1) alert US Fire Support bases in our area of the threat of enemy movement in their area. These alerts, called "TACREPS" or "Z-gram," were our most important job. And (2) write a daily summary of the location and movement of enemy troops in our area of responsibility.

Bottom line, we evaluated and summarized the work of 1,100 to 1,200 radio intercept operators, cryptanalysts, Vietnamese translators, "traffic analysts," and air units that tracked enemy activity through "radio direction finding."

The "TACREPS" went out to our units that were in immediate danger from enemy activity. Our daily summary of enemy activity went to Saigon, the "Pacific Command in Hawaii," and Washington, DC. Three men from the National Security Agency (NSA) had desks in the "reporting" section. From time to time, they would ask us what was going on and give us (pretty good) advice. We weren't privy to what else they did.

There was a lot of enemy activity in Northern I Corps. But the biggest thing that happened in the Vietnam War while I was there was President Nixon's announcement that we were getting out.

The US troops started to pull out, and South Vietnamese troops (Army of the Republic of Vietnam) took over the effort to keep the

North Vietnamese Army and Viet Cong from taking over South Vietnam. President Nixon called this "Vietnamization" of the war.

Those of us in the "reporting section" always worked as hard as we could. We weren't in much danger. I can only remember one or two rocket attacks on Phu Bai—that was it for enemy danger. But we knew that a lot of Marine and Army infantrymen "in the field" were often in danger in the area we were responsible for, so we always gave it our best. Just before I rotated back to the US, I was awarded a Bronze Star for the work I had done in Northern I Corps.[254]

I was ordered to report to Two Rock Ranch in Petaluma, California, in 1970. This was the only time I used my Thai. If I remember correctly, my "duty hours" were from 4 p.m. to midnight. I listened to recordings of radio broadcasts from Vietnam, Thailand, and Laos that had been recorded weeks earlier. My job was to scan the dial and pick up Thai voice communications that might be "Thai guerillas" operating along the Laotian and Burmese borders with Thailand. When I came across something that sounded "military," I recorded it along with the date, time, and where I had found it on the radio dial. It is possible that I actually recorded some guerillas, but I think it was just as likely I had been recording Thai border police.

I became bored with my work at Two Rock Ranch and volunteered to return to Non Sung to finish out my enlistment. I expected to work on my Thai language skills and maybe return to work in Thailand after I was discharged from the Army.

Unfortunately, I wasn't assigned to the "ChiCom" problem this time. I was assigned the "Laotian Problem" and worked there as a "reporter"—the same work that I did in Vietnam. There were no regular US units involved in the "Secret War" in Laos as far as I could tell. In fact, the US government officially denied we were involved. It seems as though we (the soldiers and Marines at the 7th Radio Research Field Station (7th RRFS) were supporting the CIA officers who were, in turn, running operations in Laos, ostensibly on behalf of the Royal Lao Armed Forces. The other side, the "rebels" in the civil war, were "Pathet Lao" ("Country of Laos") guerillas.

I came to believe that the war we were running in Laos served no one's interest and was a waste of the lives of people who were being paid to engage in a proxy war between the US and North Vietnam. We hired Hmong tribesmen to fight for our position, and the North Vietnamese supported Laotian communist guerillas with their own troops.

Over time, I came to the firm belief that what we were doing was immoral and illegal. For instance, in early 1971, I personally observed a man in civilian clothes—who I had been told was a CIA officer from the nearby CIA station at Udorn—point to a map at a supply base in Laos that was also known to contain a hospital. He talked loudly of scheduling "Arc Light" air strikes (B-52 bombing missions) against the site. At the same time, I was aware not only through the Thai people I knew who worked at our compound but also from local newspapers that we were sending Thai soldiers dressed in Laotian uniforms to fight in central Laos.

That was it for me.

I told the Marine Corps Captain Fred Parry, who I was working for, that I was not going to work on the war in Laos anymore. I told him I understood I could go to prison for refusing to do the work.

Captain Parry treated me fairly. He ordered me to go to work filling sandbags and building "bunkers."

These bunkers are best described as three-to-four-man huts made of wood and corrugated metal with several layers of sandbags on all sides (except for a small entrance) and on the roof. They were located inside the wire fence that surrounded the 7th RRFS and were intended to be manned by US troops as a second line of defense in an attack (extremely unlikely). The Thai troops outside the wire were the first line of defense.

If I was convicted of refusing a direct order, I understood I would be sent to Long Binh Jail—the US Army stockade in Southeast Asia for soldiers convicted of crimes and sentenced to a year or less.[255] (The troops referred to the Long Binh Jail as "LBJ"—the initials for President Lyndon Baines Johnson, who was the man most felt was responsible for our long-term involvement in the "Vietnam War.")

I continued to sleep in the same bunk in our enlisted barracks. I can only remember two guys who gave me a hard time. Two or three others expressed support for what I had done and said they were thinking of doing the same thing. I told them quite clearly not to do it unless they were willing to go to jail. To this day, I don't know what they did.

My father, a Marine officer who had been forced to retire after being badly wounded in action in the South Pacific in World War II, could not have been more supportive in his letters to me.

I just kept filling sandbags. After about three months, I received word that my request for an "early out" (discharge prior to the end of the enlistment date—in my case, two months early) was approved.

I don't know why the colonel decided not to court martial me. I never spoke to him. Obviously, I am glad he didn't.

I received an "honorable" discharge and left the Army in Oakland, California, in June, 1971.[256]

A 2019 Article in *Inside History* titled, "Why Laos Has Been Bombed More Than Any Other Country," gives a good summary of devastation we left behind in Laos.[257]

> The U.S. Air Force began bombing targets in Laos in 1964, flying planes like AC-130s and B-52s full of cluster bombs on covert missions based out of Thailand. The United States eventually dropped the equivalent of a planeload of bombs every eight minutes, 24 hours a day, for nine years, according to *Al Jazeera*. [my emphasis]

> By 1975, one-tenth of the population of Laos, or 200,000 civilians and members of the military, *were dead*. Twice as many were wounded. *Seven hundred and fifty thousand*, a full quarter of the population, had become refugees. . . . *Declassified documents* show that 728 Americans died in Laos, most of whom were working for the CIA. The secret war in Laos, or the Laos Civil War to many who lived through it, set a precedent for a more militarized CIA with the power to engage in covert conflicts around the world. [my emphasis]

The war in Laos, like the war in Vietnam, continues to haunt many of us who served in Southeast Asia in the late 1960s and early 1970s.

By the time of the Minh trial, I had been working as chief deputy in the Chittenden County State's Attorney's Office for approximately two and a half years. Lauren Bowerman, Chittenden County's first female state's attorney, had appointed me as her chief deputy when she took over from Scot Kline in mid-1997.

My job as Lauren's chief deputy was to prosecute major violent felonies such as murders, attempted murders, and aggravated assaults and to ensure that there was a deputy state's attorney present in court to cover arraignments and hearings.

Lauren had been Scot Kline's chief deputy. She was a great boss.

Lauren was an experienced trial lawyer who had a deep understanding of how the office should work. She made it quite clear what she expected of us. But she treated all twenty plus members of the office—secretaries, victim advocates, and lawyers—with respect and a concern for our well-being.

In 2001, Lauren's last year as state's attorney, the Chittenden County State's Attorney's Office tried 23 felony jury trials. That was 34% of all the felonies tried in the state.[258]

Lauren Bowerman resigned from her job as state's attorney in early October 2001 to take a job as an assistant attorney general. Governor Howard Dean appointed me to replace her two weeks later. I served as interim Chittenden County state's attorney until I was elected to a four-year term in November 2002.

DOMESTIC VIOLENCE CASES

When I first returned to the Chittenden County State's Attorney's Office in 1994, the most significant change that I noticed was that the office was literally prosecuting ten times as many "domestic assaults" as it was when I left in 1981.

A person commits "domestic assault," a misdemeanor punishable by up to one year in prison, when that person (most often a man) causes "physical injury" to a "household member"—someone that person has shared a home with. A person commits "aggravated domestic assault," a felony punishable by up to 15 years in prison, when he causes "serious bodily injury" to a household member or threatens a household member with a deadly weapon.[259]

In the early 1980s, police in Chittenden County, like most other law enforcement agencies in the country, rarely charged domestic assaults. Why? Police and prosecutors in Vermont, like their counterparts throughout the US, tended to treat domestic assaults as a "private" or a "family matter."

That had changed dramatically by the 1990s.

Cheryl Hanna, a professor at Vermont Law School and a nationally recognized expert in domestic violence cases, reported in the mid-1990s that:

> Police response to domestic violence has recently undergone enormous change. Aggressive arrest policies are now in place throughout the country, partially as a result of high publicity cases, most notably Tracey Thurman's. Ms. Thurman received

a $ 1.9 million settlement from the Torrington, Connecticut Police Department for its policy of nonintervention and non arrest in domestic violence cases.[260]

The Thurman case, which eventually cost the City of Torrington $1.9 million, was a shocking case of police "nonintervention" in domestic violence cases. The facts as alleged by the victim Tracey Thurman are summarized in a 1984 decision by a federal district court judge in *Thurman v. City of Torrington*—a decision which found that there was a basis for concluding that the Torrington Police Department's policy of nonintervention in domestic violence cases violated the right of domestic violence victims to the equal protection under the law guaranteed by the 14th Amendment.[261]

Over the course of eight months, multiple Torrington police officers ignored, and in at least one case deliberately refused, to consider complaints from Tracey Thurman and other witnesses who said that Tracey's estranged husband Charles "Buck" Thurman was repeatedly calling her and coming to her home to threaten her.

On June 10, 1983, Tracey called Torrington Police and reported that her estranged husband Charles was at the home she and their 8-month-old son, Charles, Jr., shared with two friends. She told police that this was a violation of her husband's probation.

After fifteen minutes without police follow up, Tracey went outside to plead with her husband "not to take or hurt the baby." Her husband responded by stabbing Tracey "repeatedly in the neck, chest, and throat."[262]

A single Torrington police officer arrived approximately 10 minutes later. Charles Thurman was "holding a bloody knife." The decision described what happened next:

> Charles then dropped the knife and, in the presence of the defendant (the officer), kicked the plaintiff Tracey Thurman in the head and ran into (the house). Charles returned from within the residence holding the plaintiff Charles Thurman, Jr. and dropped the child on his wounded mother. Charles then kicked Tracey in the head a second time. Soon thereafter, defendants (three other officers) arrived on the scene but still permitted Charles Thurman to wander about the crowd and to continue to threaten Tracey. Finally, upon approaching

Tracey once again, this time while she was lying on a stretcher, Charles Thurman was arrested and taken into custody.[263]

The judge denied the City of Torrington's motion to dismiss Tracey Thurman's lawsuit. He found there was sufficient evidence to show that the City of Torrington had denied Tracey Thurman her 14th Amendment right to Equal Protection under the law. More specifically, he found that while the evidence showed that Torrington police provided full protection to victims of abuse who were not in a "domestic relationship"; the evidence also tended to show that Torrington police had a policy of "deliberate indifference" to protection of women who were, or had been, in domestic relationships.[264]

On June 26, 1985, a jury in federal court in Hartford, Connecticut, awarded Tracey Thurman $2.3 million in damages. The jury found that 29 past and current Torrington police officers had violated her constitutional rights because they "failed to give her complaints about her former husband the same consideration as they gave other criminal complaints because hers involved a domestic dispute."[265] The City of Torrington eventually settled the case for $1.9 million after the parties agreed to drop appeals.

Charles Thurman was convicted of felony assault for stabbing his wife 13 times and kicking her in the head several times during the June 10, 1985, incident. He was sentenced to serve 15 years in prison.[266]

Domestic violence cases were often the most difficult to prosecute in the time I worked as a prosecutor. The reason for this was simple: Most domestic assault victims refused to cooperate in the prosecution.

Police across the country had ended the practice of "nonintervention" in domestic assault cases by the early 1990s. But the overwhelming majority of victims of domestic abuse still refused to cooperate in the prosecution of those who had abused them.

In my experience, more than 70% of women who called the police asking for help because their husband or boyfriend had assaulted them "took back" (or "recanted") their original complaints.

Many of these victims refused to testify at all. But some even testified for the defense. When their complaints were recorded on 911 calls, they often later claimed that they had made up the complaint because they were angry at the man who beat them (e.g., "It was my fault, I attacked him," or "It was an accident.") When the complaint was not recorded, the victim would sometimes say the police were lying.

Before I go any further, I have to say that I think I understood why many of these women changed their stories. That is why I didn't charge or threaten to charge them with a crime for lying to the police. The fact is, the reason for the "recantation" was almost always done out of fear—fear of the abuser, fear of the impact the prosecution would have on children in the home, fear of loss of income to the household, fear that what had once been a loving relationship would be lost forever. In a 2002 law review article, a law professor and an attorney—both of whom worked with crime victims—wrote that victim "recantation" was the "norm" in domestic violence cases and that these recantations were "hardly surprising" because "batterers put hydraulic pressures on domestic violence victims to recant, drop the case, or fail to appear at trial."[267]

The authors of the article said that:

> The reasons that victims do not cooperate are closely related to the victim's need for physical and emotional survival and the safety of her children.

> Victims (of domestic violence) have good reason to be afraid. Many women stay in battering relationships because when they have tried to leave, they have been beaten. Leaving a batterer is a very risky undertaking. Victims have reason to fear financial ruin. The leading cause of homelessness among women and children is domestic violence. Studies reveal that domestic violence has led to the circumstances of between thirty-five and fifty percent of all homeless women and children.

Kendall Foley, the author of a 2022 *Missouri Law Review* article, said domestic assault victims have shown a "nearly universal refusal to cooperate with prosecutors." Foley later explained the reason for the victims' refusal to cooperate.

> The core of abusive behavior is power and control over the victim. This power is gained and maintained through specific

tactics designed to damage the victim's self-esteem, keep her in a continuous state of fear, isolate her from outside support, and diminish her economic independence.

Some of these behaviors within the relationship are particularly effective at hindering the victim's willingness or ability to participate in prosecution efforts. The most straightforward of these is direct coercion, when the abuse threatens certain repercussions if the victim contacts or participates with law enforcement. After law enforcement becomes involved, batterers often coax victims to 'drop charges' or otherwise refuse to cooperate.

Similarly, more general intimidation and threats to hurt or leave the victim, commit suicide, or take other retaliatory action make the victim unlikely to challenge her abuser's power by seeking help or opposing him in court.[268]

Again, in most cases, I understood why the victims did what they did, and I did not try to force them to testify. There were often ways to convict the abuser without relying on the trial testimony of the assault victim. So, losing the victim's testimony usually did not mean the case would be dismissed.

The fact is, though, some victims and some victim advocates[269] wanted to go a step beyond refusing to cooperate in the prosecution. They believed that, as victims of the abuse who had recanted or refused to testify, they had the right to prevent the men who abused them from being prosecuted. These victims wanted "the charges dropped."

I didn't—and still don't—agree. In cases where I believed the abuser was guilty and I believed I could prove it without the victim's testimony—which was most cases—I had the obligation as the lawyer representing the people of Chittenden County to bring the case to trial. It was my job, but beyond that, to do otherwise would permit the abuser's threats to control the prosecution and undermine the justice system. I told victim advocates that I wasn't going to try to force victims to testify but I also wasn't going to let victims, or more accurately their abusers who were pressuring them, decide who was going to be prosecuted.

There were often children in the household where domestic abuse was happening. Failure to prosecute the abuser put the children in danger of physical and psychological injury. Beyond that, most of the men charged with domestic assault were not monogamous. Failure to prosecute these men put other women at risk.

In 2002, the Vermont Legislature enacted a statute establishing a "Domestic Violence Fatality Review Committee" (Committee). The Committee is composed of leaders in law enforcement, victim's services and the medical community. In 2024 the Committee published a report that said that during the period from 1994 through 2022, nearly half (45 percent of all the homicides in Vermont were "domestic violence related." At least 38 children were present during domestic violence related killings during that period.

I handled many "domestic" cases when I was a deputy (1994 to 1997), chief deputy state's attorney (1997 to 2001), and state's attorney (2001 to 2006).

I came to realize that "domestic violence cases," which ranged from misdemeanor domestic assault to murder, were among the most important cases we prosecuted. To me, this was true not only because the abusers posed a continuing threat to their victims, but also because they often scarred the lives of the children of the victims who were swept up in the violence.

I tried several domestic assault cases where the victim either "recanted" her original report of abuse or refused to testify. Basically, I approached the cases as though I was trying a homicide case where, of course, there is no victim testimony.

The police usually did a good job in investigating the case—e.g., getting photos of the victim's injuries, obtaining copies of 911 tapes, identifying witnesses, talking to neighbors, etc. The victim's first call to police, usually a recorded 911 call, and the testimony of the first police officer to come to the aid of the victim were crucial. This evidence was usually enough to convince a jury to convict the defendant—even when the victim had "recanted" and testified for the defense.

The key to these cases was the "excited utterance" exception to the "hearsay rule." The "hearsay rule" is a rule of evidence that basically says that a witness at trial cannot tell jurors what someone else said to them about something that is relevant to an issue at trial. Why? Because the person who made that "out of court statement" was not under oath when the statement was made, and the person who made that statement would not be subject to cross-examination at trial.

So, if a woman came up to a police officer and said, "My boyfriend punched me in the face," that statement would normally be inadmissible at trial unless the woman was there to be cross-examined to expose weaknesses in her testimony. If the police officer tried to tell the jury what the woman had said, the defense would object on "hearsay grounds," and the judge would normally sustain the objection.

In the example above, the "excited utterance" exception to the rule banning "hearsay" at trial would permit the police officer to testify at trial that the woman had told him that her boyfriend had punched her in the face [270]—if the facts and circumstances showed that at the time she made the statement about the "startling event" (being punched) she was still "under the stress or excitement caused by the event." So if she was crying or otherwise showing she was still feeling the stress of being punched, then the "excited utterance" exception to the hearsay rule would apply, and the jury could hear the statement even though the woman was not available to be cross-examined.

It often happened like this: A police officer was dispatched following a call about a "domestic in progress" at a specific address. The officer arrived and entered the home at the address and saw a woman bleeding from her nose and mouth, shaking and crying. The officer asked her, "What happened?" and the woman responded with something to the effect of "My boyfriend hit me; he left when he heard I was calling 911."

The statement was most likely to have been true because the evidence showed that the woman was still "under the stress of excitement" of the "startling event" and did not have time to make up a story to falsely implicate her boyfriend.

Again, I tried several domestic assault cases where the victim either refused to testify or "recanted" and testified that her husband or boyfriend was not responsible for her injuries. Six of these cases were appealed to the Vermont Supreme Court. Each conviction was based on "excited utterance" testimony. Each was affirmed by the Vermont Supreme Court.[271]

In cases where the victim testified for the defense, my closing argument to the jury would be something like: *Your common sense tells you that this woman did not tell you the truth just now. Doesn't it make sense, instead, that she told the officer the truth when he responded to her 911 call, and while she was crying and bleeding? Doesn't it make sense that she was telling the truth then, when she was still very upset about what had happened? Doesn't it make sense that she has a good reason not to tell the truth now, three months later, with the defendant, the man who assaulted her, watching and listening to her every word?"*

In my experience, when juries had to choose between police or a lay witness testimony recounting the "excited utterances" of a "recantation" at trial, the juries always went with the excited utterance. This was likely because the "recantation" was made under pressure from the abuser, and the explanation in the recantation itself usually made little sense.

Here are two brief examples.

I tried a particularly disturbing "excited utterance" case in February 1997, roughly two and a half years after I'd returned to the State's Attorney's Office. This time, the "excited utterance" testimony that countered the victim's "recantation" came not just from a police officer, as it usually did, but also from the victim's mother.

The defendant, Acel Bullock, age 24, and the younger victim lived together as boyfriend and girlfriend.

The victim's mother told jurors that on Monday, August 26, 1996, shortly before 1 p.m., the victim went to the office where her mother worked. She was "frightened and hysterical." The mom said her daughter had a split lip, a bruise near her left eye, abrasions on her neck, and bruises on her hands and arms. Mom testified further that her daughter told her that she had to get into Mom's house to get some papers that Bullock wanted. She told her mother that Bullock would beat her again if she didn't get the papers he wanted and that she was afraid he would kill her.

Mom testified that she went to her home to make sure her daughter could get in the house, but her daughter was not there. Before long, she got a call from her daughter. She had returned to Mom's office. Mom testified further that her daughter asked her to come back to her office and help her. She said again that she was afraid Bullock was going to kill her.

When Mom returned to her office, she found that her daughter, who had more bruises than before, was "cowering in a corner terrified [Bullock] would find her." Mom said she and her daughter went down the backstairs in the office building to get to Mom's car. She said her daughter laid down on the back seat, hoping that Bullock would not be able to see her. Mom then drove her daughter to the Williston Police Station, where Mom had arranged for them to meet with a police officer.

After I called the Mom to testify, I called the officer who testified that the victim was crying off and on and was terrified Bullock would show up. According to the officer, the victim said that Bullock had punched her and kicked her and "dragged her around by a T-shirt."

The judge approved admission of the photos of the victim's injuries into evidence for the jury to review.

The victim testified for the defense. Her story at trial was different from the one she had told Mom. The victim told jurors that she, the victim, had been the aggressor and that Bullock had simply acted in self-defense.[272]

This was one of the first "recantation" cases I had tried. During the trial, I lost sight of the pressure on the victim to make the defendant, Bullock, happy with her testimony. I remember that the judge (quite properly) reprimanded me when I asked the victim on cross: "How does it feel to call your mother a liar?"

After that, I focused solely on the strength and courage her mother had shown.

The jury convicted Bullock of domestic assault. It made no sense to believe, as the defense claimed, that Mom and the police officer had overreacted to what was a private dispute. The judge eventually sentenced Bullock to six to 12 months. He was to serve six months in prison, and after that he would be on probation.[273]

In one "excited utterance" case I tried, the victim called the police crying, frightened, and bleeding from a laceration on her leg. She told the Burlington police officer who responded that her husband had smashed a lamp and slashed her leg with the broken glass. Her husband, Francis "Pete" Joseph, age 49, had fled the scene.

I relied on the testimony of the officer, Pete Chapman, who recounted the victim's statement—the one she had made while she was crying and bleeding—to prove the prosecution's case at trial. The judge ruled that Chapman's testimony was admissible under the "excited utterance" exception to the hearsay rule.

The victim testified for the defense at trial. She claimed that she did not remember calling police and told jurors she had cut herself while she was in a "fight" with the defendant. She swore she had "a kind of nervous breakdown" (her first) and that she intended to contact a psychiatrist to get help.

I called a rebuttal expert on "cutters"—people who have a well-recognized condition that causes them to repeatedly "self-mutilate," often by making superficial cuts in their forearms or legs. In her testimony, the expert described "common behavioral characteristics of people who cut themselves for psychological reasons." She also testified that it was "uncommon" for "cutting" to occur in the midst of a fight.[274]

I was able to refer to this expert testimony in closing and to point out that the victim had described none of these characteristics when she'd testified. I emphasized that the victim claimed that she had cut herself.

The jury rejected the victim's claim and found the defendant guilty of domestic assault. I then introduced certified copies of the records of the defendant's prior convictions for domestic assault as well as four prior felony convictions, including an aggravated assault on a police officer. With that, jurors convicted the defendant of being a "habitual offender."

The defendant, "Pete" Joseph, had been on probation for domestic assault at the time the jury convicted him. He had also been convicted earlier of beating a female police officer until she lost consciousness and then covering her body with heavy wooden pallets in an effort to prevent her body from being found.[275] On April 10, 2002, he was sentenced to serve 15 to 25 years in prison.[276]

The Vermont Supreme Court affirmed his conviction a year later, in April 2003. The Court rejected Joseph's claim that the trial judge, David Jenkins, had committed a reversible error when he'd admitted the rebuttal testimony of the expert on self-mutilation.

Life Isn't Fair

In 2003, Robert Jones was charged with murdering Sarah, his 32-year-old longtime girlfriend. In June of that year, Emily Stone, a *Burlington Free Press* reporter, wrote a long article on the "cycle of violence" that had "trapped and eventually killed" Sarah.

Stone cited domestic violence experts who said that Sarah's experience was like that of "many battered women who return to their abusers again and again. . . . By one count it takes a woman six or seven attempts before she finally leaves for good or is killed."[277]

Robert Jones's first conviction for domestic assault against Sarah came in 1993. Jones and Sarah, a dark-haired young woman with a sweet smile, lived together off and on for the next 10 years and had two children together before he finally murdered her.

Sarah filed two complaints with police against Jones in a five-year period (from 1993 through 1998) that resulted in criminal charges. Both charges were eventually dismissed. But police involvement in the Jones-Sarah relationship intensified in January 1999.

At 3 a.m. on January 16, 1999, Sarah called 911, frantically reporting that Jones was assaulting her at her Decatur Street home in Burlington. The call was recorded, and Sarah could be heard crying and yelling at Jones. When police arrived, Jones was not there.

Burlington Police Officer Robert Haynes responded to the call and arrived within two or three minutes. He said that Sarah had "pronounced swelling" above her left eye and was crying and shaking when he spoke to her. She told the officer that Jones had punched her twice in the face with a closed fist and that he had also "kneed" her in the face twice.[278]

Three hours later, Sarah called police again and reported that Jones was outside their home banging on the door. Police arrested him, and Jones was charged with three misdemeanors—domestic assault, unlawful trespass, and violation of an abuse prevention order. Jones was released after he posted bail. He was ordered to have no contact with Sarah.[279]

A week later, on January 23, 1999, Jones broke into her apartment on Decatur Street in Burlington, "dragged her into the bedroom by her hair, stripped her naked, took off his clothes," and raped her. This was according to a statement that Sarah provided to police at the time. She said Jones then took a shower and left.[280]

Sue, a long-time friend of Sarah, told police that she had gone to the victim's home around 2 p.m. to give her a haircut. Jones was there when Sue arrived. Sarah seemed happy to see Sue, but she quickly asked Sue to help her get Jones out of the house. Sarah was crying as she was asking for help.

Jones left not long after Sue got there. Sarah began crying again while Sue was cutting her hair. By this time, twenty minutes had passed since Sue had arrived at the house. Sarah told Sue that the latter had come into the house as Jones was forcing the former to have sex when she "didn't want it." Sue said Sarah was crying off and on as she told Sue in some detail how Jones had raped her.

Sarah called Burlington Police at 2:27 p.m.—about a half hour after Sue first arrived at her home. Detective Lt. Michael Schirling responded. Sarah told Schirling that Jones had raped her, according to Schirling's affidavit.[281]

Burlington Police arrested Jones two days later on the sexual assault charge. He was held at the Northwest Regional Correctional Facility in St. Albans after he failed to post the $250,000 bail.

I was assigned the Jones rape case.

In April 1999, I offered Jones a plea agreement: He would plead "no contest" to "sexual assault" and two misdemeanors,[282] and I would argue for a sentence of six to 20 years in prison. Jones rejected the plea agreement at first, but, on July 27, 1999, he accepted it and pled no contest to sexually assaulting Sarah.

By pleading "nolo" or "no contest," Jones was not admitting he had raped Sarah. Instead, he was formally admitting that the prosecution had the evidence it needed to convict him—evidence that proved beyond a reasonable doubt that he had sexually assaulted Sarah.

The judge ordered the Department of Probation and Parole to conduct a pre-sentence investigation. Sentencing was set for October 1999.[283]

Sadly, what followed after that was at first a series of seemingly unrelated events which eventually led to Jones's early release from prison and ultimately Sarah's death four years later.

In August 1999, shortly after Robert Jones pled no contest to raping Sarah, Chris Dean, age 36, was charged with an attempt to escape from the Northwest Regional Correctional Facility in St. Albans.

Robert Jones was in the same prison in St. Albans as Dean. Jones told authorities that he had information on the Dean escape attempt. He agreed to testify against Dean. At the time of his attempted escape, Dean was awaiting trial in Federal Court in Vermont for killing a teenager. In return for Jones's cooporation, Federal prosecutors would put in a good word for Jones at his own sentencing.

On September 26, 1999, roughly two months after the escape attempt, Chris Dean of Pierceton, Indiana, accepted a plea bargain and pled guilty to causing the death of Christopher, 17, of Fair Haven, Vermont, by mailing him a package that exploded when Christopher opened it.

The killing had happened eighteen months earlier, on March 19, 1998. The victim's mother, Sheila, was standing behind her son when the bomb exploded, and she was badly injured.

Dean and his victim had never met. Dean had sent Christopher four hundred dollars to purchase a CB radio. Christopher never sent Dean the radio. So Dean looked up how to make a bomb on the internet. He built one using "black powder, a clothespin, and thumb tacks" and sent it to the Vermont teenager.[284]

Under the terms of the plea agreement, Chris Dean pled guilty to killing Christopher and severely injuring his mother. In return, prosecutors in the US Attorney's Office in Vermont, which had jurisdiction over the case because it was an interstate crime, agreed not to ask for the death penalty. Federal prosecutors also agreed not to prosecute Dean for his attempt to escape from prison in St. Albans two months earlier. Under the terms of the plea agreement, the US Attorney's Office would ask the judge to sentence Dean to life in prison without the possibility of parole. Dean could argue for a lesser sentence.

Even though the escape charges had been dropped, prosecutors in the US Attorney's Office asked Robert Jones to testify at Dean's sentencing about Dean's role in the escape attempt at his sentencing. They evidently believed Jones's testimony would buttress the prosecutors' claims that Dean should be sentenced to life in prison without possibility of parole. Under their agreement with Jones, federal prosecutors would, in turn, tell the Vermont State Criminal Court judge about Jones's cooperation with them when his own sentencing in the Sarah rape case came up.

There was a complication. Dean's sentencing was scheduled to take place sometime in January or February 2000. Jones's sentencing was to take place four months before that in October 1999. That meant, of course, that the sentencing judge in Jones's case would not hear about his cooperation because he hadn't cooperated yet.

I don't remember much about the specifics of the conversation, but I agreed to a request from Jones's attorney and federal prosecutors to ask the State Criminal Court judge to postpone the sentencing in Jones's case until after Dean was sentenced in Federal Court for killing a teenager.[285]

I don't remember giving a lot of thought to the decision to agree to postpone Jones's sentencing.

First, of course, it would help federal prosecutors get the life sentence that Chris Dean so richly deserved. He had killed a young man who had apparently "stiffed" him on a four hundred dollar business deal—nothing more.[286]

Second, Jones's decision to take the plea agreement seemed solid. He had rejected it at first and then decided to take it and plead "nolo," or "no contest," to the rape three months later, presumably after considering the advice of his court-appointed attorney.

Third, although I knew that Sarah had "taken back" complaints that Jones had abused her in the past, I thought it was likely that she was "over" the man who had repeatedly abused her for the past six or seven years. By the time I agreed to postpone his sentencing in October 1999, Jones had already been in prison for nearly nine months. This left Sarah and her two children free from Jones's abuse for the first time for such an extended period. Moreover, I was not aware that Sarah had shown any interest in "recanting" during this period.

Wrong.

On February 15, 2000, a little over a year after she was raped by Jones, Sarah filed a sworn statement saying she had lied on January 23, 1999, when she'd told her friend Sue and Lt. Schirling that Jones had forced her to have sex when she hadn't "wanted it."

Sarah gave a broad, general denial when she recanted her rape complaint a year later. She swore that Jones "did not break into her home and have non-consensual sex" with her.[287]

Ten days after the "recantation," on February 25, 2000, Jones's attorney filed a motion to withdraw his "no contest" plea to the rape of Sarah. The motion relied on her February 15, 2000, sworn statement that she had lied.

I filed a motion to keep the rape case alive, despite Sarah's new sworn statement—a statement that I was confident was itself a lie prompted by pressure from Jones, even though he was still in prison.

My argument was that I could still prove the rape through Sarah's "excited utterances" made within a half hour of the rape—first to Sue and then to Lt. Schirling. I called them both as witnesses at a hearing before Judge Brian Burgess on my motion to prevent Jones from withdrawing his plea. I do not remember much about the May 26, 2000, hearing, but I do remember that Sarah was in the audience and that she made a loud comment to the effect that there was no rape and that she ought to know. She was definitely there to support Jones in his move to withdraw his plea.

Judge Burgess ruled that Sarah's statements made while she was crying and shaking within a half hour of the "exciting event" (the rape) did not qualify as excited utterances.[288]

On June 29, 2000, not long after Sarah had withdrawn her claim that Robert Jones had raped her, a young woman named DA, 21, appeared in court in Burlington and requested a Relief From Abuse Order against Daniel Valentine, 24, of Boston, Massachusetts. Valentine and DA had lived together as boyfriend and girlfriend in Boston. They had a son together there. But DA had moved back to Vermont to get out of what had become an abusive relationship.

Valentine had broken into DA's Burlington apartment on May 20, 2000. She told the judge that Valentine had "trashed" a one-thousand-dollar stereo and threatened to take her son. She said that Valentine was "mad" because she wouldn't marry him.

Valentine denied everything—in his own way.

He didn't "break in" since the back door was open. The stereo he'd destroyed was his anyway. He'd only made one hole in the wall in DA's apartment. The hole was where the phone had been, and, after all, he had paid for the phone. He had a right to see his child.

Judge Linda Levitt granted the "Relief From Abuse" order. She found that Valentine had abused DA. She ordered him to stop the abuse and to stay away from DA.

This was all the protection the law could provide at this point, but it wasn't enough.

Sometime during the period between June 29 and July 2, 2000, DA made the mistake of letting Valentine live in her apartment until July 3 when he was scheduled to return to Boston. This mistake nearly cost DA her life. Late on Sunday, July 2, Valentine used a broken beer bottle to slash DA's face, wrists, and hands.[289] It took three hundred stitches to close her wounds. She nearly died of blood loss.[290]

DA might have died if it hadn't been for the courage of her friend and Marble Avenue neighbor, Sarah. On Sunday evening, July 2, 2000, Sarah, a longtime victim of domestic abuse herself, heard screams coming from her friend's apartment. When she went over to the apartment, Sarah saw Valentine slicing DA with the broken beer bottle. Sarah stepped in and "helped DA escape down the stairs."[291]

In fact, four months later in November, when Burlington Police held its annual ceremony honoring officers for acts of bravery during the year, they also honored Sarah for her bravery in helping her friend DA.[292]

Valentine was eventually charged with attempted second-degree murder. Deputy State's Attorney Babette Boyd, a graduate of George Washington University Law School and one of the first black prosecutors in Vermont, tried the case before a jury in May 2003.

Attorney Boyd did an outstanding job. Valentine changed his plea to "guilty" after two days of trial. In exchange for the guilty plea, Boyd agreed that she would ask that Valentine be sentenced to no more than 23 to 55 years in prison.[293] That is what Judge Ben Joseph sentenced Valentine to on September 11, 2003—twenty-three to fifty-five years to serve.[294]

Sarah's abuser, Robert Jones, had accumulated several charges in 1999 in addition to the rape charge. He remained in prison for another year after Judge Burgess denied my attempt to keep the rape charge alive.

I eventually dismissed the rape charge. There was no choice given Sarah's recantation and the judge's ruling on my "excited utterance" claim. I no longer had any evidence of the rape to present to a jury.

Jones had pled guilty to two felonies committed on Saturday, January

16, 1999—the week before the rape. He pled guilty to unlawful trespass for breaking into Sarah's home at 3 a.m. that Saturday morning and to second-degree aggravated domestic assault for punching her in the face with a closed fist that morning. Jones was released on June 20, 2001, after serving roughly 28 months in prison.[295]

Jones was jailed twice for drunk driving in the two years following his June 2001 release from prison—once in November 2001 and again in April 2002.[296]

On May 4–5, 2003, Jones had been out of prison a little more than a year. But at the time, he was still on furlough and subject to immediate imprisonment if he violated the terms of his release. Jones was living with Sarah and their two children in an apartment on Front Street in Burlington. Their home was in an area with several bars. It was also less than a mile from the Criminal Court Building on Pearl Street in Burlington.

Sarah reacted with remarkable courage in July 2000 when she'd rushed in to save DA from her longtime abuser, Daniel Valentine. But there was no one on hand roughly three years later to save Sarah from being savagely beaten to death by *her* longtime abuser—Robert Jones.[297]

Sarah arrived at Fletcher Allen Health Care shortly before 3 p.m. on Monday, May 5, 2003. She had bruises on the back of her head, her face, her chest, her back, and her legs. Sarah was in a coma when she arrived at the hospital, and she never regained consciousness. She was pronounced dead three days later on May 8th.

I had been elected state's attorney by the time police began investigating Sarah's death. On June 4, 2003, I charged Robert Jones with second-degree murder and with the separate charge of being a habitual offender, which, like the second-degree murder charge, carried a maximum sentence of life imprisonment.

I assigned myself and Deputy State's Attorney Rosemary Gretkowski to the case. Rosemary was an experienced prosecutor with a lot of experience handling cases involving violence against women.

It took another two years—until late October 2005—before we got the case to trial.

My Final Year as State's Attorney

As things turned out, I tried six jury trials in my last year as Chittenden County state's attorney (July 2005–July 2006). Five of the trials involved felonies.[298] The sixth was a misdemeanor domestic assault.[299]

The defendants in four of the five felony trials were men who had been convicted of domestic assault in the past—Thomas Sharrow, Joshua Muhammad, Stanley "Yuppie" Mayo, and Robert Jones.

The other felony trial, the kidnapping trial of Aaron Jackson, was unique because it was one of the first in Vermont that relied on "computer-generated evidence," or "digital evidence," to convince a jury of the defendant's guilt.

In early December 2005, at around 9:15 in the evening, Matt M., 17, called Aaron Jackson, 23, from a store in Burlington's Old North End. He asked Jackson to give him a ride to his home in the South End of Burlington. Matt got into the front passenger seat of Jackson's maroon Dodge Stratus.

On the ride home, Matt expected to talk with Jackson about money he owed him, but there would be no ride home to where Matt lived with his mother. Instead, Jackson made a sharp turn in the opposite direction—north—where he stopped quickly. A taller man, who was never identified, got in the back seat. That man quickly reached forward and wrapped his right arm around Matt's neck under his chin and began choking him. While his accomplice was choking Matt, Jackson accused him of breaking into Jackson's home and stealing money from him. Matt denied the charge.

What followed, according to Matt's testimony, was a terrifying hour and a half ride through towns in Chittenden County. First, north to Malletts Bay along Lake Champlain, then east to Winooski. From Winooski, Jackson turned north again to Colchester and up to Milton before coming back down to Winooski.

When they got back to Winooski, the accomplice—who Matt described as a Black man about 6'2"—covered Matt's head with a black knit hat, wrapped a belt around Matt's neck, and began choking him intermittently by tightening the tension on the belt.

Matt said that during the stop in Winooski, Jackson made a phone call asking whoever was on the other end for a "big thing." Jackson left the car briefly. When he returned, Jackson put what Matt knew from the feel was a gun up to his neck.

Not long after that, Matt made up a story to save himself. He "admitted" to robbing money from Jackson. He said a man named "Justin Finnegan" now had Jackson's money. Matt told Jackson that "Justin" lived in a second floor apartment above the Rent-A-Center on North Street in Burlington.

"Justin's" apartment was actually the home where Matt's cousin Jody S. lived with his girlfriend and their children—no "Justin Finnegan."

Jackson drove to the apartment and arrived there around 9:45 p.m. When they got there, Jackson and his accomplice, who was armed with a handgun, tried to cover their faces and followed Matt up the stairs to Jody's apartment. As soon as the door opened, Jackson and his accomplice barged in, showing the handgun. Matt took the opportunity to escape. He ran down the stairs and up North Street to Larow's Market, where he called 911. He told police that Jackson and his accomplice were in the process of robbing friends of Matt's at an apartment above the Rent-A-Center on North Street.

Jody later told police that the two men threatened him and another man at the apartment with the gun and said they were looking for "Justin Finnegan." When they were finally convinced there was no "Justin Finnegan" there, Jackson and his accomplice left.

Aaron Jackson was arrested later that evening. He denied any knowledge of the incident when he was interviewed by Burlington Detective Lieutenant Emmet Helrich.

Despite his denials, Jackson was charged with kidnapping and unlawful restraint—both felonies.

Jackson refused to identify his accomplice, and police were never able to put together enough evidence to charge the man they suspected.

To prove kidnapping, the most serious charge, I had to prove that Jackson and his accomplice had intentionally restrained Matt with the intent of putting him in fear that he would be physically injured. I called six witnesses to meet this burden.

The jury saw and heard Matt's testimony on videotape. His testimony had been taken before that point with Jackson's defense attorney and a judge present. This happened because Matt had, at his mother's urging, enlisted in the US military as soon as he turned 18, which was about three months after the kidnapping.

Jody identified Jackson as the person in the driver's seat of the maroon-colored car that had picked up Matt in front of Larow's Market not long after 8 p.m. the night he was kidnapped. This corroborated Matt's testimony. So did the fact that police had found a black knit cap in Jackson's maroon Dodge Stratus the day after the kidnapping, meeting the description of the cap Matt had described being pulled over his face.

Matt was, of course, the most important witness. But there was another key witness besides Matt. That witness was Burlington Detective Aljaray "Ray" Nails who was, at that time, one of the few Black police officers in Vermont.

Detective Nails gave testimony that showed that Jackson had lied when he'd told Lt. Helrich that he didn't know anything about Matt or the kidnapping. At the same time, Nails's testimony and the exhibit of cell phone activity that he had prepared corroborated Matt's account of what had happened.

I introduced a spreadsheet exhibit prepared by Detective Nails. Nails's exhibit contained a summary of cell phone records between Matt and Aaron Jackson during the period between 3 p.m. and 11 p.m. on December 4, 2005, the day Matt was kidnapped.

The records covered two basic facts. One, they listed the people Jackson and Matt had called and received calls from during that time period on the day of kidnapping. Two, the records showed the location of Jackson's phone during the eight-hour period between 3:45 p.m., when Jackson first called Matt, and 11 p.m.

Jackson had told Lt. Helrich that he did not know Matt M. But Detective Nails's call records showed that this was a lie. Jackson's phone called Matt's twice the day of the kidnapping—once at 3:45 in the afternoon and again at 7:02 in the evening.

At the same time, Nails's exhibit also supported Matt's testimony that he was in contact with Jackson shortly before Jackson and his accomplice terrorized him. The call records show that Matt called Jackson's phone from Larow's Market on North Street in Burlington twice just before Matt was abducted—once at 7:48 p.m. and again at 8:13 p.m.

The cell phone records also showed that Jackson had lied when he'd said he was with his girlfriend all day except for a time between 6 p.m. and 7 p.m. when he'd exchanged cars with his mother.

Nails explained to jurors using his exhibit that Jackson's cell phone had moved more than once from his home in the South End of Burlington on the day of the kidnapping, but he was at home between 6 p.m. and 7 p.m., contrary to what he had told Lt. Helrich.

Nails also told jurors that cell phone location information showed that Jackson's cell had moved from the area of his home to the North End of Burlington by 8:15 p.m.—the time Matt said that Jackson had picked him up at Larow's Market.

The records also showed that Jackson was away from his home from 8 p.m. to 11 p.m. on the night of the kidnapping. Again, Jackson had told Lt. Helrich that he was home all day except for the one-hour period between 6 p.m. and 7 p.m.

The records showed further that Jackson had made one call around 9 p.m. from the Winooski area, just as Matt had testified. It was after this—again, according to Matt's testimony—that Jackson threatened him with a gun.

Finally, phone records from Larow's Market showed that Matt had made the 911 call that alerted police to the threat to Jody and his family at 9:43 p.m. Again, this timing was consistent with both Jody's and Matt's testimony.[300]

Aaron Jackson testified in his own defense not long after I had closed the prosecution's case with Detective Ray Nails's testimony.

The cell phone records produced by Detective Nails evidently forced Jackson to come up with a version of the facts that contradicted (1) the version of events Jackson first gave to Lt. Helrich and (2) defied common sense.

Faced with the evidence that he had called Matt twice on the day of the kidnapping, Jackson admitted when he testified that he did know Matt M. after all. And faced with cell phone location evidence that he was not with his girlfriend, but was in fact moving through towns in northern Chittenden County, Jackson came up with a stunning new story.

The new version centered on the call Jackson made to the Winooski area at around 9 p.m. Detective Nails's cell phone records showed Jackson had made the call to a man named George Coleman, who had been charged in federal court with sale of cocaine two months earlier. Coleman was at home on conditions of release awaiting trial.[301]

Jackson testified that Jody and Matt had made up the story about Jackson abducting Matt. Why? Because, according to Jackson, Matt was angry with Jackson. Why? Because Jackson had not been successful in arranging for Coleman to sell Matt cocaine![302]

I argued that it made no sense to believe that this 17-year-old young man would make up a story about being abducted for an hour and a half—much less make up a story about his cousin and his family suffering an armed home invasion—simply because Jackson was unsuccessful in helping Matt buy cocaine. And it made even less sense to believe that Jody, who was unhappy with Matt for bringing armed men to his home in the first place, would join Matt in making up this story simply because Jackson had failed to arrange a cocaine buy for Matt.[303]

The story about the failure to arrange the cocaine buy provided at least some explanation—albeit a remarkably weak and bizarre one—for the call record showing Jackson's call to Coleman. But it did not explain why cell phone location records showed Jackson had actually been in the area that Coleman lived in at around 9 p.m. in the evening. Matt testified Jackson had stopped there to get the gun that was used to threaten both Matt and Jody.

Why did Jackson go to George Coleman's house at 9 p.m. on the night of the kidnapping? Again, Jackson evidently felt compelled to tailor the testimony to coincide with cell phone records. This time it was his girlfriend who provided the sworn testimony that was consistent with the phone records.

Jackson's longtime girlfriend, Latrice I., told jurors that contrary to Matt's testimony, Jackson had not gone to Coleman's home to get a gun but to help him prepare pork ribs.

Coleman had called Jackson earlier in the day (phone records say 3:14 p.m.) not to talk about drugs, guns, or money, but to get help from Jackson cooking a meal! According to Latrice, Jackson left her home about 9:20 p.m. to go out to Coleman's home to teach Coleman how to "fix ribs."[304]

The jury was not out long before it came back with a "guilty" verdict on all counts—the kidnapping and unlawful restraint involving Matt, and the two misdemeanor assault counts involving Jody and the other man in his apartment, who was also threatened with a gun by Jackson's accomplice.

The jury simply did not buy the contorted, obviously false testimony of Jackson and his girlfriend.

Judge Michael Kupersmith later sentenced Jackson to serve 7 to 13 years in prison, and Jackson's convictions were affirmed by the Vermont Supreme Court in May 2008.[305]

"He's Killing Me"

Thomas Sharrow was charged with attempted first-degree murder for repeatedly stabbing Peggy H. at her apartment in Burlington during the early morning hours of October 4, 2003.

I tried the case with Margaret Vincent in early July 2005. She was chief deputy for the more than five years I was Chittenden County state's attorney. Vincent had significant experience as a defense attorney in Middlebury before coming to work in Burlington for William Sorrell and Scot Kline. This experience gave her a helpful perspective on the work of prosecutors. She was a calm, capable trial attorney with excellent judgment who made my job as state's attorney much easier.

Sharrow had a history of assaulting Peggy. He was convicted of domestic assault against her in May 2003. Two months later, in early July 2003, he was charged with aggravated domestic assault for threatening and striking her. Two months after that, on September 3, 2003, Sharrow was arrested and charged again for assaulting Peggy.

That made three attacks on Peggy in roughly four months. But Sharrow wasn't done.

A month later, on the evening of October 3, 2003, Sharrow violated a court-imposed "no contact" requirement, broke into Peggy's apartment on lower Church Street in Burlington, and began threatening her and breaking things. Her upstairs neighbors, Dale Phillips and his wife Jennifer, heard the commotion. Dale came downstairs with his dog and knocked on Peggy's door to ask if she needed help. Sharrow told Peggy: "Don't answer the door. I'll kill you." Sharrow left not long after that.

After Sharrow left, Peggy went upstairs to the Phillipses' apartment. Jennifer Phillips had called the police. Peggy met briefly with police in her neighbors' apartment and then returned to her apartment to get some rest.

Roughly two hours later, at 2 a.m. on Saturday, October 4, 2003, Sharrow broke into Peggy's apartment again. Peggy turned off the lights when she heard the break in and tried to hide on the porch. Sharrow found her and attacked her with a knife. She struggled and cried out repeatedly: "He's killing me."

Peggy was hospitalized with multiple knife wounds. She had two knife wounds to her head and knife wounds to the back of her neck, the back of her left arm, the back of her right arm, and her lower back. The wound to her lower back was deep enough to cause an injury to her lung. Peggy also had injuries to her face and ear, which were consistent with her claim that Sharrow had punched her in the face.

The physical evidence at the scene, coupled with Peggy's account of what had happened, showed that Sharrow—who had become familiar with the apartment layout when he'd lived with Peggy—had used three knives to attack his former girlfriend.[306]

First, he'd pulled knife #1 from a kitchen drawer and began attacking Peggy with it. That knife was bent during the attack. He then went to the kitchen and got knife #2. That knife broke. Both knives were recovered at the scene. As for the third knife, when police arrived at the scene just three minutes after the neighbor's 911 call, they'd stopped Sharrow as he was fleeing from Peggy's apartment. He was clutching a "butterfly knife"—a folding knife with a sharp, pointed two-sided blade that tests later showed had Peggy's blood on it. That knife had also come from the kitchen.[307]

Once the officers had subdued Sharrow, they helped get medical assistance for Peggy, who had crawled from the porch, leaving a trail of blood toward the kitchen, where she had collapsed and was lying in the fetal position in a pool of her own blood. The officers reported that she was "twitching uncontrollably."

Sharrow's only injury was a scratch to his right index finger.

Sharrow had a weak defense. He claimed that he had acted in self-defense. He said Peggy had attacked him with a knife and that he had grabbed her arms to ward off the blows. Sharrow claimed that Peggy had unintentionally stabbed herself as she'd struggled with him.

We had three strong arguments, based on the evidence, to counter his self-defense claim.

First, the trial judge, Ben Joseph, had granted our motion to permit evidence of Sharrow's three prior assaults against Peggy in the months leading up to the October attack to show it was not likely that Peggy had attacked Sharrow as claimed.[308]

As I have mentioned several times already, in most cases, evidence of a defendant's "prior bad acts" (prior crimes, or "wrongful acts") is not admissible under Evidence Rule 404 to prove a defendant committed a crime that occurred at a later time.[309]

But there are exceptions to the evidentiary rule. Here, Sharrow claimed that he had acted in self-defense. In other words, he did not intend to hurt Peggy; he was just defending himself.

This "opened the door" for us to introduce evidence through Peggy's testimony. She could tell jurors of his prior assaults to put the attack he was on trial for in "context" to show that Sharrow had not been acting in self-defense. He had, in fact, intended to hurt Peggy, just as he had in July when he'd punched and strangled her. "Now you have something to tell the cops. I'm going to kill you."[310]

Second, although getting in evidence of Sharrow's prior assaults against Peggy tended to undercut Sharrow's claim that she had attacked him, the location of Peggy's injuries made it virtually impossible to believe his claim that she had inadvertently cut herself while struggling with him. He claimed he had been grabbing her arms to prevent her from stabbing him when she'd accidentally cut herself.

Peggy had wounds to the back of her upper left arm/tricep, two wounds to the back of her head, a wound to her neck below her left ear, and a puncture wound to her lower back on the left side—the wound that had been deep enough to injure her lung.[311]

Again, Sharrow's claim was that Peggy had *attacked him* with a knife. He had grabbed her right arm to prevent her from stabbing him. They had struggled and she had unintentionally stabbed herself.

Peggy was right-handed. I argued that it was highly unlikely—but possible—that the two injuries to the back of Peggy's head and the wound to her neck might have been caused while Sharrow was struggling to take the knife away from her. But there was no way that Peggy, who would have been swinging the knife with her right hand, could inflict a puncture wound to her right tricep. I invited jurors to try to visualize how that could even be possible. It wasn't.

Third—the recording of Peggy's neighbors' 911 call to police turned out to be our best piece of evidence.

When Sharrow came back after roughly three hours and broke into Peggy's apartment a second time around 2:15 a.m., her upstairs neighbors Dale and Jennifer Phillips made a 911 call to Burlington Police for the second time that evening. The 911 call was recorded per standard practice.

The recording was one of the best pieces of evidence I have ever had. Dale and Jennifer Phillips, the middle-aged couple who may well have saved Peggy's life, can be heard talking to the 911 operator, who questions them about what's happening with their downstairs neighbor and urges them to stay on the line until police can arrive on the scene.

In the background, you can hear Peggy screaming in terror: "Someone help. He's killing me!" She says "He's killing me" over and over.

As soon as the 911 call went through, Jennifer Phillips shouted out the window, "I called the police!" hoping that Peggy and her attacker in the apartment below could hear her. Roughly three minutes later, she can be heard calling out that the police had arrived. It is unclear whether Peggy could hear her, but Sharrow evidently did—because he tried to flee. That's when he was stopped by police on the stairs, clutching the "butterfly knife" knife with Peggy's blood on it.

During the closing argument, I used a PowerPoint slide that showed a police photo of the blood trail Peggy had left as she'd crawled in from the porch. I linked the 911 call to the slide so that jurors could hear Peggy screaming "He's killing me. . . He's killing me" as they viewed the photo of the blood trail.

To believe Sharrow's story, jurors would have to believe that Peggy was screaming "He's killing me!" while she was attacking Sharrow and unintentionally stabbing herself in her left lower back hard enough to damage her lung. Although under Sharrow's version of events Peggy was supposed to be the attacker, she did not flee when police arrived. Instead, she crawled toward the kitchen and collapsed in a pool of her own blood.

The jury did not buy Sharrow's version of events. Jurors deliberated for a few hours at the end of the trial that had taken less than a week and found Sharrow guilty of attempted second-degree murder.

Jurors found that we had not proven attempted first-degree murder, which required "premeditation." I had argued that Sharrow's decision to go back for a second and a third knife was enough to constitute "premed-itation." However, although jurors rejected the argument that Sharrow had deliberately come to the decision to kill his ex-girlfriend, jurors found that we had proven beyond a reasonable doubt that Sharrow had "recklessly disregarded" the clear risk that his actions would cause "death or serious bodily injury" to Peggy. That was enough to convict him of attempted second-degree murder.

Judge Joseph sentenced Sharrow to serve 20 years to life—the minimum for attempted second-degree murder.[312]

In retrospect, Sharrow's actions in going back for two more knives were best described as "frenzied" rather than "deliberate." In other words, the jury was right.

A FELONY SALE OF COCAINE

I tried Joshua Muhammad's case in July 2005 after federal prosecutors had withdrawn from the case.

Muhammad's case had started out as a "federal case." It was being investigated by the Federal Drug Enforcement Agency (DEA), which was working with local Burlington Police detectives who had been "cross-designated" as DEA agents. But the investigation was cut short when Burlington Police arrested Muhammad after receiving a 911 call that he had badly beaten his girlfriend.

The arrest happened before the DEA had enough "recorded buys" to prove Muhammad had sold enough cocaine to meet a federal "threshold" that would have qualified his case for federal prosecution.

I decided to take over the case and try it before a state court jury because I thought Muhammad was a threat to the community. Muhammad had come to Burlington from New York City in 2003. In less than a year, he had established a thriving cocaine distribution network.

His three-day trial for the sale of more than 2.5 grams of cocaine, a felony, was the first and only drug case I had ever tried before a jury. The trial ended with the jury convicting Muhammad on July 2, 2005.

The case was based on the testimony of a confidential informant (CI). The CI had worn a hidden "wire," which enabled investigators nearby to hear and record the drug transaction between the CI and Muhammad.

The only glitch was that I could not play the recording of the cocaine sale before the jury. The sale had taken place in Muhammad's

Burlington apartment. At the time of the sale, the case had been a federal DEA case. Under federal law, no search warrant was required to record the transaction, even though the sale had taken place in the "target" Muhammad's home.

That was not the law in Vermont. The Vermont Supreme Court had held more than 10 years earlier that a search warrant was *required* when police recorded a transaction in a target's home.[313] Since there was no search warrant, the recording was not admissible in my trial in Vermont criminal court. But the judge did permit me to let the CI listen to the recording to "refresh her recollection" the day before she testified at trial.

I had tried Muhammad before another jury three months earlier. Muhammad was charged with aggravated domestic assault (a 15-year maximum) by "attempting to cause serious bodily injury"[314] to his girlfriend by beating her repeatedly.

Muhammad's court-appointed lawyer, Harley Brown, did a good job with the evidence. As I recall, he argued successfully that there was at least a reasonable doubt that Muhammad had unintentionally caused his girlfriend's injuries while trying to restrain her. In any event, the jury found Muhammad guilty only of misdemeanor domestic assault, which carried a one-year maximum.

Judge Michael Kupersmith had sentenced Muhammad to serve 11 and half months to 12 months in prison on that conviction.

Judge Kupersmith was also the judge in the sale of cocaine trial. He sentenced Muhammad to serve six to 10 years on that conviction. He ruled that Muhammad would serve the six to 10 years to be *consecutive* to the 11 and a half to 12 months on the domestic assault.

The Vermont Supreme Court affirmed Muhammad's conviction in March 2007. The Court rejected the defense claim that permitting the CI to listen to the recording of her cocaine purchase from Muhammad prior to her testimony had violated Muhammad's rights.[315]

A "Habitual Offender"

I tried the Stanley "Yuppie" Mayo "habitual offender" case in early October 2005, roughly three weeks before Rosemary Gretkowski and I tried the Robert Jones murder case.

I charged Mayo as a habitual offender after he viciously punched and kicked Billy G., a much smaller man, while Billy lay helpless on the ground in the fetal position. Billy sustained serious head injuries as a result of the beating.

Vermont's Habitual Offender (HO) statute says that a person who is convicted of a felony and has already been convicted of three other felonies may be sentenced to life in prison. In my experience, it was rarely used by Vermont prosecutors. Mayo's trial was only the second case I tried under the HO statute. The first was *State v. Joseph*, an aggravated domestic assault case (mentioned earlier) that I tried in 2002.[316]

At the time of the trial, Mayo was 42 years old. He had spent 20 of the last 25 years in prison. He had five felony convictions, including a federal conviction for conspiracy to distribute cocaine in the Chittenden County area.

At that time (1989), investigators from the Vermont Drug Task Force had identified Mayo as the ringleader of what they called, "the largest cocaine distribution ring in Vermont history." "At least 17 people were arrested" when the network was finally rolled up.

While Mayo was awaiting sentencing in the cocaine distribution case, he was charged with two counts of "simple assault for allegedly breaking the jaws" of two other inmates in separate fights at the Vermont Correctional Facility in St. Albans.[317]

Mayo was released from federal prison on February 25, 2000, after serving 10 years of his 12-year sentence on the cocaine conviction. He was back in federal prison within three months for a parole violation.

The parole violation that sent Mayo back to federal prison for another 15 months stemmed from the report of a witness who told Burlington Police that he had seen a woman, who had been a passenger in what turned out to be Mayo's truck, fall into the roadway. The woman, who had several "open wounds" according to Burlington Police, did not cooperate in the investigation. Mayo told police that the woman had been driving his truck because he had been drinking all day. His federal parole officer evidently did not buy Mayo's claim that the woman had fallen out of the moving truck because "the door accidentally opened."

On September 3, 2002, Mayo was back in jail—this time on a state charge. I charged him with aggravated domestic assault for repeatedly punching and kicking his girlfriend while she lay helpless on the ground. His girlfriend suffered a broken nose, a ruptured spleen, and a fractured orbital bone (the base of the eye socket).

Aggravated domestic assault carries a maximum of 15 years in prison. My best recollection is that I offered to recommend a 10-to-15-year sentence if Mayo pled guilty to the charge.

It was at that point that I lost control of the case.

Judge Ben Joseph, who I knew and respected, told Mayo's attorney, Mark Kaplan, that he would sentence Mayo to a sentence of 18 months to 7 years "split" to serve 18 months in prison if Mayo would plead "guilty" to the aggravated domestic assault and obstruction of justice. Pleading "guilty" to the obstruction of justice charge meant that Mayo had to admit that he had told the victim, NS, that he would kill her if she told police that he had assaulted her.

The practical effect of the plea deal Judge Joseph offered would be that Mayo would serve no more than 18 months in prison. After that he would be on probation.

Mayo took Judge Joseph's deal and pled guilty to the aggravated assault on NS. He also pled guilty to obstruction of justice for threatening to kill her if she called the police. He was released from prison in February 2004.

I do not know why Judge Joseph decided to settle the case himself and cut me, the prosecutor, out of it completely. It was the only time I can remember a judge doing something like that.

Whatever the reason, I think it was a bad decision. Mayo was not entitled to a break. He had shown he had no respect for the law and no interest in following it. NS's case was a good example of Mayo's disdain for the law. When he was arrested for beating and kicking her, he told the Colchester detective who arrested him: "I can get four people who will say the bitch fell."

He was true to his word. He produced four witnesses. I deposed all of them. They all gave a variation on the same theme. Each said they were present when NS became angry at Mayo and grabbed a gold chain he had on his neck. The chain broke, and NS fell and hit her face on a nearby cinder block. The fall, as described by the witnesses, might account for the broken nose—but not the ruptured spleen.

In any event, Mayo left these witnesses behind—witnesses who had lied to protect him—when he took Judge Joseph's deal. Mayo admitted that he had seriously injured NS when he punched and kicked her while she was lying on the ground. (No mention of a gold chain or a cinder block.)[318]

In December 2004, roughly 10 months after he was released from prison for beating and kicking NS, I charged Mayo as a habitual offender for beating and kicking Billy G. while Billy lay helpless in the parking lot of a Colchester bar.

Charging someone as a habitual offender is a two-step process.

In Mayo's case, for example, I charged Mayo first with aggravated assault—a 15-year felony—for "recklessly causing serious bodily injury" to Billy. Then I upped the charge to habitual offender by citing three other felonies that Mayo had been convicted of.

The actual trial of a habitual offender is also a two-step process.

Mayo would be tried first for aggravated assault. If the jury found we had proved the aggravated assault case beyond a reasonable doubt and convicted Mayo, they would then be asked to decide whether he had been convicted of three earlier felonies. This, of course, was a formality.

If the jury found Mayo guilty of aggravated assault, I would introduce certified copies of Mayo's convictions for aggravated assault (NS), obstruction of justice (NS), and one of the burglaries he had committed in Chittenden County. The jury might be asked to go through the formality of voting on whether Mayo had been convicted of these offenses, or more likely, Mayo's lawyer would "stipulate," or admit that Mayo had been convicted of these offenses. The judge would then certify that Mayo had been convicted as a habitual offender and was liable for a potential maximum penalty of life in prison.

Not long after 2 a.m. on Friday evening, November 19, 2004, Billy and his friend, GP, were preparing to leave the Edgewater Pub, which was located near the shore of Mallets Bay on Lake Champlain in Colchester. Billy had identified as a female named "Julie" as an adolescent. He was now a 36-year-old man with a slight build. As Billy looked out at the parking lot in front of the pub, he saw AV, a man he had known when they were both school age.

AV, who was 35, had visited Billy's family on a regular basis more than twenty years earlier. Billy's family had been kind to AV, sometimes even sharing meals with the teenager. AV had gone on to become a skilled welder. But he was also an alcoholic who had multiple drunk driving convictions. AV was on probation with a condition that barred him from drinking on the night Billy was attacked.[319]

When he saw AV in the parking lot, Billy offered him a ride.

There were three cars side-by-side, facing up against the curb in the parking lot in front of the Edgewater Pub. GP, Billy's friend, was still in the bar, but he would be driving AV and Billy in Car 1, which was his car. A young married couple who were also Billy's friends were already in Car 2. Mayo and several friends were standing along the curb not far from Car 3.

GP got in the driver's side and prepared to drive away in Car 1. AV was already in the rear passenger seat. Billy, who was feeling good about the evening, broke into what he called a "happy dance"—a hop and a skip with arms outstretched—on the sidewalk in front of Car 1 before getting into the right front passenger seat.

The "happy dance" triggered something in Mayo's group. I later told jurors it was like "throwing chum in the water" for Mayo and his entourage.

Robert Roche, a tall, dark-haired man who was drunk, moved from Mayo's group and leaned into the driver's side window of Car 1 and began challenging GP and making homophobic slurs. AV urged GP to drive away, but GP rolled down the window in order to speak to Roche. Roche responded by punching GP repeatedly in the face through the open window.

Billy had gotten out of Car 1 when he saw GP being attacked. He had intended to go back into the bar to call for help. But as Billy got to the sidewalk in front of Cars 1 and 2, someone hit him from behind,[320] and another man, who was later identified as Mayo, punched him in the face.

Billy collapsed to the ground and Mayo began to beat him savagely. Mayo started by kicking Billy repeatedly in the left side of his face. Then he straddled Billy and punched him repeatedly in the face. Billy was helpless. He got into the fetal position and tried to protect his head with his arms for two to three minutes. He said later that he had thought he was going to die.

He might have if it hadn't been for AV.

Roche continued to beat GP after GP got out of the car to defend himself. AV got out of the car on the right rear passenger side to come to GP's aid. He went around the rear of the car, and he and another man subdued Roche. This was all happening on the sidewalk in front of Car 1.

After AV helped subdue Roche, he looked to his right and saw Billy being attacked on the sidewalk in front of Car 2 by two men. AV recognized one of the men who was attacking Billy. He was a man AV had known for years—"Yuppie" Mayo. He saw Mayo kicking Billy in the face. AV immediately went to help Billy. As AV approached him, Mayo backed off. But by that time, Billy had lost consciousness and had already been seriously injured.

(Dr. Peter Gunther later testified that the beating had caused Billy to suffer a broken nose, broken left eye socket, the loss of two teeth, and loss of hearing in his left ear. According to Dr. Gunther, the beating had also caused brain damage.[321])

For his part, GP kept a close eye on Roche after AV and others had pulled Roche off of him. As AV was moving to help Billy, GP watched Roche stumble away from the melee and back toward the entrance to the Edgewater Pub. Roche was 10 to 15 yards away from the spot where Billy was being beaten, and he was headed in the opposite direction.

I called seven witnesses over the course of what turned out to be a two-and-a-half-day trial—October 4–6, 2005. I called GP, Billy, and AV, as well as two police investigators and two medical experts who had treated the men.

Although I was certain that Mayo had been one of the two men who had beaten Billy, I was concerned at first that the jury might have trouble with the case.

"Yuppie" Mayo had a reputation for intimidating witnesses and anyone else who might cross him. He was about five foot 10 with a stocky, muscular build and a pugnacious attitude. Billy was shorter than Mayo, who outweighed him by 30 to 40 pounds, but, unlike many others, Billy gave no indication at any time during the trial and the events that led up to it that he was intimidated by Mayo.

Billy came across as an open, honest, and angry victim—but there were portions of his testimony that the defense could exploit.

One was that Billy had not identified Mayo right away as one of his attackers. AV had told him that Mayo was one of the men who'd assaulted him. Three weeks later, when Billy was shown a "photo lineup"—a series of eight photos of men fitting the general description of the man who'd straddled him while beating him—Billy picked two photos. One of them was Mayo, but Billy said he wasn't "100 percent" sure.

In addition to questions about his identification of Mayo, there was an additional potential problem with Billy's testimony: He had a condition that I learned was called Dissociative Identity Disorder (DID), also known as "Multiple Personality Disorder," which is a result of trauma an individual has suffered in childhood.

I called Dr. David Boedy, the therapist who had been treating Billy for two years, to testify at Mayo's trial. Dr. Boedy confirmed that Billy did indeed have multiple "personalities" or "identities," and they came out at different times. In addition to Billy, the social worker mentioned other identities that might come out in speaking with Billy: "Damian," "Steven," and "Julie."

Mayo's attorney, Mark Kaplan, had taken Billy's deposition and questioned him about his DID. Kaplan argued that Billy had told him that the different identities "remember things differently or view things differently or understand things differently." Dr. Boedy said that this had not happened in his experience with Billy, and he had been treating him since 2003.

I do recall that Billy did indicate at trial that another one of his identities—"Damian"—was somehow involved in his trial testimony. I recall asking for a "bench conference" between Attorney Kaplan, Judge Michael Kupersmith, and me. Out of an abundance of caution, I suggested that "Damian" should be sworn in as a witness just as "Billy" had been.

Judge Kupersmith rejected my suggestion after Kaplan objected that I was just trying to get "sympathy" for Billy.

While Billy had said at one point that he was not "100 percent sure" that Mayo was one of the one men who had assaulted him, AV had always been 100 percent sure. AV was over six feet tall and powerfully built. He had known "Yuppie" Mayo most of his life, and he was certain that Mayo was one of the men who had beaten Billy. AV had seen Mayo beating and kicking Billy when he had gotten out of the car to help, and he had gone to confront Mayo, who had backed off when AV had approached him.

But AV had his own "baggage." At the time of Billy's beating in December 2004, he had already been convicted of giving false information to a police officer for giving a fake name when he was arrested for one of his DUIs.

AV had not hesitated to come to the defense of GP and Billy. But, at first, he was reluctant to come forward as a witness in the Mayo case. He was on probation for multiple drunk driving cases.

The night of the assault on Billy, AV had "clocked out" at just after midnight at Hazelett Strip-Casting on Lakeshore Drive in Colchester, where he worked, and had gone to the nearby Edgewater Pub for what the bartender later testified was "one or two drinks." This was a violation of the terms of his probation. It would probably have been in AV's best interest not to draw attention to the fact that he had been at the Edgewater Pub that evening.

AV relented, though, after Billy asked him to come forward and tell police what he had told him. AV was certain that Mayo was the man who he had seen kicking and punching Billy.

It was "the right thing to do." It was a decent, selfless act—an act that turned out to be crucial in the conviction of "Yuppie" Mayo. It was also an act that brought AV little but trouble. AV was sent to prison on a probation violation after he came forward to tell what had happened in the parking lot of the Edgewater Pub around 2 a.m. on November 20, 2005.

AV had asked police to put in a good word for him at the Probation Department for stepping up to protect Billy and GP. They had. But it did not have any impact.

I can still remember AV lifting up his feet during the trial and putting them on top of the "witness box" to show the jury his ankle restraints. Mark Kaplan, Mayo's attorney, had suggested that AV received a benefit in the State's handling of his own probation violation case in exchange for his testimony against Mayo.

This gave me the opening on my redirect questioning to ask AV about how he had benefited from his testimony. His answer was that he hadn't. The fact was that sheriff's deputies had brought AV to the trial from prison to testify, and they were going to bring him back to prison after he was finished testifying. He showed jurors the ankle restraints he was required to wear when he was traveling in the deputies' custody to make it clear he had received no favors for telling the truth about what happened.

No doubt AV was a key witness for the prosecution. But, I believe, oddly enough, that the testimony of the two defense witnesses that Mayo called to give "his side of the story" also turned out to be most helpful in making our case.

When he was first interviewed after the assault, Mayo had said that he *had not been at the Edgewater Pub* the night Billy was attacked. Anyone who claimed he was there was either lying or mistaken. But once Mayo was charged and multiple witnesses had put him at the pub, Mayo gave notice through his attorney that he was going to call two witnesses who, the defense claimed, would tell jurors that Mayo *was at the scene of Billy's beating.*

The two witnesses, Tanya, Mayo's girlfriend at the time, and Renee, the wife of one of Mayo's friends, would testify that Mayo was there while Billy was being beaten and kicked into unconsciousness. But, according to the two women, Mayo *was not beating Billy,* he was *protecting Billy* from Robert Roche!

Renee and Tanya testified that it was Robert Roche, not Mayo, who was belligerent and drunk, who went after GP and then went after Billy.

According to these women, Roche was the one who was hitting and kicking Billy ("the smallest guy of all"). Renee said that at one point, Roche was on top of Billy. She testified that it was around the time that Mayo got out of the car and went over to his friend, Roche, and said, "This isn't cool, [Billy] has done nothing wrong to you." She said that Mayo's only role in the situation was to go over and try to get Roche off "the little guy."

Tanya's version of events was slightly different, but she, too, said that Mayo's sole role was as a peacemaker.

There was no question that Billy was the victim of an aggravated assault. Someone had beaten and kicked him into temporary unconsciousness. Someone had broken his nose and left eye socket. The sole issue for the jury was whether the prosecution (me) had produced evidence that proved beyond a reasonable doubt that Mayo was the one who had kicked and beaten Billy.

Defense attorney, Mark Kaplan, had done a pretty good job of undermining Billy's identification of Mayo as the man who had kicked and beaten him. But that was before these two women testified. They put Mayo there at the scene with Billy while Billy was being beaten.

The defense no longer said that Billy had been mistaken when he'd identified Mayo because Mayo wasn't anywhere near Billy at the time he was being beaten. No, there was no question Mayo was there. Now, absurd as it sounds, the issue for the jury was whether Billy had been wrong when he'd thought Mayo was kicking and beating him when, in fact, according to the defense, Mayo had been protecting Billy by pulling Robert Roche off of him.

My argument to the jury was: "To believe the defense, you have to believe that Billy mistook being kicked and beaten for being protected and saved."

The jury deliberated for only 90 minutes before sending a message to Judge Michael Kupersmith that they had reached a verdict. The verdict had come in relatively quickly, and I wasn't sure what to expect. But the verdict was "guilty."

Billy told reporters that he was happy with the verdict and the "upgrade" to habitual offender. "That's the justice I am seeking. Praise to God. Now maybe he can't hurt anyone else anymore."

Mayo's attorney Kaplan was critical of the jury—particularly the fact that the jurors had only deliberated for 90 minutes before finding his client guilty: "I question how the jury could have carefully considered the facts in this case in such a short time."

Kaplan had "stipulated" that Mayo had been convicted of three earlier felonies. This meant Mayo could be convicted as a habitual offender, and Judge Kupersmith confirmed and certified the conviction.

Mayo was sentenced in July 2006, some nine months after the jury had convicted him. I asked the judge to sentence Mayo to 25 years to life. I cited his long criminal record and put particular emphasis on the viciousness of his crimes in the five years since he was released from federal prison. I argued the sentence was necessary "to protect the community."

Although Mayo did not testify at his trial, he had plenty to say at his sentencing. He spoke for 15 minutes and continued to proclaim his innocence and insist that he had been there to help Billy—who, according to Mayo's trial witnesses, had actually been assaulted by Robert Roche.

The fact was that Robert Roche was nowhere near Billy at the time he was being beaten. GP, the man who *had been attacked by Roche*, had watched Roche walk toward the entrance of the Edgewater Pub after AV and others had pulled Roche off of him.

For his part, Roche had told me in a deposition prior to the trial that he was very drunk the night Billy was beaten, and he remembered little of what happened. But, importantly, his friend "Stan" Mayo had told him that he, Mayo, had intervened to *protect Roche* who, according to Mayo, was being beaten by several people.[322]

But that isn't what Mayo told Judge Michael Kupersmith at his sentencing. He insisted he had intervened to help Billy: "For once in my life, I thought I was doing the right thing. I just don't feel I deserve to go to jail for a very long time for something I didn't do."

Judge Kupersmith was not moved. "It's only fate or luck you didn't kill [Billy]. I don't think we as a community have to wait until you kill somebody to put you away in a place where you can't hurt somebody."

He then sentenced Mayo to serve the 25 years to life that I had requested. At that point, Mayo "snapped," as the *Burlington Free Press* put it. As he was being dragged from the courtroom, he shouted obscenities at Billy, who had asked that he be sentenced to life in prison without parole.[323]

Robert Jones's Trial

During Robert Jones's trial for the murder of Sarah, I worked closely with Rosemary Gretkowski, who was experienced in handling domestic assaults. I did the opening, and she did the closing and rebuttal closing. I would cross-examine Jones in the event he gave up his Fifth Amendment right and took the stand to defend himself. We split the direct examination in half. We would each be responsible for presenting the testimony of 10 of our witnesses to the jury.

We had a strong, largely circumstantial evidence case. I recall that Burlington Police Sgt. Shawn Toof had done an exceptionally good job in putting our case together—e.g., identifying, finding, and scheduling the 20 witnesses and their statements that Rosemary Gretkowski and I needed to prove the case.

Jones was represented by Kate Moore, an experienced defense attorney, who had been retained by the State on Jones's behalf.

We picked the jury in one day—Monday, October 24, 2005—with Judge Michael Kupersmith presiding. I don't remember any problems or anything unusual.

The next day, Tuesday, October 25, 2005, was the first full day of trial. I gave the prosecution's opening statement.

I told jurors that first we would call witnesses who would give a brief description of the events leading up to the murder. Then we would begin proving three basic facts that we were confident would convince jurors of Jones's guilt beyond a reasonable doubt: (1) Jones was the only adult present in the apartment when Sarah received the beating that killed her; (2) Jones had abused Sarah repeatedly and cruelly throughout their eleven-year relationship; and (3) Jones had given several explanations for Sarah's injuries, which the Vermont Supreme Court later described as "palpably false accounts"[324] in attempting to explain why something or someone other than Jones himself was responsible for the injuries that killed Sarah.

Jones had another longtime girlfriend besides Sarah—MB. She told investigators that she and Jones did not hide their relationship from Sarah. Their relationship lasted for a year and half in the late 1990s. They had been broken up for several years, but MB and Jones had gotten back together again in January 2003.

In May 2003, MB lived in Bristol, Vermont, a little under an hour's drive south of Burlington.

MB and Kellie, a friend of Sarah from their school days, testified on the first day of what turned out to be a five-day trial. They told jurors their recollections of what had happened during the hours leading up to the savage beating that ended up killing Sarah.

Jones had spent Saturday night, May 3, 2003, at MB's home in Bristol. When he left for Burlington on Sunday morning, May 4, Jones told her that he would be back later that evening. But that did not happen.[325]

Sarah's longtime friend, Kellie, told jurors that around 8 p.m. on Sunday evening, she and Sarah left the apartment that Sarah and Jones shared. They were just going to get more beer at a nearby store in Burlington's Old North End.

This left Jones alone with their 2-year-old daughter. It meant that Jones would be unable to get away to see MB in Bristol until Sarah returned.

According to Kellie's testimony, on the way back from getting the beer, she and Sarah decided to stop at the Old Northender—a bar that was nearby on North Street in Burlington. While there, the two women drank shots of "Dr. McGillicuddy's Liqueur." By the time they left, Sarah was intoxicated.

Kellie testified that when they returned to the apartment from the Old Northender, it was around 10 p.m. The two-hour delay caused by the beer run and the trip to the bar angered Jones. He immediately began arguing with Sarah about her detour to the bar. He pushed her in the chest with both hands, knocking her to the floor. Kellie helped Sarah to her feet but left soon afterward at approximately 10:30 p.m.

Kellie testified further that at the time she left the couple's apartment, Sarah was intoxicated but had not been in any fights—other than being pushed by Jones—and showed no visible signs of injury.

MB picked up what happened after that. Her testimony was based on what Jones had told her over the phone on the evening of May 4 and the morning of May 5.

MB told jurors that Jones had called her in Bristol around 11 p.m. on Sunday night and said he wouldn't be there that night. According to MB, Jones told her that Sarah had come home drunk and had been in a fight. Jones said that Sarah, who he said was very drunk, had passed out and fallen onto the bathroom floor. Jones told MB that at that point, he had put Sarah to bed.

MB went on to testify that around 1 p.m. the next day, Jones called her and asked her to come to Burlington and help him because he "could not wake Sarah." She said she got to the home at 82 Front Street in Burlington around 2 p.m.[326]

I questioned MB during the afternoon of the first day of trial. Her direct testimony went pretty well until we got to the point where she got to the Jones-Sarah residence on Front Street on Monday afternoon.

We had transcripts of prior interviews of MB, including one that Rosemary Gretkowski and I had conducted. MB's testimony tended to track what she had said in the interviews until I asked her about the conversation she and Jones had after she had viewed Sarah's bruised and comatose body for the first time.

At that point, my questioning of MB became what the *Burlington Free Press* described as "strained and testy."[327]

My problem was that during interviews with witnesses, she had said that as soon as she saw Sarah, she told Jones that they (MB and Jones) had to take Sarah to the hospital right away. She had gone on to tell us that she had told Jones that he should "stay away from [Sarah] so you don't kill her." MB had also told us that Jones hadn't wanted to take Sarah to the hospital for treatment because there were likely to be questions about how she had gotten the bruises on her body.

But when I asked her about this at trial, MB had a failure of memory. She said she couldn't remember the conversation she had with Jones when she first got to the apartment at 82 Front Street.

I asked Judge Kupersmith for a brief recess, gave MB a copy of one of the prior sworn statements, and asked her to review the passages where she talked about what she had said to Jones when she had seen the condition Sarah was in for the first time. The courtroom was virtually empty.

Judge Kupersmith called the jury back as soon as MB had reviewed the documents. I got permission to treat her as a "hostile witness." This meant that even though I had called her as a prosecution witness, I could cross-examine her about her conversation with Jones when she'd first seen Sarah's condition.

One of my first questions was: "Isn't it true you told the defendant to stay away from [Sarah] because if he didn't he was likely to kill her?" MB admitted that she said that after seeing Sarah bruised and comatose. "Isn't it also true that the defendant did not want to take [Sarah] to the hospital at first because he was concerned there would be questions about how she had received her injuries?" She admitted that was true. "You had to talk him into it, didn't you?" She admitted that, too, was true.[328]

MB testified that she had ultimately convinced Jones to take Sarah to nearby Fletcher Allen Health Care. They'd arrived at the hospital with Sarah's comatose body at around 2:45 p.m. on Monday, May 5, 2003.[329]

The testimony of Burlington Police Sergeant Shawn Toof was the key to proving Robert Jones was the only person who could have given Sarah the beating that had killed her. His testimony came early on the first day of the trial. Rosemary Gretkowski handled his direct testimony before the jury.

As I mentioned earlier, Sergeant Toof was the lead investigator in this case. His work was crucial. He took a recorded statement from Jones while he was at the hospital pretending to be concerned and puzzled by Sarah's condition. Jones told Toof that he had been the only one in the apartment with Sarah—aside from their 2-year-old daughter—from the time Sarah returned from drinking at the Old Northender bar with her friend to the next morning when, according to Jones, he discovered Sarah was non-responsive and making "gurgling sounds."

In fact, Sergeant Toof's testimony made the point that Jones was the only adult with Sarah in the nearly 16-hour period between 10:30 p.m. on Sunday—when, according to Kellie, Sarah had no injuries—and 2 p.m. on Monday, when MB convinced Jones to take the bruised and comatose Sarah to the hospital.

When he got Sarah to the hospital, Jones spoke first to an emergency department nurse, then to the doctor who was in charge of the ED, and finally to a neurosurgeon who had also seen Sarah in the ED.

We called all three at trial.

The ED nurse testified that Jones had told her that Sarah had "gone to Montreal" the night before (Sunday night). She had gotten into an "altercation" there and returned home late. When he'd tried to wake her Monday morning, he couldn't.[330]

The medical director of the ED told jurors that when she'd seen Sarah, she was in a "comatose state" and had bruises on her chest wall, lower neck, face, and arms. She testified that Jones had told her that Sarah had been out with a friend in Burlington the night before and that "she may have been in a fight or overdosed on Klonopin"—an anti-seizure drug that was being abused by some in Burlington at the time.[331]

The neurosurgeon, who was called in to assist in the ED when Jones and MB brought her to the Medical Center, testified that Sarah had "bruising of various ages on her head, chest, arms, and legs." He told jurors that Jones's story was that after she'd come home with her friend (Kellie), Sarah had passed out in the bathroom and fallen to the floor. Jones had said he'd picked her up and put her in bed. Jones had insisted that Sarah's condition was caused by drugs and alcohol and not "trauma."[332]

Expert testimony from Vermont's chief medical examiner and a consulting neurologist later showed that all three of the explanations that Jones had given people in the ED for Sarah's death were false.

Dr. Steven Shapiro, Vermont's chief medical examiner, was the next-to-last prosecution witness. He had conducted his autopsy of Sarah's body on May 9, 2003, the day after she died.

Dr. Shapiro told jurors that Sarah had suffered a savage beating. She had injuries to the back of her head, her face, her chest (a "4x11 inch bruise"), her arms, and her legs—a total of 16 separate injuries.

In his opinion, Sarah's injuries simply could not have been caused by a single fall. In fact, it would have taken five separate falls, given the location of the injuries on different "planes" of her body. For instance, while a single fall might have caused the "2x4 inch purple bruise" on the back of head, the same fall could not have caused the injury to her right temple or the injury to her lower jaw. And *no fall* could have caused the injuries to her chest, which had resulted in 12 broken ribs.[333]

In Dr. Shapiro's opinion, Sarah's death was caused by a "beating"—more specifically, "blunt impact injuries to her head." There were four such injuries. The "manner" of her death, in his opinion, was "homicide," not an accidental fall in the bathroom—the explanation the defense settled on at trial. There was no drug overdose as tests showed no Klonopin, no cocaine, nor any other dangerous drug in her system. Simply put, Sarah was beaten to death.

Dr. William Pendlebury, a consulting neurologist assisting Dr. Shapiro, had examined Sarah's brain following the autopsy. He explained to jurors that the blunt force blows to Sarah's head had caused her brain to swell. The swelling compressed her brain stem and "led to disrupted cardiac and respiratory function, resulting in death."[334]

The defense had tried to make the case throughout the trial that Sarah's death was an "accident."

The truth was that Sarah had died as a result of five blows to the head. But could we prove Jones did it? We had Sergeant Toof's testimony that Jones had admitted he was the only adult with Sarah from 10:30 Sunday night to when she arrived at the hospital comatose and badly beaten. Simply put, no one else could have done it.

But jurors were likely to ask: "Why would he do it?" After all, he and Sarah had been together for 11 years, and Sarah was the mother of his two young children. As far as what the jurors were concerned, there was no reasonable explanation for Jones to savagely beat her to death as the prosecution claimed. This might be enough to create a "reasonable doubt" in jurors' minds.

At the time of his trial for murdering Sarah, Jones already had 11 felony convictions and three convictions for domestic assault, including two for assaulting Sarah. But the jury knew nothing of these "prior bad acts."[335]

Fortunately, we could introduce evidence that dispelled any notion that Jones was a peaceful loving partner who was not capable of beating the mother of his children to death. We could call witnesses who could describe for jurors how Jones had repeatedly beaten Sarah, the mother of his children, throughout their time together.

As mentioned in the discussion of the *Sharrow* trial, in most cases, evidence of a defendant's "prior bad acts" (prior crimes, or "wrongful acts") is not admissible under Evidence Rule 404 to prove a defendant committed a crime that occurred at a later time [336]

The rationale is that the prosecution has to prove the crime that is charged against the defendant beyond a reasonable doubt based on the facts and circumstances of the specific crime they are charged with.

Beyond that, there's a concern that if jurors hear evidence that the defendant committed earlier unrelated "bad acts" in other places against other victims, it will give the prosecution an unfair advantage by easing its burden of proof. That is, jurors will see that evidence as showing that the defendant is a "bad actor" who has a "propensity" to commit crimes (e.g., "If he did that one, he probably did this one, too.").

This case, as in Sharrow, we were able to rely on an exception to the rule that would normally bar admission of evidence of a defendant's "prior bad acts."

In cases where the defendant claims the injuries the victim sustained were the result of an *accident* and not an intentional assault, the prosecution is entitled to introduce evidence of incidents when the defendant did, in fact, intentionally assault the same victim in the past. The theory is that these prior incidents of intentional assault against the *same victim* tend to make it less likely that the injuries the defendant is on trial for are an accident.

On September 8, 2005, a month and a half before the trial, Judge Kupersmith held a day-long hearing on whether we could call witnesses at trial to introduce evidence of 11 incidents of prior assaults by Jones against Sarah. Our "motion in limine" (at the "threshold") had been filed months before the scheduled trial date in order to give the defense an opportunity to object to the "404(b) evidence" we intended to introduce at trial.

It was to everyone's benefit to have the issue decided before trial to avoid delay and enable the prosecution and defense to plan and organize their cases.

As expected, the defense objected to admissibility on the grounds that (1) they had not raised accident as a defense and (2) any tendency this evidence had to show the "pattern of abuse" by Jones against Sarah was "substantially outweighed by the prejudicial impact" the evidence of prior abuse would have against the defendant in the eyes of the jury.[337]

We had proposed calling 10 witnesses. Judge Kupersmith ruled that we could call five witnesses at trial who could describe seven incidents.

We called Robert Haynes to testify. He was the Burlington police officer who, as noted earlier, had responded to a hysterical Sarah's 911 call from her Decatur Street home in January 1994. He told jurors that when he'd arrived, he'd found Sarah crying and shaking with a "golf-ball-sized lump" over her left eye. The officer testified that Sarah had told him that Jones had punched her twice in the face with a closed fist and "kneed" her twice in the face as well.

Sarah's sister-in-law told jurors about an incident in 1994 when Sarah had called her after she had been beaten by Jones. Sarah was crying, and the side of her face was bruised from her "eyebrow to her chin."[338]

Sarah's brother, Rob, testified that after he had seen her bruises, he had confronted Jones when he'd seen him in a parking lot in Winooski. "My intention was to blacken his eye the way he'd blackened my sister's eyes." But according to Rob, Jones began crying and apologizing. Rob told jurors that he had given up his plan to give Jones a beating. "With him bawling, I couldn't do it."[339]

DA, the woman who Sarah had protected when her boyfriend was attacking her with a broken beer bottle, told jurors that Sarah had often come over to her apartment while she and Sarah were neighbors on Marble Avenue in Burlington. She had testified at the deposition that she had seen Sarah with a black eye on three occasions during these visits. DA said that she had heard "banging and screaming" from the Jones-Sarah apartment three or four times per week. DA testified that she thought Sarah saw DA's home as a "safe haven."

DA told jurors of one incident in which she'd seen Jones push Sarah out the door of their apartment. Sarah had a black eye and blood coming from her eye. She had been "hysterical." But she did not want DA to call the police. Sarah had said, "That would just make it worse."[340]

Sheryl, a longtime friend of Sarah, told jurors about three incidents during the period from 1995 to 1997 in which Jones had brutalized Sarah.

There was an incident in 1995 when Jones had become angry with Sarah for wanting to go out with friends. Sheryl told jurors that Jones had responded by grabbing Sarah by the hair and dragging her away from the door and toward the bedroom.

There was another incident where Jones had dragged the mother of his children by the hair neanderthal style. This one occurred during the summer of 1996. Jones and Sarah were with friends, including Sheryl, at North Beach on Lake Champlain in Burlington. Jones had decided he wanted to leave. When Sarah had said she wanted to stay, Jones had again grabbed her by the hair. This time he'd dragged her by her hair across the beach toward his car.

Finally, Sheryl told jurors that she'd hosted a barbecue at her home on Memorial Day, 1997. Sarah had attended the barbecue; Jones was not invited. Jones and his brother Chris had come anyway. Sheryl said that when Sarah saw Jones drive in, she became frightened and ran upstairs. Jones had followed her upstairs, found Sarah in the bathroom, and grabbed her by the throat. Sheryl testified that she had seen the "indents" of Jones's fingers on Sarah's throat.

Jones and his brother had refused to leave Sheryl's home until Sarah left with them. She eventually did.[341]

Closing arguments were held on Saturday, October 29, 2005—the fifth day of the trial. It had taken us three days to put in our evidence. The defense took less than a full day. Jones exercised his Fifth Amendment right not to testify.

Rosemary Gretkowski did the prosecution closing: "This was not a tragic accident. The defense wants you to believe this is a tragic accident. But the evidence will not let you believe that."

She told jurors that Jones had become enraged when Sarah and her friend Kellie had stopped at the bar and left him with their 2-year-old daughter because this meant he could not go to Bristol to visit MB as he had planned. She went on to tell jurors that after Kellie left, Jones "started to assault Sarah and didn't stop."

Defense Attorney Kate Moore told jurors that Sarah had come home intoxicated and fallen. She said that medical evidence did not conclusively prove that Sarah had died as a result of blows to her head. She said the evidence on the cause of Sarah's injuries showed that some of her injuries, including her 12 broken ribs, could well have come after she'd arrived at the hospital.[342]

The jury began its deliberation at 1 p.m. It deliberated for only three and a half hours before announcing its verdict. Jurors found Robert Jones was "guilty" of both charges—second-degree murder and habitual offender. Each conviction carried a potential life sentence.

Roughly six months later, on May 3, 2006, Judge Michael Kupersmith sentenced Robert Jones to serve 50 years to life for being a habitual offender—the assault on Sarah and three other prior felonies. It was the sentence that Rosemary Gretkowski had argued for.

Jones maintained his innocence to the end: "What happened to Sarah that night was not my fault. She did fall in the bathroom. I did not beat her to death. . . . I loved that woman."

Judge Kupersmith had the final word. He told Jones that he was a dangerous man with a record for violent behavior spanning two decades. The judge told Jones: "I think the most important factor is to protect other people from you."

CLOSING

When I was elected in 2002, I decided that I would only serve one term as state's attorney. I left office in early August 2006 and took a job in the Civil Division of the Vermont Attorney General's Office where I worked less than a year before I retired from service for the State of Vermont at age 62.

I was proud of what the members of the Chittenden County State's Attorney's Office had accomplished over the roughly five years I had served as state's attorney.

Violent crime—murder, rape, robbery, and aggravated assault—had declined in Vermont[343] in the 1990s. By 2006, crime was on the rise in Vermont as a whole, but *it was still down* in Chittenden County.[344]

Although crime was down in Chittenden County, our office was still by far the busiest in the state. When I was interviewed for a newspaper article on my retirement, I bragged that our office was a "bargain for taxpayers" because we prosecuted 35 percent of all felonies in Vermont and 29 percent of all criminal cases in the State while being allotted only 17 percent of state funds allocated for state prosecutors.[345]

I went back to the State's Attorney's Office in 1994 because I wanted to get back to trying jury trials. I am glad I did.

What did I like about jury trials?

First, I enjoyed preparing a case for trial. That meant identifying the witnesses I would need to prove the case beyond a reasonable doubt. It also meant meeting with these witnesses and going over the questions I was going to ask them at trial. And it meant drafting and memorizing "opening" and "closing" arguments and writing questions that could be used in cross-examination of defense witnesses. I got particular satisfaction out of identifying pieces of evidence that I might have trouble getting in (e.g., "excited utterances," or "prior bad acts") and doing the research and planning I needed to take my best shot at getting this evidence admitted.

Second, I took pride in actually trying my case and convincing jurors who came from all parts of the community that I could prove my case. These were people who owned and operated all types of businesses; they were military retirees, lawyers, teachers, and even retired judges. They had left their daily lives to do their civic duty to serve as jurors. I knew they expected me to do my job and put on a clear, compelling case that overcame the presumption of innocence and proved the defendant's guilt beyond a reasonable doubt.

I knew from experience that they had no qualms about telling me when I had not done my job and I had failed to meet my "burden of proof." Of course I was disappointed with a "not guilty" verdict. But that didn't happen often, and I got a feeling of satisfaction when, as usually happened, jurors came back with a "guilty" verdict.

The feeling of satisfaction after a "guilty" verdict didn't happen much when I first started trying cases in the 1980s and was mainly handling DWIs and burglaries. Then it was: "Okay, you did your job. What's next?" But when I began trying mostly violent felonies (1994–2006) it's probably no surprise that I took particular satisfaction when juries held men accountable for beating people who were usually smaller and weaker than they were.

The third reason I liked doing jury trials was that I got to work with people I liked and respected.

I always met with the police officer(s) who had actually put the case together. These were remarkable people who often don't get the credit and respect they deserve. They were smart, dedicated, and willing to help. We would go through the investigation and identify key witnesses and key pieces of evidence. They would let me know what to expect from the "civilian" witnesses I was going to call. I always came away from meeting with these men and women with a much deeper understanding of the case and what I needed to do to make the most of the evidence.

When I was trying cases, I often came in contact with another group of remarkable people. They were people from the community who "stepped up" to help others who were victims, or about to become victims, of crimes.

You saw an example of this in the *Bevins, Bissonette* fraud trials. Neighbors stepped up to testify and tell what had happened to Clara Carlson, the 93-year-old woman who the con men cheated out of $1,800. These neighbors had been watching over Mrs. Carlson and her 87 year-old sister, "Nellie" Irish, hoping to protect them.

You saw it again in the *Sharrow* attempted murder case where neighbors kept close track of, and probably saved the life of, a downstairs neighbor who was being beaten by her ex-boyfriend. And again, when Sarah put herself in danger by stepping in to protect her neighbor, DA, who was in the process of being beaten to death by her boyfriend. "Billy"—the man with multiple personalities—was helpless and being kicked repeatedly in the head by "Yuppie" Mayo when AV came to Billy's aid and forced "Yuppie" to flee. Minh Nguyen's victims, Duyen and Dung, were staggering home after Minh hacked them up with a meat cleaver when a neighbor called 911—a call that probably saved their lives.

I saw examples of this—people selflessly stepping up to help someone who was in danger—over and over again, particularly when I tried domestic assault cases.

Why are jury trials important?

On the most basic level, jury trials are absolutely necessary to protect citizens from an oppressive government in the form of corrupt or overzealous prosecutors. Any person who feels they have been wrongfully charged with a crime has an absolute right under the US and Vermont Constitutions to require the prosecution to prove that person's guilt by convincing an "impartial jury"[346] of the defendant's guilt "beyond a reasonable doubt."

I can't imagine people in our country being content with a justice system that is completely controlled by lawyers and judges. Thankfully, in our system, jurors continue to be the ultimate "judges of the facts."

But juries are also important because they can help build public confidence in the criminal justice system. There is a level of distrust in the justice system in the community. Many feel they have no control over the system because it has become the exclusive domain of lawyers and judges who work in the "courthouse bubble," where they are isolated from the concerns and values of the community.

This book has given examples of cases where jurors have used the power the law has given them to ensure that those who have been caught up in the criminal justice system, victims and defendants alike, are treated fairly.

When they are speaking with friends and neighbors, former jurors can point to examples of when the system works and tell of the courage and skill of police (*Sharrow; Minh Nguyen*) in arresting suspects and conducting investigations that ultimately led to convictions. They can also describe for others the courage of child witnesses who come to court and tell their frightening stories to strangers (*Hamlin; Koveos*).

But these former jurors can also tell of times when the system faltered, and the law gave the jury the power to correct mistakes and right wrongs. Again, you've seen examples of this in the book. For instance, the murder case where the prosecution failed to prove the defendant was "guilty" (*Sorrell* trial). Or the murder case where jurors found the defendant guilty of manslaughter because they were convinced the evidence showed the defendant had caused the victim's death but were not convinced that the prosecution had proved the more serious charge—"murder" (*Norton* "quarry killing"). They can also point to the case where a judge had made a preliminary ruling that a defendant's statement was "voluntary," but jurors later found that the statement was "not voluntary" and refused to consider it when reaching their verdict (*Koveos* trial).

Former jurors can point to these examples as evidence that the criminal justice system has not lost touch with the community because jurors won't let that happen.

After I retired as a Vermont state employee in 2007, I began teaching full time as the director of the criminal justice program at Champlain College, a small, private college in Burlington. I had been teaching part time (nights) at Champlain as an adjunct instructor since 1990.

I developed and taught "traditional" courses and online courses in criminal law, criminal procedure, juvenile justice, and family violence. But the work I enjoyed most was developing courses in a relatively new field—the law of searching for and seizing "computer-generated evidence." This is the evidence that was crucial in the *Jackson* trial.

I got approval from the College Curriculum Committee to develop and teach a required course for students working toward a BS in criminal justice that focused on "digital evidence." The course focused not only on the importance of "digital evidence," but also on the laws that criminal investigators must know and follow in order to ensure that this important evidence was ultimately admitted at trial.

I retired from full-time work as program director in 2011. But before I retired, I developed and began teaching an online course called Legal Principles of Digital Investigations for what was to become Champlain's master's degree program in digital forensic science.

Teaching online was more work for me than "traditional" teaching in a classroom because I had to give regular, detailed written feedback to each student's online responses to weekly "discussion questions" that was based on assigned reading. In contrast, when I taught face to face, I simply answered student questions on the assigned reading as they came up in class or spoke individually with students who had questions when the class was over.

There was no textbook. Instead, I selected law review articles and other scholarly articles dealing with digital evidence as well as state and federal appellate court decisions dealing with computer-generated evidence for class members to study. When the European Union's computer data protection law—the General Data Protection Regulation (GDPR)—went into effect in 2018, I began to include scholarly articles and cases dealing with provisions of the GDPR as well.

The students in this class were exceptional. They were older than the students I had taught in undergraduate classes at Champlain. My guess is that most were in their 40s. They participated from all over the world. Most posted from states throughout the US, but some posted responses from where they were stationed in the military in Western Europe and the Middle East. I even had a student who participated from Hong Kong and another who participated from Singapore.

The last Legal Principles of Digital Investigations class I taught was in the summer of 2022. The range of experience of the twelve members of that class was typical of that of many of the earlier classes in the course that I had taught. For instance, one class member worked in cybersecurity for a "defense contractor"; one had been in computer forensics for just one year and before that had served in the Navy as a sonar-technician on a submarine; one was an FBI agent who had been an Air Force intelligence officer; one was a Secret Service officer stationed in Washington, DC; and one had retired after 20 years in the Air Force and worked as an "IT Specialist" for the US Department of Agriculture.

While I was teaching at Champlain College, I also ran a solo law practice out of my home. That work ranged from testifying as an expert witness[347] in cases involving claims of "ineffective assistance counsel" in criminal cases to serving as a hearing officer[348] and "conflict counsel" for several Vermont state administrative agencies.[349] I also conducted independent investigations for the Vermont Department of State's Attorneys, the Vermont Attorney General's Office, and the Vermont Professional Responsibility Program, the program set up by the Vermont Supreme Court that disciplines lawyers.[350]

I gave up my law license in 2022 around the same time I stopped teaching. By that time, I was 77 years old.

ENDNOTES

1   I was an "E-5," which is the equivalent of a "Buck Sergeant"—the lowest level sergeant.

2   Ronald H. Spector, "Vietnam War" In Encyclopædia Britannica. February 17, 2025. https://www.britannica.com/event/Vietnam-War.

3   Colgate University in Hamilton, New York, 1967–Vermont Law School, South Royalton, Vermont, 1978.

4   Shari Seidman Diamond and Jessica M. Salerno, "Reasons for Disappearing Jury Trials: Perspectives from Attorneys and Judges," Louisiana Law Review 81, no. 1. (2020) https://digitalcommons.law.lsu.edu/lalrev/vol81/iss1/9.

5   Marco Poggio, " 'Coercive' Prosecution Drives Trial Penalty, Defense Attys. Say," *Law 360*, March 30, 2021.

6   Vermont Model Jury Instructions - http://www.vtjuryinstructions.org/criminal/MS24-031.htm

7   13 VSA 1023(a)(3).

8   Many of my memories of Louie Hamlin's case are clear even now, 40 years later. But I have reread portions of *Death or Innocence*, a book written by Peter Meyer that was published in 1985, to help me remember important details. For example, the quotes from Judge Connarn in the section on Hamlin's threat against the college student were taken from Meyer's book. Peter Meyer, *Death of Innocence: A Case of Murder in Vermont*, G. P. Putnam Sons, 1985, pp. 88–95.

9   *Death of Innocence*, pp. 69–74.

10 Joe Mahoney, "Parents Say Their Daughter Was 'So Spunky' In Nature," *Burlington Free Press*, May 17, 1981, pp. 1, 14

11   Death of Innocence, pp. 110-112.

12   Strusinski's composites, *Burlington Free Press*, May 17. 1981, p. 1.

13   *Death of Innocence*, pp. 107, 118.

14   *Death of Innocence*, pp. 134–35.

15   Rule 41.1 - Vermont Rules of Criminal Procedure.

16   *Death of Innocence*, p. 138.

17   *Death of Innocence*, pp. 143–46.

18   *Death of Innocence*, pp. 148–158.

19   *Death of Innocence*, pp. 159–60.

20   *Death of Innocence*, p. 163.

21   *Burlington Free Press*, August 10, 1981, p. 17.

22   *Death of Innocence*, pp. 198–99.

23   *Burlington Free Press*, May 23, 1981, p. 14.

24   *Death of Innocence*, pp. 173–175.

25   Joe Mahoney, "Anger Launched Petition Drive," *Burlington Free Press*, June 25, 1981, p. 6.

26   *Burlington Free Press*, July 18, 1981 pp. 1, 9.

27   Title 33 Vermont Statutes Annotated Section 5204.

28   *Burlington Free Press*, April 23, 2015 p. C9.

29   Laura King, "Court to Rule on Via's Role in Essex Murder Trial," *Burlington Free Press*, January 28, 1982, p. 11.

30   *State v. Hamlin*, 141 Vt. 190-91 (1982).

31   Davis and Valsangiacomo both went on to successful, distinguished careers in the law. Davis served on Vermont's Ethics Commission for many years.

32   State v. Hamlin, 146 Vt. 97 (1985).

33   I saw this happen in cases I tried as a prosecutor, e.g., *State v. Koveos*, 169 Vt. 62 (1999) and *State v. Roy*, 140 Vt. 219 (1981). Father Emmanual Koveos and "Chippy" Roy were each convicted by juries of criminal sexual abuse of a child. I tried the Roy case in 1980 with Susan Via. I tried the Koveos case in 1998.

34   Jane Smith, "Hamlin Found Guilty by Jury," *Burlington Free Press*, May 15, 1982, pp. 1, 14.

35   *State v. Orlandi*, 106 Vt. 165, 171 (1934); *State v. Miller*, 146 Vt. 502 (1985); 13 VSA 3.

36   May 6, 1982–May 14, 1982.

37   Jane Smith, "Hamlin Found Guilty by Jury," *Burlington Free Press*, May 15, 1982, p. 1.

38   Annemarie Christensen, "Hamlin Sentenced to 45 Years to Life," *Burlington Free Press*, July 16, 1982 p. 1, 9.

39   William Braun, "Jamie Savage Changes Name in Arizona," *Burlington*

Free Press, May 30, 1984, pp. 1, 9.

40   Timothy O'Neal, Obituary, *Burlington Free Press*, April 12, 1982, p. 16. Timothy O'Neal, Funeral Notice, *Burlington Free Press*, April 17. 1982 p. 3.

41   Sorrell and Miller, NCIC Entry Form for "Wanted Persons," April 1982.

42   "Police Ask OK on Plan in Winooski," *Burlington Free Press*, March 15, 1982, p. 14.

43   William Braun, "Winooski Police Officer Faces Three Perjury Charges," *Burlington Free Press*, June 18, 1982, p. 17.

44   "Man's Body Found in Winooski River," *Burlington Free Press*, April 10, 1982, p. 5.

45   13 VSA 2301.

46   Vermont Model Jury Instructions can be found here: http://www.vtjuryinstructions.org/criminal/MS24-101.htm

47   *State v. Orlandi*, 106 Vt. 165, 171 (1934); 13 VSA 3.

48   Mike Donoghue, "Arrest Warrants Issue in Slaying," *Burlington Free Press*, April 14, 1982, p. 1.

49   "2 Murder Suspects Surrender," *Burlington Free Press*, May 12, 1982, p. 1.

50   Don Melvin, "Witness Says She Saw Blood on Pants," *Burlington Free Press*, December 10, 1982, p. 18.

51   William Braun, "Witness Says Ex-Cop Threatened Murder Suspect," *Burlington Free Press*, December 9, 1982, p. 18.

52   William Braun, "Former Officer is Key Defense Witness," *Burlington Free Press*, December 10, 1982, p. 17.

53   William Braun, "Circumstantial Evidence to Play a Big Role in Trial," *Burlington Free Press*, December 8, 1982, p. 16.

54   William Braun, "Sorrell Found Innocent of Murder Charge," *Burlington Free Press*, December 12, 1982, pp. 15, 18.

55   William Braun, "Former Winooski Police Officer Sentenced for Perjury," *Burlington Free Press*, December 14, 1982, p. 13.

56   "Ex Winooski Police Officer Pleads Guilty to False Swearing," Burlington Free Press, November 12, 1982, p. 13.

57   "Miller Murder Trial Continues Amid Tight Security," Burlington Free Press, March 18, 1983, p. 16.

58   March 4, 1983, letter from me to Miller's attorneys, Robert Keiner and Michael Kupersmith, notifying them that Tobler would be a witness for the prosecution.

59   Written statement of Daniel Tobler given to Attorney General's Investigators Moran and Ravenna.

60 *State v. Miller*, 146 Vt. 164, 168 (1985).
61 Peter Freyne, "Brother Describes Bloodstained Pants," *Burlington Free Press*, March 20, 1983, p. 18.
62 *State v. Miller*, 146 Vt. 164, 168 (1985).
63 William Braun and Alexandra Marks, "Jury Declares Timothy Miller Guilty in Winooski Beating-Drowning Death," *Burlington Free Press*, March 23, 1983, p. 13.
64 Ibid.
65 William Braun, "20 Years-to-Life for Miller," *Burlington Free Press*, June 2, 1983, p. 13.
66 Ibid, p. 15.
67 State v. Miller, 146 Vt. 164 (1985).
68 Ibid, pp. 175–77.
69 13 Vermont Statutes Annotated 2002.
70 William Braun, "Bevins Fraud Trial Opens," *Burlington Free Press*, April 26, 1983, page 13; William Braun, "88-Year-Old Testifies in False Pretense Trial," *Burlington Free Press*, April 27, 1983, p. 16.
71 Rule 404(b), Vermont Rules of Evidence.
72 13 VSA 2002.
73 *State v. Orlandi*, 106 Vt. 165, 171 (1934); *State v. Miller*, 146 Vt. 502 (1985); 13 VSA 3.
74 William Braun, "88-Year-Old Testifies in False Pretense Trial," *Burlington Free Press*, April 27, 1983, p. 16.
75 "Jury Finds Bevins Guilty in Roofing Fraud Case," *Burlington Free Press*, April 29, 1983, p. 24.
76 "Bissonette Trial Now Underway," *Burlington Free Press*, May 18, 1983, p. 16.
77 Patrick Leahy was Chittenden County State's Attorney from 1966 to 1974. In 1974, he was elected to the US Senate. He served Vermont in the US Senate from 1975 to 2020.
78 William Braun, "Bissonette Found Guilty in Roofing Fraud Case Involving Elderly Women," *Burlington Free Press*. May 19, 1982, p. 13.
79 "Roofer Gets 1 and ½ Years for Cheating Elderly Sisters," *Burlington Free Press*, July 19, 1983, p. 16.
80 "Roofer Gets 3 to 6 Years for Fraud," *Burlington Free Press*, August 10, 1983, p. 12.
81 *State v. Bissonette*, 145 Vt. 381 (1985).
82 *State v. Bevins*, 146 Vt. 129 (1985).
83 There are twelve towns in Washington County. Barre and Montpelier are on the southern border of the county.
84 Dorothy Richter, Barre Granite Quarries, Barre, VT, Geological

Society Centennial Guide 1987. https://www.uvm.edu/~gdrusche/Classes/GEOL%20110%20-%20Earth%20Materials/Richter%20-%20Barre%20quarry%20field%20guide.pdf.

85   147 Vt. 225-226 (1986).

86   147 Vt. 227.

87   Ibid.

88   "Suspect Takes Stand in Murder Trial," *Burlington Free Press*, March 30, 1984, p. 17.

89   Vermont Standard Jury Instructions for involuntary manslaughter can be found here: https://www.vtjuryinstructions.org/criminal/MS24-251.htm

90   "Man Sentenced in Quarry Death," *Burlington Free Press*, May 25, 1984, p. 17.

91   147 Vt.223 (1986).

92   The community of believers led by Elbert Spriggs has been known at times as: The Twelve Tribes, Vine Christian Community, Northeast Kingdom Community Church, Messianic Communities, and Community Apostolic Order.

93   "Judge Denies State Custody Request," *Burlington Free Press*, June 23, 1984, p. 4.

94   "Island Pond Raid Raises Constitutional Issues," *Burlington Free Press*, June 26, 1984, p. 10.

95   *Case of Wetjen and Others v. Germany* (Applications nos. 68125/14 and 72204/14), European Court of Human Rights, Final Judgment, June 22,2018, ¶85. https://hudoc.echr.coe.int/fre?i=001-181583.

96   The Village of Island Pond is named after Island Pond, a pond that borders the village. The pond itself got its name because there's a 20-acre island located in the pond.

97   Luke O'Neil, "Twelve Tribes: The Church Preached Child Abuse & Slavery," *The Daily Beast*, July 17, 2016.

98   Essex County, Vermont, had a population of 6,306 in 2010. It increased by 7 to 6,313 in 2018. It is the "least populous county" in New England. It is in the northeast corner of Vermont and is separated from New Hampshire by the Connecticut River. https://en.wikipedia.org/wiki/Essex_County,_Vermont.

99   The efforts of White, Leene, Braithwaite, and Cloutier to get state help in executing the warrant were set out in a *Burlington Free Press (BFP)* article by reporters Mike Donoghue and Leslie Brown titled "Attorney Initiated the Raid Plan," on June 23, 1984, p 4A, and in articles in the July 1, 1984 *BFP* detailing events leading up to the decision to apply for the order to temporarily seize the children. *BFP* 1B, 3B, 4B.

100 Pineles went on to become an excellent trial judge and one of the founders of the innovative Drug Court Program in 2000. He told reporters at the time that he did not know why Keyser had reversed himself. *Burlington Free Press*, July 1, 1984, p. 3B.

101 33 V.S.A. § 4915.

102 Transcript of Jeff Jencke interview, March 16, 1984, pp. 6–7.

103 Moran's work had been crucial in putting together the case that led to Timothy "Pucky" Miller's murder conviction in 1983.

104 Moran affidavit, p. 10, CHINS process is now in 33 VSA Chapter 51.

105 Definition—https://legislature.vermont.gov/statutes/section/33/051/05102

106 There were also allegations that the children were receiving inadequate education and, in some cases, inadequate medical care.

107 Braithwaite affidavit, p. 7.

108 Interview with Ira Sawyer (IS), a member of the Northeast Kingdom Community Church (Twelve Tribes) on August 23, 1983. IS was a member of the church from September 1977 when the church was in Chattanooga, Tenn., until 1981 (after the church had moved to Island Pond).

109 Braithwaite affidavit, p. 3.

110 Braithwaite affidavit, pp. 1–2.

111 Moran affidavit, p. 4.

112 Moran affidavit, p. 7.

113 Braithwaite affidavit, p. 3.

114 Ibid, pp. 3–4.

115 Ibid, p. 7.

116 Ibid, p. 12.

117 18 VSA 5211, *State v. Chambers*, 144 Vt. 234 (1984).

118 144 Vt. 234 (1984).

119 Affidavit of Christopher Braithwaite, June 8, 1984 (Braithwaite) at p.1.

120 Braithwaite affidavit p. 4.

121 "State: Church's Tenet Constitutes Child Abuse," *Burlington Free Press* July 1, 1984, p. 3B.

122 Ibid, p. 3B.

123 Ibid.

124 Braithwaite affidavit, p. 6.

125 *State v. Cantrell*, 151 Vt. 130 (1989).

126 Moran affidavit, pp. 13-14, endnotes 58–60.

127 State v. DelaBruere, 154 Vt. 237 (1990).

128 Moran affidavit, p. 14.

129 Moran affidavit, pp. 14–15.

130 Moran affidavit, p. 15.

131   Moran affidavit, p. 16.

132   Robin Smith, "Secrets from Island Pond's Chilling Raid," *Caledonian-Record*, August 4, 2017. https://www.caledonianrecord.com/news/secrets-from-island-ponds-chilling-raid/article_5637dcda-12a6-51ea-9b9f-3e43cffd463d.html.

133   33 V.S.A. § 632(a)(12).

134   *In re: Neglected Child*, 130 Vt. 525, 296 A2d 250 (1972).

135   Braithwaite affidavit, pp. 3–4

136   Bill Gray died of leukemia in 1994 at age 52 before he could serve on the Second Circuit.

137   33 VSA Chapter 12, now 33 VSA Chapter 51, Moran affidavit, p. 10.

138   *In re: Neglected Child*, 130 Vt. 525, 296 A2d 250 (1972).

139   Decision dated June 25, 1984, holding that the State's Petition for Temporary Detention was "properly denied," pp. 3–4.

140   387 U.S. 523 (1967).

141   387 U.S. 538-39.

142   387 U.S. 538-39.

143   *Morris v. US Department of Labor*, 439 F. Supp. 1014, 1018-19 (S. D. Illinois, 1977).

144   August 6 decision; Mahady's decision granting church parents motion to suppress, p. 7, section E.

145   Order granting parent's Motion to Dismiss the State's Petition, p. 7 section E.

146   Alek Fleury, "The Day 140 Officers Raided Island Pond," *Burlington Free Press*, August 19, 2020, pp. 1, 5A.

147   Luke O'Neil, "Twelve Tribes: The Church Preached Child Abuse & Slavery," *The Daily Beast Online*, July 18, 2016, https://www.thedaily-beast.com/twelve-tribes-the-church-preached-child-abuse-and-slavery.

148   The opinion is in the case Wetjen and Others v. Germany (Applications nos. 68125/14 and 72204/14). https://hudoc.echr.coe.int/fre?i=001-181583

149   Article 8–Right to respect for private and family life:
"1. Everyone has the right to respect for his private and family life, his home and his correspondence.
2. There shall be no interference by a public authority with the exercise of this right except such as is in accordance with the law and is necessary in a democratic society in the interests of national security, public safety or the economic well-being of the country, for the prevention of disorder or crime, for the protection of health or morals, or for the protection of the rights and freedoms of others."

150   Opinion of the Court ¶ ¶ 1, 3.

151   Opinion ¶ 84.

152   Opinion ¶¶ 8–10.

153   Opinion ¶ 11.

154   Opinion ¶¶ 18, 23.

155   Opinion ¶¶ 85–87.

156   Steven Rosenfeld, "Order Sought to Stem Coal Tar Flow in Barre," *Burlington Free Press*, February 2, 1985, pp. 13, 17.

157   Steven Rosenfield, "State Near Settlement of Barre Coal Sludge Lawsuit," *Burlington Free Press*, March 14, 1985, p. 2; Steven Rosenfeld, "State Engineers Ready to Begin Plan for Clean Up of Barre Spill," *Burlington Free Press*, April 13, 1985, p. 1.

158   *Re: Southview Associates*, Permit No. 234 Docket No. 634034; WO-634-Decision of the Vermont Environmental Board, June 30, 1987, pp. 1–3.

159   Southview Associates, Ltd. V. Bongartz, 980 F2d 84, 91 (2d. Cir., 1992).

160   *Re: Southview Associates*, Permit No. 234 Docket No. 634034; WO-634-Decision of the Vermont Environmental Board, June 30, 1987, pp. 9, 12.

161   *In Re Southview Associates*, 151 Vt. 373 (1989).

162   151 Vt. 378–79.

163   *Southview Associates, Ltd. V. Bongartz*, 980 F2d 84, 100 (2d. Cir., 1992).

164   Mark Johnson, "Jury Hears Hunt Confession," *Burlington Free Press*, February 26, 1985, pp. 1B, 2B.

165   Laura King, "Barre Man Shot Dead; Youth Held," *Burlington Free Press (BFP)*, April 21, 1982, pp. 1, 10A.

166   James J. Dunn, *Breach of Trust: The Ethics Scandal that Challenged the Integrity of the Vermont Judiciary*, Onion River Press, 2018, p. 11.

167   "2 Sides Judges Reject Plea in Murder Case," *Burlington Free Press*, August 12, 1983, pp. 1, 9.

168   *State v. Hunt*, 145 Vt. 34, (1983).

169   Ibid. and *State v. Hunt*, 485 A2d 109, 145 Vt. 24 (1984).

170   James J. Dunn, *Breach of Trust: The Ethics Scandal that Challenged the Integrity of the Vermont Judiciary*, Onion River Press, 2018, p. 11.

171   *Breach of Trust*, pp. 18–19.

172   *Breach of Trust*, p. 21.

173   13 VSA 4801 *a.

174   13 VSA 4801 (b).

175   Mark Johnson, "Prosecutor Portrays Hunt as a Cold-Blooded Killer," *Burlington Free Press*, February 23, 1985, pp. 1B, 4B.

176   Mark Johnson, "Doctor Gives His Testimony," *Burlington Free Press*, February 24, 1985, p. 1B.

177   Mark Johnson, "Jury Hears Hunt Confession," *Burlington Free Press*, February 26, 1985, pp. 1B, 2B.

178   Mark Johnson, "Psychiatrist Says Hunt 'Compelled' to Kill," *Burlington Free Press*, February 27, 1985, p. 11.

179   Mark Johnson, "Hunt Murder Trial Testimony Ends," *Burlington Free Press*, February 28, 1985, p. 16.

180   Ibid.

181   Ibid.

182   Page retired as State's Attorney in 2014.

183   Mark Johnson, "Insanity Defense Unsuccessful Hunt Found Guilty of Murder," *Burlington Free Press*, March 1, 1985, p. 15.

184   Mark Johnson, "Chester Man Found Innocent of Murder Due to Insanity," *Burlington Free Press*, February 28, 1985, p. 1.

185   18 VSA 7101 (17) and 18VSA 7601-29.

186   Mark Johnson, "Hunt Sentenced to 30 Years to Life for Barre Murder," *Burlington Free Press*, April 27, 1985, pp. 17–18.

187   *State v. Hunt*, 150 Vt. 483 (Vt. 1988).

188   Richard Cowperthwait, "Parolee Charged in Woman's Death," *Burlington Free Press*, May 7, 1985, p. 8.

189   Ibid.

190   "Brattleboro Man Held for Murder of His Wife," *Burlington Free Press*, November 16, 1964, p. 1.

191   Ibid.

192   Nancy Crowe, "Jury Selection Falls Short For Hanson Murder Trial," *Burlington Free Press*, November 4, 1986, p. 4.

193   Ted Tedford, "Murderer of His Fiancée Sentenced," *Burlington Free Press*, Jul 25, 1987 p. 17.

194   Ted Tedford, "Parolee Pleads No Contest to Murder," *Burlington Free Press*, February 4, 1987, p. 11.

195   Ted Tedford, "Murderer of His Fiancée Sentenced," *Burlington Free Press*, Jul 25, 1987 p. 17.

196   *In re Green Mountain Power*, 162 Vt. 378, 381–84 (1994).

197   *In re Petition of 24 Vermont Utilities* 159 Vt, 339, 358, 360–61, (1992); *In Re Petition of 24 Vermont Utilities* 159 Vt, 363, (199); and *In Re Petition of 24 Utilities*, 160 Vt. 227 (1993).

198   758–551=207/551=38%   https://www.disastercenter.com/crime/vtcrime.htm.

199   Danielson spent 32 years as a lawyer for the State of Vermont—first as deputy state's attorney in Chittenden County, then at the Vermont

Attorney General's Office with the Department of Children and Families, and finally as a deputy state's attorney for the Orleans County State's Attorney in Newport, Vermont, where he retired from state service in April 2020. https://newportdispatch.com/2020/04/15/deputy-states-attorney-phil-danielson-retires/.

200   Mike Donoghue, "Heroin Death Draws Manslaughter Charges," *Burlington Free Press*, October 7, 1994, pp. 1–3.

201   From the Vermont Standard jury instruction on involuntary manslaughter.

202   Mike Donoghue, "Drug Victim Left Unaided State Claims," *Burlington Free Press (BFP)* April 12, 1995, p. 15.

203   Mike Donoghue, "Witness to Overdose Returns to the Stand," *BFP*, April 14, 1995, pp. 19, 21

204   Mike Donoghue, "Officer: Defendant's Story Changed," *BFP*, April 15, 1995, p. 15.

205   Mike Donoghue, "Jurors Deliberate Drug Death," *BFP*, April 19, 1995, pp. 17, 19.

206   Mike Donoghue, "Jurors Deliberate Drug Death," *BFP*, April 19, 1995, p. 17.

207   Mike Donoghue, "Woman Injected Friend with Heroin," *BFP*, June 29, 1996, p. 1.

208   Candace Mertz, "Methadone Clinic Fills to Capacity," *BFP*, May 11, 2003.

209   18 VSA 4250.

210   *US v. Shawn Gibson*, D. Vt., Docket No. 2:02, -cr-106-1 Decision on Defendant's Motion For Reduced Sentence (Document 72) pp. 1–6.

211   Drug Overdose Deaths by State—2021/Drug Overdose Mortality by State.

212   Mike Donoghue, "Services Canceled After Priest's Arrest," *Burlington Free Press*, January 25, 1997, p. 17.

213   Sam Hemingay, "Koveos Verdict Rests with Details," *Burlington Free Press*, February 6, 1998, p. 13.

214   Mike Donoghue, "Koveos Trial to Open," *Burlington Free Press*, February 3, 1998, p. 13.

215   Helen Simon, "Court Prepares to Hear Trial of Priest," *Burlington Free Press*, January 29, 1998, p. 11; *State v. Koveos*, 169 Vt. 62, 67–68 (1999).

216   Mike Donoghue, "Koveos Guilty of Fondling Girl," *Burlington Free Press*, February 7, 1998, p. 9.

217   *State v. Koveos*, 169 Vt. 70.

218   Mike Donoghue, "Koveos Trial to Open," *Burlington Free Press*,

February 3, 1998, p. 13.

219   At the close of the trial and before the beginning of deliberations, two jurors would be selected by lot as "alternates" and excused.

220   *In Re Petition of Koveos*, 178 Vt. 485–86 (2006); Mike Donoghue, "Priest Admits Fondling, Police Say," *Burlington Free Press*, February 4, 1998, p. 11.

221   My notes on Lt. Wark's cross examination.

222   Mike Donoghue, "Priest Admits to Fondling, Police Say," *Burlington Free Press*, February 4, 1998, p. 11; my notes on Koveos's testimony.

223   Mike Donoghue, "Priest Denies Fondling Preteen Girl," *Burlington Free Press*, February 5, 1998, p. 1B, 6B; *In Re Koveos*, 178 Vt. 485–86 (2005).

224   *State v. Koveos*, 169 Vt. 62, 70 (1999).

225   Mike Donoghue, "Koveos Jurors Rehear Testimony," *Burlington Free Press*, February 6, 1998, p. 13.

226   Mike Donoghue, "Koveos Guilty of Fondling the Child," *Burlington Free Press*, February 7, 1998, p. 9.

227   *State v. Koveos*, 169 Vt. 62, 64 (1999).

228   Mike Donoghue, "Son of Convicted Priest Pleads Innocent," *Burlington Free Press*, February 11, 1998, p. 9.

229   Mike Donoghue, "Priest Sentenced in Sex Case," *Burlington Free Press*, May 22, 1998, p. 19.

230   Rev. Gary Kowalski, "Truth Unclear," *Burlington Free Press* (Letter to the Editor) July 2, 1998, p. 9.

231   Mike Donoghue, "Priest Sentenced in Sex Case," *Burlington Free Press*, May 22, 1998, p. 15, 19.

232   Abbey Duke, "Koveos Maintains His Innocence in Fondling Case," *Burlington Free Press*, June 17, 1998, p. 13.

233   Christopher Graf, "Turmoil Continues For Vermont's Highest Court," Nashua Telegraph, April 14, 1988, p. 6.

234   13 VSA § 1028.

235   "The terms blackjack, cosh, and sap refer to any of several short, easily concealed club weapons consisting of a dense (often lead) weight attached to the end of a short shaft." https://en.wikipedia.org/wiki/Baton_(law_enforcement)#:~:text=The%20terms%20blackjack%2C%20cosh%2C%20and,from%20the%20swing%20to%20it.

236   *State v. Desjardins*, 142 Vt. 255. 256–58 (1982).

237   "Man Sentenced for Attempted Murder," *Burlington Free Press*, December 26, 2000, p. 13.

238   "Two Men Injured Third Charged," *Burlington Free Press*, November 27, 1999, p. 15.

239   Vermont Rules of Evidence 403, 404(b).

240   Videocassette recorder last manufactured in 2016.

241   My notes on my Sentencing Memo, December 2000.

242   *State v. Minh Nguyen*, 173 Vt 598–599 (2002).

243   My notes on witness "lineup" for the trial.

244   The account of what happened before Minh went downstairs for the meat cleaver was taken from my notes on Aly's statements and my closing.

245   My notes on Dr. Leffler's proposed testimony as well notes on the closing and notes on the statements of Dung, Aly, Duyen, and Minh.

246   The account of Minh's testimony, the cross-examination, and the closing are taken from my notes on the closing, the cross-examination, and the reports of Lt. Helrich and Detetive Cyr.

247   Vermont Standard Jury Instructions for attempted second-degree murder can be found here: https://www.vtjuryinstructions.org/criminal/MS24-151.htm.

248   "Man Sentenced For Attempted Murder," *Burlington Free Press*, December 26, 2000, p. 13.

249   13 VSA 9(a).

250   13 VSA 2302(d).

251   13 VSA 2303.

252   Now Ho Chi Minh City.

253   Elijah Alperin and Jeanne Batalova, "Vietnamese Immigrants in the United States," Migration Policy Institute, September 2018. https://www.migrationpolicy.org/article/vietnamese-immigrants-united-states-5#:~:text=In%201975%2C%20about%20125%2C000%20Vietnamese,end%20of%20the%20Vietnam%20War.

254   Army DD214 (military service record), Robert Vose Simpson, Jr.

255   The Long Binh Army base was in the southern part of South Vietnam—around 20 miles from Saigon. It was the largest US Army base in Vietnam (60,000 men and women), headquarters for the US Army in Vietnam, and the home of the 9th and 24th Evacuation Hospitals.

256   US Army, DD-214, Robert Vose Simpson, Jr., June 13, 1971.

257   Jessica Pearce Rotondi, "Why Laos Has Been Bombed More Than Any Other Country," *Inside History*, December 5, 2019. https://www.history.com/news/laos-most-bombed-country-vietnam-war.

258   23/1156= 2%; Vermont Judiciary Statistics for FY 2001, Table 3(e).

259   13 VSA 1042, 1043.

260   Cheryl Hanna, "No Right to Choose Mandated Victim Participation In Domestic Violence Prosecutions," 109 *Harvard Law Review* 1849,

1858 (1996).

261   *Thurman v. City of Torrington*, 595 F. Supp.1521, 1525 (D. Conn., 1984).

262   595 F. Supp 1525–26.

263   595 F. Supp. 1526.

264   595 F. Supp. 1526–30.

265   "Officers Must Pay $2.3 Million to Wife Maimed by Husband," *The New York Times*, June 26, 1985, p. 34.

266   Ibid.

267   Douglas Beloof and Joel Schapiro, "Let the Truth Be Told Proposed Hearsay Exceptions to Admit Domestic Violence Victims Out of Court Statements As Substantive Evidence," 11 *Columbia Journal of Gender and Law*, 1, 4 (2002).

268   Kendall Foley, "The Prosecutorial Problem of Non-Cooperative Domestic Violence Victims and Overcoming its Evidentiary Complications in Missouri" 90 *University of Missouri Kansas City Law Review*, 885–887, 891 (2022).

269   Emily Stone, "Domestic Abuse: When to Back Off," *Burlington Free Press*, August 10, 2003, pp 1–6.

270   Federal Rules of Evidence 803 (2)—"Excited utterance. A statement relating to a startling event or condition made while the declarant was under the stress of excitement caused by the event or condition."

271   *State v. Joseph*, Supreme Court Docket No. 2002-213, April 2003, *State v. Bullock*, Supreme Court Docket No. 97-295 (1998); *State v. Bergeron*, Supreme Court Docket No. 99-209 (2000); *State v. Lawrence*, Supreme Court Docket No. 2003-288 (2004); *State v. Seerveld*, Docket No. 2006-070 (2006); *State v. Shea*, 2008 Vt. 114 (2008) (court trial tried in 2006).

272   *State v. Bullock*, Vermont Supreme Court Docket No. 97-295 (1998) p. 1 (three justice panel).

273   *Burlington Free Press*, April 24, 1997, p. 19.

274   *State v. Joseph*, Supreme Court Docket No. 2002-213 (3 justice panel), pp. 1–2.

275   Emily Stone, "Domestic Abuse: When to Back Off," *Burlington Free Press*, August 10, 2003, pp. 1, 6.

276   *Burlington Free Press*, April 11, 2002, p. 16.

277   Emily Stone, "Abuse: Pattern Nothing New in Genest Case," *Burlington Free Press*, June 8, 2003, p. 4.

278   Notes on the transcript of the State's May 26, 2000, Motion Limine hearing in the Jones sexual assault case, pp. 16–20.

279   The description of Jones's sexual assault charge and Sarah's eight

months later are based on my recollection and my notes of witness statements as well as Emily Stone's article, "Abuse: Pattern Nothing New in Genest Case," in June 2003 and an article by Adam Silverman, "Twists Let Abuser Out to Kill," *Burlington Free Press*, May 28, 2006, pp. 1, 4.

280   Adam Silverman, "Twists," *Burlington Free Press*, May 28, 2006, p. 4.

281   My notes on Sue Holton's testimony in the May 26, 2000, hearing and my notes on Schirling's affidavit.

282   The maximum penalty for sexual assault is life in prison. 13 VSA 3252 (a) and (f) (1). The maximum penalty for the two misdemeanors is 18 months.

283   Silverman, "Twists," *Burlington Free Press*, May 28, 2006, p. 4.

284   Tamara Lush, "Bomber: Dean Accepts Plea, Avoids Death Penalty," *Burlington Free Press,* September 28, 1999, pp. 1, 5.

285   Silverman, "Twists," *Burlington Free Press*, May 28, 2006, p. 4.

286   Dean was sentenced to life without possibility of parole on February 11, 2000, two days after Jones testified in Dean's sentencing on February 9, 2000. Silverman, "Twists," *Burlington Free Press*, May 28, 2006, p. 4.

287   Ibid.

288   My notes on the transcript of the May 26, 2000, hearing before Judge Burgess.

289   "Slashing Victim in Fair Condition," *Burlington Free Press*, July 5, 2000, p. 9.

290   Sam Hemingway, "Relief From Abuse Orders Can Go Only So Far in Preventing Abuse," *Burlington Free Press,* July 7, 2000, p. 11.

291   "Abuse: Pattern Nothing New in Genest Case," *Burlington Free Press*, June 8, 2003, p. 4.

292   *Burlington Free Press*, November 28, 2000, p. 15.

293   "Sentencing Begins in Assault Case," *Burlington Free Press*, August 27, 2003, p. 17.

294   "Man Gets 23 to 55 Years for Attempted Murder," *Burlington Free Press*, September 12, 2003, p. 18.

295   Silverman, "Twists," *Burlington Free Press*, May 28, 2006, p. 4.

296   Ibid.

297   Emily Stone, "A Pattern of Abuse," *Burlington Free Press*, June 8, 2003, p. 1.

298   The jury convicted in all six trials: (1) *State v. Sharrow*, 2008 Vt. 24—Attempted Murder; (2), *State v. Muhammad*, 2007 Vt. 36—Sale of Cocaine defendant; (3) *State v. Mayo*, 2008 Vt. 2—Aggravated Assault/Habitual Offender; (4) *State v. Jones*, Murder, 2008 Vt. 67; (5) *State v.*

Jackson, Kidnapping, 2008 Vt. 71.

299   *State v. Seerveld*, Domestic Assault (misdemeanor), 2006 WL 58838215—victim testified for the defense.

300   My notes on proposed closing, proposed opening, and Detective Nails's exhibit.

301   Nails exhibit; my notes on proposed closing argument; Coleman search warrant request.

302   *State v. Jackson*, 2008 Vt. 7 Vt. ¶¶ 33–35.

303   My notes on proposed closing argument.

304   Jackson's attorney's Notice of Alibi; My notes for trial prep.

305   2008 Vt. 7 Vt. ¶¶ 33–36.

306   Trial exhibit photo of three knives—one bent, one broken, and one butterfly knife.

307   *State v. Sharrow*, 2008 Vt 24 (2008) ¶ 2, 3; my notes on Sharrow's closing argument.

308   2008 Vt. 24 ¶ 2 Sharrow's conviction was reversed in 2017. The Vermont Supreme Court found that Sharrow's defense counsel at trial had been "ineffective" because he had failed to object to the trial judge's error in failing to instruct the jury that Sharrow could have been found guilty of the lesser charge of attempted voluntary manslaughter. *In Re Thomas S. Sharrow*, 20 Vt. 69.

309   Vermont Rule of Evidence 404 (b) says:
"b) Other crimes, wrongs, or acts. Evidence of other crimes, wrongs, or acts is not admissible to prove the character of a person in order to show that he acted in conformity therewith. It may, however, be admissible for other purposes, such as proof of motive, opportunity, intent, preparation, plan, knowledge, identity, or absence of mistake or accident."

310   Vermont Rule of Evidence 404 (b). My notes on Peggy's proposed testimony.

311   My trial notes and an exhibit with a diagram of the location of Ms. Peggy's injuries.

312   13 VSA 9 and 2303 (a)(2)(A).

313   *State v. Blow*, 157 Vt. 513, 518 (1991).

314   13 VA 1043 (a)(1).

315   State v. Muhammad, 2007 Vt, 36, ¶ 8.

316   The other was an aggravated domestic assault case—*State v. Francis Joseph*, Vermont Supreme Court Docket No. 2002-213 (2003).

317   Sam Hemingway, "Assault Conviction Upgraded," *Burlington Free Press*. October 7, 2005, pp. 15, 17.

318   My State's Sentencing Memo, July 2006, pp. 1–3.

319   My notes on the opening statement in the Mayo Habitual Offender
trial.

320   This person was never identified.

321   *State v. Mayo*, 2008 Vt. 2 ¶ 2; My notes on Gunther testimony.

322   My notes on August 3, 2005 deposition of Robert Roche.

323   Adam Silverman, "Mayo Snaps at Sentencing," *Burlington Free Press*,
July 25, 2006, pp. 13, 15.

324   *State v. Robert Jones*, 2008 Vt. ¶ 20.

325   MB testified at deposition and at transcribed interviews in the months
leading up to the trial. My account is based on my notes on these.

326   Transcribed pre-trial interview that Rosemary Gretkowski and I did
with MB, pp. 6–7.

327   Adam Silverman, "Trial: Jones Pleads Not Guilty," *Burlington Free
Press*, October 26, 2005, p. 16 (4B).

328   Adam Silverman, "Trial: Jones Pleads Not Guilty," *Burlington Free
Press*, October 26, 2005, p. 16 (4B).

329   *State v. Jones*, 2008 Vt. 67 ¶ 4.

330   *State v. Jones*, 2008 Vt. 67 ¶ 5.

331   *State v. Jones*, 2008 Vt. 67 ¶ 6.

332   *State v. Jones*, 2008 Vt. 67 ¶ 7.

333   The summary of Dr. Shapiro's testimony is taken from the Supreme
Court Opinion—*State v. Jones*, 2008 Vt. 67 ¶ 8 and PowerPoint
slides that I created for the trial. The order in which witnesses like Dr.
Shapiro, MB, and others appeared was taken, in part, from a "witness
lineup" that Rosemary Gretkowski and I prepared shortly before trial.

334   *State v. Jones*, 2008 Vt. 67 ¶ 8.

335   Emily Stone, "Police Charge Boyfriend in Woman's Death,"
Burlington Free Press, June 4, 2003, p. 1.

336   Vermont Rule of Evidence 404 (b) says:
"b) Other crimes, wrongs, or acts. Evidence of other crimes, wrongs,
or acts is not admissible to prove the character of a person in order
to show that he acted in conformity therewith. It may, however, be
admissible for other purposes, such as proof of motive, opportunity,
intent, preparation, plan, knowledge, identity, or absence of mistake
or accident."

337   Vermont Rule of Evidence 403 says:
"Although relevant, evidence may be excluded if its probative value is
substantially outweighed by the danger of unfair prejudice, confusion
of the issues, or misleading the jury, or by considerations of undue
delay, waste of time, or needless presentation of cumulative evidence."

338   *State v. Jones*, 2008 Vt. 67 ¶ 13; my notes of proposed testimony of

Leah Genest.

339   Adam Silverman, "Trial: Jones Defense Takes Over in Murder Case,"
      Burlington Free Press, October 28, 2005, p. 1B, 3B.

340   *State v. Jones*, 2008 Vt. 67 ¶ 13; my notes on proposed testimony of
      DA based on Ms. DA's deposition, which was taken on June 24, 2005.

341   *State v. Jones*, 2008 Vt. 67 ¶ 13; My notes on the proposed testimony of
      Sheryl Vuley.

342   Victoria Welch, "Guilty: Jones Convicted of Killing his Girlfriend,"
      Burlington Free Press, October 30, 2003, p. 4A.

343   By the end of the 1990s, annual reported violent crimes had declined
      by 12 percent, from an annual average of 758 per year in the 1980s to
      an annual average of 664 per year by the end of the 1990s.

344   2006 Crime Report, Vermont Crime Information Center (VCIC)
      Vermont Department of Public Safety, p. 1.

345   Adam Silverman, "Simpson: Prosecutor Leaves at Top of His Game,"
      Burlington Free Press, August 2, 2006, p. 6A.

346   Vermont Constitution, Chapter I, Article 10.

347   *In re Roger Clinton Brown v. State*, S. Ct. Docket No. 2015-084 (2015)
      (3 Justice Panel).

348   *In re Stephanie Taylor*, 2016 Vt. 1982 (2016).

349   Vermont Agency of Education; Vermont Department of Health
      Access; Vermont Criminal Justice Training Council; Vermont
      Department of Financial Regulation; Vermont Medical Board
      (regulation of physicians); Vermont Department of Professional
      Regulation; Vermont Board of Health.

350   *In re Glenn Robinson*, 2019 Vt. 8 (2019).

www.ingramcontent.com/pod-product-compliance
Lightning Source LLC
Chambersburg PA
CBHW021718120626
46545CB00004B/1614